To Mother

Christmas 1954

Love, Jane

Born Catholics

BORN
CATHOLICS

Assembled by
F. J. SHEED

Sheed & Ward · New York

1954

Contents

page

v

Born Catholics

Assembler's Note

This Note is not one more essay to add to the nineteen which make up the book. Its purpose is simply to tell readers what the contributors were asked to do and to underline certain limitations within which they were necessarily working—in other words to make various explanations and disclaimers which belong to each essay, but would be monotonous repeated eighteen times.

We outlined it to the contributors in these terms: "Converts are continually and usefully telling us why they joined the Church. In this book born Catholics (which term includes those who came in in small childhood) tell us why they are still in the Church. The last phrase puts it too crudely, of course. What I mean is that they should try to convey what the experience of living in the Church has been—what is most valuable in it, and also, if they wish, where the shoe pinches."

In fact, every Catholic knows he is in the Church by the grace of God. One of the writers, Clare Nicholl, puts it for all of them. "The answer can be given in a sentence: I am still a Catholic owing solely to the patience, the mercy and the infinite love of God." That is hardly enough for an essay; yet from our end, there is no more to say. Only God could write it at length and in detail—if He did, not one of us but would get some sharp surprises: what God is doing in the depths of the soul, He knows and we don't: we only know that we should be lost without it. But there *is* a human experience of the Faith, mind and will and emotions are not simply passive. It is this experience, different for

3

everyone, that the writers of these essays have tried to set down in words.

Thus what each is concerned with is the Church as he has experienced it. What they have written binds no other Catholic or the Church, it is valid only as a statement of their own thoughts and feelings. They do not claim that this is what Catholicism is, but only that this is what it has been to them. If some fellow Catholic tells them that they have got it all wrong, that they have missed some particular point, or even the whole point, they would (I imagine) be happy to be put right. Meanwhile this is how they see it and feel it. (One remembers the people who said that Newman had been converted in quite the wrong way, and his answer that it was too late to do anything about it, he *had* been converted and that *was* the way.)

Without exception the writers are dissatisfied with what they have managed to get said. The experience of the Faith is so rich and touches intimately so many elements in us, that any statement seems meagre, almost unbearably so. There is not only the impossibility of uttering all that is in the mind, but the sense of all that lies deeper than known knowledge. For the Faith is not simply a set of dogmas to be accepted, though it has its dogmas, or a code of laws to be obeyed, though it has its code. Essentially it is a life to be lived. To be asked why one is still in it is like being asked why one has not committed suicide—easy enough to write an essay about as a jeu d'esprit, but to be answered seriously only by conveying one's whole life experience. I remember asking one friend why she was still in the Church, and she answered instantly "It's so cold outside"—which is good jest, and good earnest too, but only a tiny fragment of the answer.

We shall better appreciate the difficulty, and so better appreciate what the writers of this book have achieved, if

4

we ask ourselves how we should have gone about it had we been invited. As it happens I was not invited, I issued the invitations. But I could not avoid both being relieved that I need not write and wondering what I should have written.

My central certitude that in the Church one has for the taking all the gifts of truth and life and union with Himself that Christ meant men to have—that would have had to be said. That the gifts are there I know because Our Lord said they would be; I know it again because the saints, in all ages from the beginning to now, have found them there in such plenitude; but I know it most unshakably by what is objectively the scantiest evidence of all, namely what I have found there myself—for in the matter of the gifts of Christ, most of us ration ourselves pretty stringently, satisfied if we do not fall below subsistence level; yet the little we let ourselves take is still so much, and it is a living fact in ourselves, known to us as the mightier experience of the saints cannot be known. So we are back where we started: it is not any one element taken in isolation, it is one's whole life as a Catholic that keeps one in the Church, the whole mass of experience, certainties and difficulties, elations and depressions, things remembered and things forgotten. There is simply no way of conveying it. The best we can do, probably, is draw out one strand that seems dominant, and be content if we can approximate to an utterance of that. This in general is what the contributors have done. They have not said all, or perhaps more than a small fraction, but what they have said is so.

What does the book prove? I do not know. Need it prove anything? It is witness, not apologetic. By the end of the book you will have met some Catholics. That is all. They were not chosen as typical. They were hardly chosen at all. We wanted born Catholics, or as the precisians prefer to

5

call them cradle Catholics, people, anyhow, who simply found themselves in the Church, as distinct from converts who have made their own way in: actually the list contains two who were brought in very young by parental decision, rocking-horse Catholics (as Caryll Houselander puts it) rather than cradle Catholics. We wanted lay men and women, because the clergy's experience is necessarily different. We had to have people with enough skill in writing to get their experiences down on paper.

In the event the contributors, all but two, are friends of mine—I know them well enough to ask them to do something Catholics are not much in the habit of doing. And I could not resist ending the book with one essay not written for it—an essay Hilaire Belloc wrote on the same theme a quarter century ago and published in a different context.

I have said they were not chosen as typical Catholics. I doubt if there is such a thing. Here you will meet nineteen people, quite unlike one another. There are three hundred million more. And each of them has his own way of being a Catholic. All the same they have something in common, The Catholic Thing, so to speak. It is in this book. For you to find.

F. J. SHEED

Riley Hughes

*Riley Hughes has been teaching English in the George-
town University School of Foreign Service since 1946. For
nearly 23 of his 40 years he has been publishing book
reviews. Since 1951 he has published a monthly column of
reviews in* The Catholic World, *for which he is fiction
critic. He contributes a quarterly column on reprints and
new editions to* Books on Trial. *A graduate of Providence
College, he did graduate work at Yale, Brown, and Georgetown Universities, and he has held various teaching posts
since 1938. From 1940 to 1942 he was with the Connecticut
WPA Writers Project, first as an editor and then as Director. Out of this experience came a book,* Our Coast
Guard Academy: A History and Guide, *published in 1944.
He has also written a novel,* The Hills Were Liars, *and is
at work on another. He is married to a "non-born Catholic";
they have four children.*

"The times," says Hopkins in an untitled fragment,
"are nightfall." The times are always nightfall, and
always their light grows less. But one could scarcely
have chosen to be born at a darker time and more ambiguous hour than in the last months of the soon to be shattered
peace of 1914. To be born then, in the first year of the Victorian war—as Scott Fitzgerald calls it—was to be a mere
chronological contemporary of the expiring days of the last
Golden Age, and to be heir to an apocalyptic-seeming time.
This Prisoner's Base, to use the term of one who became a

7

leading spokesman for this generation, was, one learned later, to colour all our thought. From the womb of time we went to the nursery of holocaust. In certain ways we could never take our century and its pretensions seriously.

If one became a prisoner of time, one was also cabined in space. One was committed to a fierce and embattled heritage in being born to a Catholic family in New England. One was Irish, a member of an "adroit and melancholy race," as Evelyn Waugh puts it. Issues of which one would only slowly become aware had long been joined. In this country of group alliances and of tensions between the regional majority and minorities, to be a member of a minority group is to be born into a condition, not a culture. To be a "hyphenated American" in the first decades of this century was to bear a peculiar burden; or perhaps, in masochism, to assume it. Heywood Broun, with his eye sternly on the American scene, was to characterize the Irish as "the cry babies of the western world." The evidence was inescapable, and all around; it would be the work of years to fight off bitterness and truculence. To be born to a condition, to feel oneself the special target of malice domestic, was to be predisposed to make of it a "cause."

"Celtic you'll live, and Celtic you'll die," the Monsignor in *This Side of Paradise* tells the hero. And one came at things the wrong way at first. The very core of identity, the statement that seemed to exist before time was—"I'm a Catholic"—was nonetheless qualified by, subsumed in, the Celtic sense. As a child one thought that everybody was Irish. The shocked discovery that this was not so was the first, hushed, far-away intimation of the Fall. That one was oneself part English and part Scots could be, somehow, conveniently forgotten. Gradually the circumference of knowledge grew to include the "French Church," the "Ger-

man Church" and, dimmest of all, the "Italian Church"—all
of these were in town; years later one heard the term "Irish
Church." The first person to utter it was looked upon as
being willfully paradoxical. Still, being Irish in New Haven
could never be the career it had always been in Boston;
one was, after all, almost at immigration's western edge.
(Chicago was another matter; in fact, another country.)

One was meant, one soon felt, to be forever alien in the
land. The "forefathers" of public school reverence, of holiday oratory, were patently not one's own. In sepia tints the
alien Yankee of un-Irish name looked down from framed
reliquary in public buildings. The names of streets and
parks were a reproach, or so one often thought. Was there
ever anywhere before such an aristocracy of place, such a
geographical Jansenism, a context which conferred lineage
for nothing beyond the achievement of fifteen generations
beside a river of Indian name without any rise or change
in the social scale? In subtle, unseen ways one accepted;
one conformed to a climate of attitudes and a vocabulary.
One became a Puritan of sorts, but always the background,
insistent, inescapable, was Gothic or Romanesque.

There was always the long past to inhabit, but to claim
citizenship there meant a recourse to books and to dreams.
There was life, and then a thing apart—was this not the
traditional Celtic dichotomy?—there was the dream. In a
landscape, at any rate, where an edifice or plot of ground
which could lay claim to two hundred years was reverently
labelled "ancient," one had to look beyond landscape to
the paleolithic era. Anything more remote than 1620 cast
no shadow; it was inoperative and unreal. Perhaps an almost
ingrained habit of reading had its origin here; one sought
identity and found it in voices silent, in a web of time forever broken. In reading and in sympathies one always followed lost causes. "They always fought, and they always

fell." Of one's ancestors this was written; it applied too to all the ancestors of one's spirit. And so one read on, regretting the Reformation, regretting (almost equally) the fall of the Stuarts. One preserved a pained silence over the Boyne, fateful river. Oddly enough, one was drawn to Macaulay, whose *History of England* was the first book of length and substance one ever read; into it one read losses and gains the Whig historian never intended. It was all a search, over long years, for a lost Golden Age. It was a dangerous business too, as one at length understood. Like Burke, one inclined to regret the plumage and forget the dying bird. One was well on the road to joining those whom Yves Simon deplores as "amongst the most dangerous of nihilists," those who "project their sublime ideal into the past, into a good old time whose virtues are unverifiable, into the conventional Middle Ages imagined at the dawn of the Romantic period by writers ill adapted to the modern world." Intellectually one arrived at the very pre-Raphaelitism that he aesthetically abhorred.

This was the inner world, the world that cast no shadow. Here one could gobble up time in voracious mouthfuls. One recalls childhood games with one's brother in which one was Charlemagne, completely out of century and contemporaneous, in fact, with Napoleon; one solved the problems of church and state by declaring Charlemagne pope as well as emperor. It was always the problem of *imperium in imperio,* of finding circumference for worlds within the world. One was a Victorian, living within the nineteenth-century time lag. God was never the gentleman with a long white beard, of course, but somehow the concept of cosmic policeman hovered. One associated religion with mustard-colored pews, with dampness, with statues mockingly, repellently unreal, and with the flickering glow of gaudy lamps accentuating the darkness. Well within the

10

dim religious light was the recurrent event that gave so much to the character of those early years, the wake. One shrank from these events, so close to family piety, so removed from oneself. One had no sympathy for those, old, dim, remote, who slipped from the family circle; to die was their *métier*. One's task (in a bet with oneself, always lost) was to kneel in prayer, eyes closed, praying rapidly, in a sincere swell of self-pity and callow wonder, without ever once looking into the face of death. One had never heard keening, of course, or indeed become aware of any strong emotion. The calm and the jovial undercurrents of these occasions were always an offense; one found it hard to assume a Chestertonian attitude toward such "manly materialism."

The truth is that one was a romantic fallen among realists. Through accident or intent, one had committed oneself to editing the cosmos. Space was impersonal or depersonalizing; one fled backward into time. With persistence and with pessimism (neither of which one could summon for long) one could have become, along with Henry Adams, a "conservative Christian anarchist." There was always the possibility, of course, of effecting on the cultural level the political compromise one saw everywhere: "If you can't lick 'em, join 'em." But neither surrender nor the unceasing belligerence, the calculating nosism of the politician (one's cousins, one's other self) quite fitted the romantic position. Yet this position, one came at length to know, was itself essentially secularist. The pose of the balanced eclectic could not be held for long. Although one little deserved it, one was saved, God be thanked, from the ruthless logical consequences of the impressionist dalliance. "You talk to me," says Stephen Dedalus, "of nationality, language, religion. I shall try to fly by those nets." This was perhaps one's temptation, but one was, somehow, incapable of the final

11

arrogance. The flight into the sun was time and again put off; one never really got to fitting on the wings.

Meanwhile, one had got through, somehow, the prison house of public school. School meant sitting at assembly, with one's often Irish and Catholic teachers, through readings of the King James Version from a book held in thin Protestant hands. One stood silent as the multitude went on with "for Thine is the kingdom." Islands of prayer and islands of silence. Always after that, the cry for separation of church and state seemed a Catholic issue; one could never, in later years, accustom oneself to the fact that those claiming to speak for Protestants could comfortably make it their own. (One remembered the charred remains of the Klan's burning cross, seen the morning after, marking a spot not far removed from the cave that had given refuge and protection to the regicides of Charles I.) And all this time one's older cousins fled to the professions to seek unreality there, unreality in its most abstract, Byzantine forms.

From this Emersonian world of gnostic platitude, of complacency in being the Land of Steady Habits, as Connecticut is called, escape, though necessary, seemed as uncertain as it was over-long delayed. But escape did come, and with it a rebirth for which one can never leave off being grateful. One left Carthage, sullen city, and one arrived at last in Rome. However feebly, then and since, one had come at last to one's connatural home. To Providence, the city and the college, and behind both The Unfamiliar Name, one's steps were now directed. What could, perhaps, have been the final withdrawal, the descent into the toils of the Middle Ages, became instead an integration. If one fled to the past, through it one faced, for the first time, the present. By a happy chance, one set out, all unknowing, for thirteenth-century Paris, only to discover twentieth-century New York and Chicago. One could never claim to be a neo-Thomist,

12

certainly not in the fullest sense, but one had come, at a time when Neo-Scholastic philosophy was becoming fashionable, to the only place where a layman could go and find Thomism at the source, where it was fully and triumphantly traditional. The Puritan and secularist, knowing nothing, himself least of all, came and sat under the sons of St. Thomas, the Dominican Fathers.

It is now some twenty years since one first came to the city of Roger Williams; of Roger Williams still, as a faint tradition and as a sense of breadth in public order, but now inescapably the city of Thomas too. For four years as a student (and then, after a time, for an equal number of years as an instructor) one came to experience at first hand in the lives of devoted men the rule of reason and the rule of holiness—and to know that these are one. How mild the rule of reason is (and how essentially un-Victorian) one learned from the friars in a white flowing in medieval formlessness. One could be right, one discovered now, without falling back upon New England rigour. Though the college was younger than oneself, it went back seven centuries in the tradition of the Order. The atmosphere of raw newness in a young college contrasted pleasantly with the icon-laden ease of the tradition; and it was the tradition that gave off vigour. The profoundly Dominican sense of innovation, of dogmatic combativeness, and of adaptability was what one needed; one was, one cannot doubt, liberated at the hands of those careless regarders of a past merely to be located in the material order.

One caught at Providence College, slowly but with mounting satisfaction and excitement, what Chesterton calls the Angelic Doctor's "exaltation in the blaze of Being." (Slowly, because the public schools had done their work well; one came with the Inquisition and other matters stuck firmly in one's craw.) From the beginning the atmosphere

13

was metaphysical. Sermons as well as classroom lectures were philosophical and theological discourse, with almost never the touch of *ferverino*. Thus was another Victorian heritage sloughed off. Slowly, fighting many a rearguard action, the impressionist, the eclectic gave way. A private consciousness, incommunicable yet burning to communicate, was by degrees replaced by a kind of public consciousness. Mood became mind. It is a confession of how much one lacked to say how much one was remade then. "Seldom confirm, never deny, always distinguish." These words were a slogan to be bandied about, half laughed at. Yet one could never be the same again after having heard them and having daily undergone the discipline of mind that lay behind them. If a man's wit, says Bacon, "be not apt to distinguish or find differences, let him study the schoolmen." One had found the schoolmen, not only in books, and they were very much alive.

One had come to college with little more than a mood, and one had found what Chesterton calls the "mind surviving a hundred moods." But one was never to lose (and this would make one an academic maverick) the conviction that the work of the world was not done in college classes, that it could not be neatly cut up into the tidy dimensions of college courses. We all know those, too many, whose entire libraries, after college, consist of the textbooks they had used. In those who later taught, the attitude was merely professionalized; competence and authority were limited, and attested to, by the courses that had been taken. Independent reading, voracious and random reading, reading as breathing—for this there was little professional use. The lover of books was to remain the mere amateur, or worse, the despised journalist. In one who had been appearing (pontifically at first) in print well before he was twenty and handing down literary decisions in the public press

14

throughout his undergraduate years, there had been built up a vast resistance to formal learning, and a counter-snobbishness with which to oppose it. Luckily, and long before such terms and concepts as "general education" and "core curriculum" became fashionable elsewhere, Providence College required a coming to grips with reality on terms other than one's own. Before Providence one had been, in one's sensibilities, able to deny the principle of contradiction when the wind was north-north-west. One left something of an impressionist still, but an impressionist with bias.

The habit of writing, it is said, leads to a search for something to say. And the new habit of thinking led to a quest for sustenance. "Books That Have Hindered Me" is the title of one of Agnes Repplier's delightful essays, and one knew how much one had been hindered by the books one had read, and still more by those one had read for review. To Newman, and More, and the Chesterbelloc one reached out to add Maritain, and Eric Gill and Dawson. One deserted Dickens (though not quite Henry James) for Mauriac, Waugh, and Greene. At about this time one drifted aimlessly to Yale and Brown, ancient campuses both. (Ever the academic alien, one would attend seminars in Tudor drama or the literature of Colonial America armed with the latest *Commonweal* and a murder mystery for review.) One discovered later that one had been born too soon: Browning and Matthew Arnold were still, in the late Thirties, the final word in poetic thought and practice. Donne was "period" only, and Gerard Manley Hopkins went unmentioned. Once again one entered the arena of conflict and tensions, but this time armed and wary. As one struggled now not only for identity but for status in the world, one was freshly conscious of being among those who, as Belloc puts it, "are condemned by their Faith to exclusion and exile." One had embraced secular competence, gathered from some years of

15

writing for the public press, but one was told that one could never look, at least in New England, to become a responsible editorial voice. What may be called the professions of opinion were to remain closed, unlike those of advocacy or those which touch men's bodies merely. In the realm of ideas, in teaching or in newspaper editorial work, "Catholic ideas"—the absolutes, the broad metaphysical bases of human thought since the high days of Greece— were limited, contentious, parochial, "exotic." They could never, it was contended, become public ideas in New England.

One remained for a time on the fringes of such a world, and learned much. For a time, through accident, one assumed responsibility, rather near the top, in a government bureaucracy of sorts, the Writers Project. But if one were not to remain forever hopelessly subordinate, perpetually embattled idealogically, and always tempted to retaliation, one would either have to meet this world completely on its own terms or leave it. As D. W. Brogan observes in *The American Character*, published here in 1944, "from the political and social point of view, the Catholic problem is one of segregation, voluntary or involuntary." One did not wish to become the deferential tool, what Negroes call a "handkerchief head." And one had seen too much of, and suffered too much from, the Catholic chowder and marching society mentality of belligerent reaction to wish to become part of that either. As for temporary allegiance to hare and then to hounds— one persuaded oneself that this had not in fact already occurred—that was not to be borne.

In writing for the Catholic press, an activity one entered only after a decade of writing for what we call the "secular" press, one found at last something of a mission, a minor apostolate. Moving and working, with equable temper, among those of like mind one could employ, as best one

16

could, the techniques and professional standards of writing learned in the secular scuffle. One could at least return to one's original concept and program: that shoddiness in prose and thought refuses due honor to God, that the fresh truths of religion deserve fresh seeing and fresh-minted words. As a book reviewer (and a veteran, now, of perhaps some five thousand reviews over more than twenty years) one could encourage high standards of utterance where they were singularly little known. Or at least sentence could be independently pronounced; one could attempt to testify with honesty to performance, to be sparing of such labels as "great," "classic," and "masterpiece" and yet look hopefully for authentic finger touches and resounding rings of what Donat O'Donnell calls "the great Catholic bell." One could distinguish between a complex body of doctrine or reflection of the perennial philosophy and an individual contextual employment. One could (and often had to) withhold from the *bonum* the quality of *bene,* and pass the judgment *male.* Again, as one swam through two decades and more of fiction, often a moral *malum,* one could not in truth withhold the *bene.* One could agree with Mauriac's contention that literature today is determined by a false metaphysics, one "which girds at everything," accept Mauriac's own literature "based upon psychology," and yet still hope for a literature based upon a sound metaphysics.

Many times it would be the work of quiet desperation to employ thoughtfully and with justice Eric Gill's great dictum for art, "the well doing of what needs doing." There was room to work, and if at times one seemed to be almost alone in the demand for literary quality and in a refusal to practise critical benevolence at the expense of the integrity of form, that was, after all, Othello's occupation. It was an occupation best practised alone; for society one had the classroom and the public lecture platform. In the college

17

teaching that was the other half of one's writing activity (in that it allowed independence from commercialism and the more debilitating forms of hack work) one was extremely fortunate. When one came to Georgetown especially one found that integration of soul and soil that one long had sought. Georgetown is almost unique, and certainly pioneering, in its articulation of the American tradition and the Catholic tradition. Bearing, by Congressional grant and favour, the national eagle on its seal, Georgetown has been since 1789—and in the spirit of John Carroll, its founder and the first American bishop—a profoundly American institution. From the beginning non-Catholics have come to Georgetown in great numbers; thus one could find on this campus not alienation and withdrawal but a reflection of America's pluralist society. Here, in a national and international university, one encountered what one did not find in any university in New England: an institution of higher learning of truly generous spirit, of tolerance, in the best sense, instinctively practised. Here, at the centre of the nation's sometimes disordered mind, the *esprit de finesse* is given scope and function.

All the while one sought a space to occupy, time was moving forward at a terrifying speed. Concern with a private world had always been projected against the larger world. Through all personal problems one was aware of being a contemporary of this century's great popes, of being united with the historic Church, of being part of a larger Catholic context. And however far one moved back in time, the context was the same. One spoke, through faith, that first and greatest gift, the *lingua franca* of the anonymous ones of early and medieval Christian literature as well as of the great saints. One could look into the true medieval mirror and see "a fair field full of folk," all holding what one had always held. These were the things to shore up against the ruins of

18

time. One had, too, entered the past in another way; through one's children one became no longer a descendant only, but an ancestor. One could not therefore, be the times ever so nightfall, face whatever final overwhelming catastrophe lay before the worlds of wanwood with complacence or a facile fatalism. With Jeremias, having read much in the book of life and in other books a little, one could say: "In very deed the hills were liars, and the multitude of the mountains; truly in the Lord our God is the salvation of Israel."

Bernard Wall

Bernard Wall *was educated at Stonyhurst and Brasenose College, Oxford, and has lived much abroad, mainly in France, Italy and Switzerland.* He edited Colosseum, *1934–1939, and* The Changing World, *1947–1949. During the war, he was head of the Italian Section of the Foreign Office Research Department and in Intelligence, Rome Area, Allied Command. His books include* These Changing Years, Rome and South Italy, Northern Italy and Tuscany *and* Alessandro Manzoni. *He has contributed to most literary periodicals of the United Kingdom. He married Barbara Lucas, a granddaughter of the Meynells, and they have two daughters.*

A comment on one's own life is always partial. I can think of about four different ways in which this piece could be written, and each way would provide another aspect of the truth which is a dialogue or a trialogue or more, and can take metaphysical forms or historical forms or affective ones. So this version, which I might call "The De Profundis of a Highbrow," is only one among many that are possible.

I was educated by Jesuits at Stonyhurst, and the ideas prevalent there in my youth were of the Chester-Belloc kind. By this I mean a rather aggressive and boozy Catholicism. The Chester-Belloc followers, at least in those days, seemed

to think of drink as a kind of eighth sacrament. As a reward
for being good at examinations we would be allowed to go
off to the Cumberland lakes in charabancs, accompanied by
a Jesuit. There we sometimes rowed on the water, but the
main fun consisted in drinking in the pub, and we were
always rather boisterous and sometimes sick during the
journey back to school. Letting the boys drink and smoke on
feast days is an old Jesuit tradition. There was a lot to be
said for the general spirit; it fostered an atmosphere of cheer-
iness that precluded homosexuality—and this, I gather, is
most unusual in an English school. Another basic idea of the
Chester-Belloc idealogy was worship of France and other
Latin countries where people were gay and drank wine. This
survives in me. I still incline to think that life begins at
Calais, but the idea has become widespread since I was a
boy.

Another survival of my Chester-Belloc school-days was
perhaps less fortunate. It consisted in a complete contempt
for systematic learning and for University dons. From this
I suffered all the time I was an undergraduate at Oxford. I
refused to conform in anything to the ideas of my tutors.
After my second term I stopped attending tutorials except
for philosophy, the only subject that interested me—though
I was not even interested in this in a conventional way, for
I read St. Thomas Aquinas when I was supposed to be reading Kant, and though I refused to consult the books on our
syllabus, I had already a certain mastery of the ideas of such
different writers as M. Maritain, Unamuno, Eugenio d'Ors,
Joseph de Maistre and Eric Gill. At the same time I developed a contempt for all "salaried" or "bourgeois" occupa-
tions. Of course money was more plentiful in those days, but
even today I value independence from money interests very
highly. For the rest at Oxford at the end of the twenties, we
led something of the gay social life described in Mr. Evelyn

Waugh's novels. With some friends I started a society for lectures that had three thousand members, and we entertained famous men of the day, including G. K. Chesterton, Dean Inge, Lord Russell, a great authority on vegetarianism and constipation whose name I have now forgotten, and others. Also from my lodgings we planned a balloon society. A huge balloon was borrowed and filled with gas at the gasworks and a friend of mine took off after being kissed by Tallulah Bankhead and blessed by Sir Nigel Playfair. The silly twenties will never come again. And how we loved quoting Cocteau to prove that the decayed canals behind the gasworks were more beautiful than the colleges.

But I don't intend to write a piece of autobiography at this point, only to give a general atmosphere. Where that boring subject, the Ego, comes in is as a coat-hanger for some of my ideas and reactions about Catholicism. Mostly we learn by trial and error in ideas as in actions. We develop an idealogy that we find afterwards to be worthless, just as we fall hopelessly in love with the wrong girl. That at least was the way it was with my generation, and the main difference between most of my English friends and me was that they had their experiences and ideas before a Protestant, or what Stephen Spender calls a "lapsed Puritan," backcloth, whereas mine was Catholic.

By the time I reached my early twenties and was living with an Austrian professor in a chalet outside Fribourg in Switzerland, I had amassed a very substantial knowledge of literature of a largely continental type, especially French, but my ideas were undisciplined and sometimes scatterbrained. It was at this time that I helped to start and subsequently edited a quarterly review called *Colosseum*. The critic, Martin Turnell, was a co-founder. *Colosseum* was a Catholic review and also one of extreme *jeunesse*. Yet when I look through its pages now I realize that it was extremely outspoken and free. We attacked Catholics for their stuffy attitude to sex, we were anything but "clerical" in our comments on Christianity, we supported many of the best contemporary writers, especially French; and our attitude to the social question and *le monde bourgeois* was entirely anti-conformist. Martin Turnell was responsible for the pure literary criticism; I barged off into fields such as philosophy, sociology—and art and industrialism. The writers we printed included Maritain, Eric Gill, Mauriac, Valéry, Léon Bloy, Berdyaev, Christopher Dawson.

The worst thing about *Colosseum* was its acrimoniousness. It trounced the *bourgeoisie,* Nazis, Communists, *bienpensant* Catholics, liberals and pretty well everyone except the contributors, and it recited a rosary of quarrels. In other words it was extremely un-Christian. The idea that Christianity meant *caritas,* love, had never been brought to my notice in a full and living way. It is a grave thought, but there it is. And I think it *is* the experience of many born Catholics in Europe, and the cause of their weakness. Eventually I did find out something about this, though only after the bitter experience of the war that ended my youth.

As I look back I see I merely had some dim ideas about generosity, some formal practices which were external and resembled a gesture of burning incense to the established Gods of our fathers, and for the rest I was spasmodically carefree and pagan. I think many English readers may find this paganism in Catholics quite astonishing. The state of mind I am describing, however, has nothing novel about it. One French writer, Valéry Larbaud, has described it brilliantly. Montherlant, that perpetual adolescent, comes near to the same thing. I now see that there was a kind of doublethink going on inside me. Or even a quadruple-think. I have only to enumerate the writers and persons I was most impressed by to show this. These included Eric Gill and the little anti-machine colony of Christians at Piggots, Maritain, Christopher Dawson, Laforgue, Pound, Valéry—but I could go on and on mentioning ultimately irreconcilable influences, Greeks and Jews. I have never known the tranquillity of order; these tensions exist in us all as long as we are alive, we never become complete and integral persons though we wrestle this way and that to do so. The tension between conflicting aims now seems to me characteristic of European civilization itself. But we feel it hardly in these unsettled times of enormous destruction, for civilization has lost its form and style, with uniformity of belief.

The Spanish civil war brought things to a head for everyone of my generation in a way that now seems fantastic. The folly from which the great public was to suffer a few years later afflicted writers over the Spanish business. We quarrelled, we couldn't speak to one another, we stayed awake at night fighting battles in the fields of La Mancha. We had absolutely no business in Spain except as stretcher-bearers, but we all interfered. My own reaction was exactly the opposite of that of my contemporaries. When I saw them signing manifestoes for the International Brigades, attending mass-meetings of protest against Franco's bombers which attacked women and children (in those days that was what was said—nowadays we know how impossible it is for bombers to single out women and children while leaving the aggressive sex hale and hearty) I began to see the virtues of the ancient Spaniards; I set Ferdinand and Isabella against Largo Caballero and La Passionaria; the peasants of Navarre against the townsmen of Catalonia (who were commercial hangers-on anyway, and not noble) and began flirting with the Maurrasiens. This was easy as we were living in Paris at the time. Maurras was by then old and deaf, but he was pouring out more venom than had been known in France since the Dreyfus case. Unquestionably he was a great

24

writer of French prose, but I can only compare his works to a beautiful and deadly rattlesnake. Maurras loved everything about Catholicism except its religious content; the forms were Greco-Roman and harmonious, whereas the moral ideas were revoltingly Jewish. The basis of his doctrine was essentially aesthetic, and to some extent "decadent"; unfortunately it involved an attitude to practical life. In this he resembled Nietzsche and poor D'Annunzio. English people have no idea of the influence of Maurras over Frenchmen of my generation and older, and over Catholics outside France. There are still plenty of "atheist clericals" around whose ideas have been warped by Maurras. At this period I quarrelled with Maritain, and the only newspaper in English in which I could ventilate my ideas was, perhaps significantly, *The Tablet*.

Came the war. Once more I apologize for introducing the Ego, but our ideas grow and die with events. I learnt what an absurd and undignified thing Fascism was in Rome during the phony war; I became bitterly anti-Fascist and have remained so ever since. During all those years I strengthened my contacts with Italy and the Italians which I had had since boyhood—first of all in the Research Department of the Foreign Office, where I was put in charge of the Italian section by Professor Arnold Toynbee, and subsequently in Italy itself.

I suppose we all read much more during the war than at any other time because there were far fewer distractions. I elected to make extensive studies in Italian literature—especially Dante—on the one hand, while on the other I felt the impact of Kierkegaard, who was just then being translated by Alick Dru (an impossible dualism once more). Out of these two conflicting influences I developed the ideas that I expressed in the review I started up with the Harvill Press soon after the end of the war—*The Changing World*.

25

The Changing World was in all things different from *Colosseum*, and a lot of readers wrote saying they missed the full-bloodedness of the old review (but of course nothing makes for vigorous writing better than denouncing others— it's irreducible facts that spoil one's sentences). We were living in a different epoch. Polemics and intolerances had been, I hoped, washed away in the sea of blood; if they had not, at least the very thought of them sickened me. Plainly we had to go much deeper. We were like children in very thin daylight, everything seemed tenuous, the very foundations of the world we had been born into were cracked, even the most elementary securities seemed open to question. The important thing was to seek for every means of conciliation, to examine our ruins and see how we could live again. I myself was no longer "the man who knows" but a humble knocker at the door. It seemed to me that in our New Middle Ages, which Berdyaev had prophesied and which had now come upon us, the ideal was that of the "clerk" who managed to carry through the traditions of civilization in a brutal age by the association of religion and culture. What I mean is, it seemed plain that culture could never survive in the old nineteenth-century pride that we had inherited; for we had forgotten that *pietas* and respect for created things, not to say persons, that "liturgical" contact with the seasons and nature, that sense of myth and symbol and childlike awareness of mystery which were really the foundations of life.

I don't pretend I thought out all this by myself, or that it came purely through Dante studies (for in fact Dante is, in my impression, already moving along the highway that leads to Boccaccio, Petrarch and the Renaissance, and certainly not the "mystic" that Charles Williams said he was); much of what I thought was worked out with my old friend David Jones by his gas-ring, where the tea-kettle used to simmer on interminable evenings, and in his books he expresses the awareness I was looking for. The collaborators of *The Changing World* represented many different kinds of opinion, for what we demanded was not idealogical pundits but sincere human beings who could feel our tragedy. David Jones, Gabriel Marcel, Lewis Mumford, Ungaretti, Auden . . . I have copies by me as I write and these names jump to my eye. Above all, by now, I distrusted writers who "knew all the answers," "know-alls," as Eric Gill used to call them, and it seemed to me that whatever one's beliefs there was no alternative for a sane European but to adopt wholeheartedly the principle of religious and political toleration and to reject its opposite. I am against every form of totalitarianism and will have no connivance with that spirit. No one subscribes to the principles of our Committee for Cultural Freedom more wholeheartedly than I do. The crows have come home to roost at last.

Now some jottings about Catholicism.

Perhaps it is already plain that it has never occurred to me that I could call myself anything but Catholic—in this I am in a situation similar to that of countless millions of other Europeans. For them, as for me, Catholicism is something inevitable—like nationality. But this, though important, is a very broad statement. It merely covers what, in traditional Catholicism, apparently differs from Protestantism. Protestantism (I speak subject to correction) is first and foremost a *moral* position. This difference causes interminable misunderstandings. There are many Catholics in gaol, there are many Catholic drunks, and think of all the Catholics who cause scandals in Protestant countries by their love affairs.

So if I say that I'm a Catholic I don't mean to claim any kind of moral pre-eminence for myself, and I don't suppose

27

for a moment that I'm in a position to judge other people. Far from it, what I write is definitely a bleat from the black sheep's pen. It is the attitude of the

> *povre petit escholier*
> *qui fust nommé François Villon.*

But besides lacking Villon's talent, I lack his deep religious feelings—at least the ones he had when he was in a blue funk.

In addition I don't claim moral pre-eminence for other Catholics. In the enormous rosary of this thing that has gone on so long there has been every kind of person. Montaigne was a Catholic, so were the Borgias, so was Francis of Assisi. Here I have to say something about Catholicism and Clericalism.

With English-speaking people this word "Clericalism" doesn't find a clear echo. It is a mysterious thing that Frenchmen get worked up about like the Dreyfus case. All Latin countries seem divided into Clericals and anti-Clericals who are as constant as the two sexes, and one is tempted to think they are the two inevitabilities of institutional religion as men and women are the inevitabilities for producing children. People are disagreed about who started "Clericalism." Some say it was Pio Nono. Others say it began at the Council of Trent and is a Counter-Reformation phenomenon. I don't want to go into this. There seems to me something deeper.

This is the confusion between *ends* and *means*. An institution comes into being for a certain purpose. The purpose is liable to be forgotten and the institution itself turned into the purpose. A classical example of this is the Soviet Union. The original idea of Russian revolutionaries, however twisted their minds were by oppression, was to bring freedom to workers and peasants. The excuse for the Soviet Union was simply that. BUT the institutionalists got busy and the means and ends were reversed. The Soviet Union became the *end,* and the workers and peasants became the *means.*

Now the Catholic Church, as an institution, could hardly escape this *Drang.* A huge hierarchy exists to administer the business of Christianity. What matters is the religion, not the hierarchy. "Faith is the substance of things hoped for, the evidence of things not seen." But the "Clerical" doesn't see things this way. When I look at a Catholic newspaper I see a huge mass of material which has nothing to do with Christianity at all. You find out what a bishop eats for breakfast, if that be your anxiety; you find the doings of Catholics boosted and the doings of people who aren't Catholics deprecated. Surely this is a monstrous reversal of values.

What I mean is that the "Clerical" Catholic adopts a tone towards Catholicism that makes people think of a Communist talking about The Party. What The Party does is right: what The Party says ought to be forgotten is forgotten. And even the instinct to re-write history, so as to abolish the unpleasant side of the past and keep all in rosy light, has its place. Catholics have done ghastly things to other Catholics, and above all to non-Catholics. The Spanish Inquisition was absolutely out of the tradition of the Beatitudes. So was the use of excommunication by Popes for personal ends, such as weakening an enemy state before attacking it, or (the case of Alexander VI) preventing a mistress from going back to the husband the Pope had married her to for cover. "Unedifying" is, I believe, the cliché. But such things are not determinant in a theology. It is only the "Clerical" who causes confusion, for he seems to make his religious belief dependent on the hypothetical moral superiority of Catholics; whereas he should join with all men in saying *mea culpa*—with the Protestants for the burning of Servetus, the hangings at Tyburn, the burnings of witches and the elimination of Red Indians by the Puritans. After all, it is only comparatively recently that the fundamentally Christian idea that people shouldn't be tortured for their opinions has become at all accepted in society, and still only in part of the world. The defence of Catholics as though they were Party members is sectarian and corrupted with materialism.

Perhaps here I should remember the distinction between Catholicism as it exists in the old Catholic countries, and the spirit of Catholics where they are in a minority—though this distinction is rapidly diminishing with modern times. Some English and American Catholics have something of the "Protestant" in them; they sound, as it were, like "protestants" against Protestantism. But the subject is too complicated to discuss in detail.

I find the Party attitude refreshingly absent from medieval writers. It would never have occurred to Dante that he was less a Catholic because he put popes in his Hell, for it is abundantly clear that he distinguished the office of the Papacy from the person of the occupant. It would never have occurred to Boccaccio that he was less a Catholic because he loved Maria di Aquino.

There is an excellent story in the first book of Boccaccio's *Decameron* which bears on the same point. It is about how a Jew called Abraham was converted to Christianity. Abraham lived in Paris and became interested in discussions about religion with some Italian merchants. After a while he told them that he intended to visit Rome. His Italian friends tried to dissuade him because they foresaw how shocked he would be by the behaviour of the Romans, and when he set off they thought he would never become a Christian. But just the opposite happened, and when he returned to Paris they were astonished to hear that he had been converted. For, he said, when he saw the prevalence of every sort of vice in Rome, and in the Papal court itself, he was forced to the conclusion that there must be some kind of divine intervention at work, for otherwise the Church would surely collapse.

Abraham's destiny was one thing, mine is another. As I was born and bred in the Catholic tradition, and I am the accumulation of my own past, now I review the times gone by, I see more and more what Montaigne meant: "Since I am in no position to choose, I follow the choice of others, and remain in the rut in which God has set for me. For otherwise I would roll and roll without end . . ."

Mary Reed Newland

Mary Reed Newland. Born 1915 in Kalamazoo, Michigan. She spent her growing-up years in and around New York, and was at an art school for awhile. She married William Joseph Newland as her essay recounts. They live in Monson, Mass., and have a daughter and five sons.

I am a Catholic because God has infinite love and pity and said, when He knew me long before the beginning of time, "She's a nice girl and We love her, but she will learn slowly, so We will put her *in*."

It is as simple as that. I have been saying thank-you for years, and I'm not being one bit coy about any of this. If I had not been born a Catholic I have no confidence I'd have found my way in. Not that there would be any lack of grace or opportunities, but considering the ways I have squandered the graces I've been given while in, I shudder to think what I'd have done if out.

It's a hard thing to explain why you are still a Catholic when you have always loved being one, always have had the kind of faith that was easy, never any moments of wishing you were anything else. But then if one understands about faith being a gift, it is easy to understand too that it was graciousness on God's part that He should give me this kind of faith. That there should be a hunger, too, is as easily understandable, because He gave the hunger. Then at Baptism one receives infused (along with all the other gifts and virtues) the gift of Wisdom, and Wisdom operates in the most remarkable way in the young. Before they are too cluttered up with a lot of silly notions it usually accounts for some very clear movements on their part toward the end for which they were created.

For instance, I remember the house where we lived long ago on the day I asked my mother, "What do you have to do to be a saint?" She said you must not do anything naughty, so I decided that that was for me. It would be easy, because all you had to do was be good, and all children *want* to be good, which doesn't mean they are, but they continue to want to be. As far as I knew, to be a saint was the best and highest you could go, and all children want to be the best and the highest of something. Like choosing whether to be the best fireman or policeman or dancer or teacher. Saints were higher than these, I reasoned, so that was what I would be. And that lasted for a while, until I forgot, probably because nothing followed to explain how to go about it.

Then one time we had a children's mission. The missionary did some very unorthodox things, by our standards, like walking up and down the aisle when he preached and confusing us mightily about his relationship to God at the Consecration. We staggered out of church that day reeling with the announcement that at the moment the bread and wine were changed into the Body and Blood of Christ, the priest became God. Confused as we were, we understood in a vague way that he really didn't mean *that*. He had been trying to drum into our heads that something terrific happened, and although he'd missed by a hair's breadth, we all understood that it had been a good try. He had at least startled us, and that was something in those days of sitting through instructions which went in one ear and out the

33

other. Then the next day he did it. We returned for the last
session, half suspicious, half curious, not knowing exactly
whether he was as good as he made out or had just tricked
us into coming back, and he gave a conventional wind-up
sermon about which I remember nothing and then walked
down to the altar rail and said, "Well, anyway—let's all
remember to pray every day that we'll be saints."

There it was again. I have no idea how the rest of them
took it. My impression was that they considered it another
of his ghastly exaggerations (this was very presumptuous
of me). But I went home hugging to myself the terrible
secret. I wanted to be a saint. I must never tell anyone. It
would sound so frightful to want something so big. And because I never told, and never brought the subject up, no one
ever thought to explain (if they did know it) that of course
I *should* want to be a saint. All Catholics should be saints.

This was the first time I had a reason why I was glad to
be a Catholic. I had never thought about being glad before—
just was one and quite happy to be. Failing to turn into a
saint after that time so long before, I had decided, I guess,
that certain people were *picked* to be saints and wanting
had nothing to do with it. Now revelation. Wanting did have
something to do with it. Everyone was supposed to want it
(the missionary assumed we did) and everybody was supposed to try. O joy! It was a wonderful thing to be a Catholic
and to be the best kind you had to aim for the top, the
hardest thing of all. That's what I would be.

Which just goes to prove how things go with the young
and what fools we are to give them easy goals. And of course
it is quite the most sensible thing in the world that this
should be, because God created no one to be anything but
the best. He doesn't make mediocre people. He has no law
of averages which picks out a percentage to enjoy His bliss
and marks the rest Expendable. And when I asked a *very*

patient priest one day, years later, "How about Hitler?" and he said, "You have to love Hitler," I nearly yelled. This was why it was so wonderful to be a Catholic. No matter what you sprung on the Church, she answered it with the impossible, which was the only answer which made any sense. Asking you to love Hitler was asking the impossible, but it explained the Cross. Suppose you weren't asked to love him? Suppose the horror and nightmare on Calvary, the Man Who was "a worm and no man," had done it only for some and not all? How would *He* be any match for the devil, who had access to all? What it meant was that the devil was free to drive a man to the depths of loathsomeness, and when the man had gone as deep as he could go and looked on the face of his victim, it would be Christ. "Whatsoever you do. . . ."And the face of his victim was the face of Love, Who, though your sins be as scarlet, could make you as white as snow.

Then I asked for the first time out loud: "Is it presumptuous of me to say I want to be a saint?" And he said: "Of course not. You're supposed to be."

That was my first conversion. This book may be the other side of the conversion coin, but the paradox is that born Catholics still have to discover the Church. And if conversion is a long road with many difficulties, so is discovering what the Church is when you are born in it. It's like your father's house and the comforts you are used to. You don't open your eyes the day you are born and say, "Ah, I have a home and a family. See how I am blessed." You simply take it for granted, and now and then become quite critical when your father loses his temper, your mother gets cross, and you have to share things, like chocolate ice cream, with your sisters when you'd far rather go off and eat them all yourself. You don't go around saying, "Consider the sanctity of the family. I've got one, it's a miniature Mystical

35

Body and I am so grateful that nothing will bother me much, not even having to share the ice cream."

The Church is your house too, which you take for granted. And the sacraments are the furniture of your life. There they are: you are used to them and you don't rock and reel with their impact.

Now things were different for me, however. Being born *in* was not a matter of merely being inside the house instead of out. It was clear that having been inside since my beginning, I'd been sitting doing nothing; wondering, from time to time, if there wasn't something one was supposed to do, but never discovering what. Knowing at last what I was supposed to do (or at least *one* of the things I was supposed to do), made all the Catholic things I had taken for granted (the way people take food for granted, eat it, then do up the dishes and complain about *them*) brand new wonders. Now frequent Confession and Communion were more than things you did because you were a "good Catholic" and went often if you were. Confession was where you went at the sins that kept you from being a saint, and Communion was food for the saint you were supposed to be. Very self-centred, this, but closer to the point than before. Now there was beginning to form a concept that promised to describe how you were supposed to feel and act, and love everyone and everything, and it hinted that *everything*, not just "religion," had a meaning in relation to God. As for the Mass— but I had only the littlest sense of what the Mass really meant. What I did know in a vague way was that the Mass was the most important thing in all the world, and next to it nothing else really mattered. Someone said: "Oh? So no one else really matters? Only God and the Mass?" And I had to groan, because I couldn't make it clear, but knew, that when you felt this way about the Mass, everybody else mattered more than they'd ever mattered before.

God teaches you in the strangest ways. For instance, this conviction about the Mass. He will stir it up, once it begins to simmer, and goad you to think about it until your mind aches. Like the time Gimbels' sold the Hearst art collection. (I think it was Hearst.) It was incredible seeing in Gimbels' (where I once worked as a sales clerk) such a hodge-podge of medieval armour, furniture, rugs, diptychs, triptychs, saints in paint, in stone, in wood, gold and silver, enamels, porcelain, and lovely majolica, and to see people shopping for culture. There was one great long table of what looked like remnants, and the bits of tapestry, damask and brocade were being snatched up by a lot of curious women who rubbed and pinched them, held them to the light, searched them over with the air of finding something fine and old and beautiful with which to cover a cushion. Such conversation pieces they would make—"My cushion covered with a piece of sixteenth-century brocade." I was as intrigued as the rest, and poked and sorted until my heart stopped beating entirely at the sight of one woman clutching a rose chasuble. Little did I know of Laetare Sunday then, or why rose, or even that it was called a chasuble, but I knew what it was and my fun slammed to an abrupt stop right there. Here in a pile of marked-down art treasures was a vestment which had been worn for the Mass. I thought insanely: "*I'll* buy it." But that was ridiculous because I had no money to buy it. And I thought: "What should I do? It has been used for the Mass. You can't just stand here and let them paw at it like that." In the end I did nothing but go away and sit on the Long Island train all the way home and want to cry, because back there in Gimbels' women shoppers were yanking back and forth between them something a priest had worn long ago when he offered the Mass; and the Mass was the most important thing in the world.

Now once this sort of thing begins to grow, it plays terrible havoc with your nice neat plans. Daily stirred by little signs and wonderings which could not remotely qualify as full-blown understanding but which were more a sharpening of instinct, I decided to change my life to accommodate them—at least change the outside (the inside is not so easily changed). So the first step was to write, from my desk in an advertising agency, to the only Catholic publishing firm I knew anything about and announce that I wanted to work for them more than anything else in the world. It made sense. If I wanted to learn, why not get in where there were books written about the things I wanted to learn? I would be glad to take any job they had for me if it paid carfare and lunch money. I would sharpen pencils, empty wastebaskets, sweep the place out if only I could work for them. As it happened, the news had not penetrated my world that this particular firm had been bombed out in London and did not, at the moment, have any pencils to sharpen, though I daresay they had plenty of trash to carry out in wastebaskets. And while I waited for a reply, it was noised about to friends of friends of the firm that I dreamed night and day of working for them. The shattering reply to this (*not* from the firm itself, I hasten to say) was: "Well—er—I'm afraid, how shall I say it—she really isn't the type they'd be interested in hiring."

Too much lipstick. Those were the days of the Joan Crawford mouth and *Vogue* editorials featuring a passionate pout being painted by a fashionable claw over the caption: "Her red badge of courage!" It was proof that my new outlook was beginning to bear a little fruit that I, always a loyal devotee of *Vogue,* hesitated to be convinced that all the war widows whose beloveds were being shot to pieces over Germany would be comforted by painting their mouths. But then it showed how far I had to go when, hearing a friend of my sister say with some awe, "Isn't your sister a

38

model?" I was flattered to my fashionable toes. The friends
who did know what a sterling character I was under all my
Max Factor were still greeting me with, "Ah! Dracula's
daughter!" and I was still laughing it off and doing nothing
about it. One does not relinquish such securities as these
(make-up, nail polish, dressing "well") easily. I am as convinced now as I was then that being a Christian has more
to do with your inside than your outside, and people who
dismiss the worldlings as "not the type" trample on a lot of
good intentions. You can't convince me that Mary Mag-
dalene fell in love with God because she washed her face.
She fell in love first, and then she washed her face—because
she had discovered something more important than her face.
So, knowing only one thing for sure—that I wanted to be a
saint—and still in the process of discovering what it meant
to love, and be loved by, God, I substituted for face washing and working in the publishing firm, working at night to
help a friend who ran a Catholic bookshop.

All those books! This was the most frustrating thing yet;
to know that on shelves in front of you was all you wanted
to know, and not to know where to begin. Every time I went
into that shop I had the same terrible desire to read them
all at once. The *Summa*—that covered everything, I'd heard
—I'd begin with the *Summa*. I took one volume down,
looked through it, and returned it as quickly, with a horrible
feeling that it was far too complicated for me and if anyone
saw me they would know it was and be either amused or
outraged that I had dared disturb it on its shelf. That is one
of the things hungry Catholics have to battle all the time—
an excruciating sense of inferiority and ignorance in the
presence of, in this instance, their Catholic college friends.
There persists in the minds of the unknowing a strange conviction that, not knowing, it is too late now ever to know.
Which shows they do not understand the least thing about

grace, for all the memorized Catechism lessons and their familiarity with the thing known as "the state of grace."

So there I was, stymied. I wanted to know everything right from the beginning. How to prove the existence of God and how everything had a place and a purpose under God like all the stones in a pyramid. (I was sure it was so.) Then I wanted to know all about my soul, because it was making its existence more and more clear. Whenever I would start to pray, all that would come out was "Teach me!" And I was in a terrible stew because even when I got myself jockied into position among books and people who could teach me, I either lost courage or didn't have enough sense to come right out and say what I wanted.

My patient priest patiently worked many wonders, like explaining the Holy Spirit so that I sat there and cried when he was done. He helped me drag my feet through the *Confessions of St. Augustine,* and it made me very happy to discover that, for all his good head, he learned late too. Then one time I had an opportunity handed me on a silver platter and muffed it out of sheer stage fright. I was making a retreat at the Cenacle (these helped ever so much) and discovered that Fr. Leen was there, resting between lectures. I took my just-purchased copy of *In the Likeness of Christ,* approached him where he sat under a tree, begged his pardon and asked for his autograph. I have never had a particular craving for autographs but it was the only excuse I could think of for getting near him. I wanted so badly to say to him, "Tell me about being a saint. What do you *do?*" And what did I say? "Father, all these short stories and plays by Irish writers are so terribly anti-clerical you get the idea the Irish are losing the Faith. Are they?" And he smiled and said quietly, "No, they aren't." And that was that.

Of course anyone who knows anything about how God loves you knows that what seem to be blind overtures are

40

never without some meaning and always accomplish something, but the wretched state of the one making the blind overtures is simply blindness. Nothing looks like anything. You make these gigantic efforts to pierce the mystery, and when they get you nowhere, apparently, you return to doing what you have been taught "good Catholics" do. The latter are excellent for the over-all effort, but they can sometimes be without much flavour.

I joined the Legion of Mary in our parish, and together with the other girls walked miles to distribute pamphlets, take the parish census, visit the sick. We prayed together and read the Legion handbook and Grignion de Montfort at the meetings, but these didn't seem to shed much light on what *I* wanted to know. I loved Our Lady and was as hungry to learn more about her as I was about everything else, but all I felt, listening to these holy writings, was that my edges were curling like an oyster in hot milk at every repeated "ineffable." At the bookshop there were hints of great things hatching in France in something called the Lay Apostolate, talk of the Catholic Workers and of another group in Harlem under the banner of someone called the Baroness, and all this made me more than ever glad I was *in*, because look what other Catholics were doing; but I was envious because it didn't mean for me what it meant for these others. So whenever anyone would say it was admirable to walk all those miles as a Legionary and work those after-hours at the bookshop, I would make a joke and say: "Didn't you know? I am pursuing sanctity." Isn't that too bad—that people will want something so badly and not dare be serious about it?

It was Caussade and his "sacrament of the present moment" that made everything different. And discovering the significance of every moment made me wonder if there might not be something more for me to do with my moments than sit behind a desk and type out promotion on Duz and

41

Ivory Soap. This was obviously going the long way round for one who was in such a tear to be up and off, doing the will of God. My Aunt Bess, who is a Franciscan and a love, had said sweetly but firmly: "No, dear, you do *not* have a religious vocation." She had been a mistress of novices and was in a position to know, and she was so *right*. Then one time I had raved on to a friend (who is a Dominican now) about the kind of man I wanted to marry, and her answer was "Well, you're out of luck. All those men are priests." And when at last I was in love and marriage seemed like a *very* good idea, I couldn't decide if getting married were God's will for me, or staying unmarried in order to discover God's will. What an idiot! My patient priest said finally: "Look. If you are waiting for some handwriting on the wall, it isn't going to come. You are *still* going to have to make up your mind for yourself." As though God couldn't have a will for me in whatever state I decided, as best I could, was the right one. And my patient beloved repeated patiently that *he* had no doubts, that he knew, too, we were supposed to be saints, and he couldn't see what all the fuss was about. If you got married to someone you loved, it simply meant you were supposed to be a married saint. As this is not supposed to be the story of my romance, suffice it to say that we were married and I was more glad than ever to be a Catholic, because God had designed a sacrament in His Church which bound together, forever, love for Him and for someone else, serving Him and someone else, and from now on learning how to love and serve Him would begin with loving and serving this very dear someone else.

Then, thick and fast, came one reason after another why I was glad. Waiting it out in the delivery room for every baby, I was glad I had learned from a Catholic grandmother long ago that suffering was holy. She died of cancer refusing opiates because she wanted to give the pain to God. And when we were very poor I learned, at last, what St. Francis meant about poverty who was so beautiful under her rags that he made her his mistress—because never before had we felt God's arms so tight about us, had Him choose what we were to eat and wear, when we were to be warm or cold. Then there was the day Our Lady made it so clear that she was catching in her lap all the strange assorted things we were trying to toss up to her Son. There was such a lot of smelly washing saved up, and no hot water for weeks, and making a kind of grim fête of it I composed a terrible poem to her and sang it very loud so the smell wouldn't seem so bad. "O dear Blessed Mother, with joy and with mirth, I greet thee with washing . . . " what would rhyme with mirth? . . . "to honour thy birth." It turned out to be her birthday—but I didn't know it at the time.

Then we discovered the liturgy. *To be part of Christ,* of His Body, to be as close as *that,* as important as *that!* No one but God could care so much and use all your uselessness like that, and no one but a Church that was divine and in *authority* would dare teach something so impossible.

This Church you were born in, this "political institution," they love to call her, bends daily with every Mass to caress every pebble and stick and kiss every child, stroke every feeble hand, bless the good passion of the married, count the tears of the sorrowing, the pains of the suffering, put a precious price on the fears and worries and joys and longings of everyone everywhere. Time falls away at the Mass; and He is still thinking the same thoughts He did that day when He looked through the blood in His God's eyes and saw the screaming, yelling, howling ones who wanted Him for their love and didn't know it; when He saw every thorn and weed and blossom and far-away hill and cloud and bird and little grub in the soil where they dug the hole to plant His tree. And He loved them so because they were all conceived in His Father's mind before sin came, and they were all so holy and good. So He hung quietly and let the blood drip and the water gush, and it has never stopped. At every Mass He pays His Father back all over again, and then—incredible!—He sends us out to fill up what is wanting in *that!* No wonder a child will want to be a saint—when Baptism grafts him to the Body of Christ. No wonder I am not a saint, when it means all this and is so terribly, terribly hard. It is the hardest thing in the world to be a Catholic, but I get cold chills thinking, "I might have been born *out. . . .*"

Clare Nicholl

Clare Nicholl *was born in Darjeeling and lived the first eight years of her life in India. She has been in England ever since, and earns her living typing in all sorts of offices.*

The answer to the question why am I still a Catholic can, of course, be given in a sentence: I am still a Catholic owing solely to the patience, the mercy and the infinite love of God. But a sentence, unfortunately, will not pass muster for an article, so the bald statement must be amplified by describing some of the landmarks on one particular road to "the City of Truth, whose maze of paths enchanteth the heart."

There is a pious legend that St. Peter was crucified upside down because, in his humility, he felt himself unworthy to suffer exactly the same form of death as Our Lord. This is probably true, but I am sure there was an even profounder reason for this death-in-reverse. I believe St. Peter was crucified upside down in spiritual as well as literal fulfillment of Christ's words to him, "Amen, amen, I say to thee, when thou wast younger, thou didst gird thyself and didst walk where thou wouldst. But when thou shalt be old, thou shalt stretch forth thy hands, and another shall gird thee and lead thee whither thou wouldst not. And this He said, signifying by what death he should glorify God." The inner meaning of

45

this parable may well be that St. Peter had to learn that his own ideas, even his own best ideas, were not Christ's ideas. He had to be emptied of himself: he had to be turned upside down. And what was true of St. Peter is true for many other Christians, perhaps for *all* Christians who would follow their Lord in spirit and in truth.

To be turned upside down is a painful and protracted process, particularly if one is obstinate: in the initial stages it seems to be an utterly destructive process, a series of disasters creating nothing but havoc, what Chesterton described as "strange-visaged blunders, mystic cruelties." But the first glimmer of enlightenment, the first indication that what seemed to be upside down is in fact right side up, is the recognition that what, in one's childishness and ignorance, one mistook for stumbling-blocks have been in reality stepping-stones on the way to God. The shape and substance of the stumbling-blocks will differ with each individual; the essence of their impact is the same for all.

We cradle Catholics suffer from all the disadvantages of our tremendous advantages, and we are apt in our dark hours to dwell on these, the reverse side of the medal. The disadvantages vary more or less from one generation to another, and one can only speak from one's own experience and quote a few of the more obvious difficulties as a sort of common denominator for Catholics of one's own age.

To be born and bred as children of the household of the Faith can result in a sort of purblindness. The Church of Christ, from its very familiarity, becomes something "far too plain for sight"; its dogmas are as much the stuff of our early days as the nursery furniture; they are part of the background and, like the background, we are inclined to take them for granted and never really examine them. There is a grave danger that the truths of faith, swallowed whole-sale and never properly digested by a child's mind, may be

CLARE NICHOLL

the focal point of misunderstanding in the adolescent and
do far-reaching damage to the whole spiritual system, damage that will need half a lifetime of painful "unlearning" to
rectify. Baptismal grace is a life which should keep pace
with the development of physical life, and a faith which is
not exercised in the intelligence and free will, and so
strengthened, is almost more dangerous than no faith at all,
because it breeds darkness and confusion where there should
be increasing light: it hampers the development of grace,
and suppressed or neglected grace is at the root of most
neuroses.

> Acceptance is not all, and Amen is more than an affirmative.
> The faith a man has is to be expressed, and that is the work of
> a lifetime. It is not a single declaration, once made and then
> to be forgotten. Rather is it a lasting habit of mind, a constant
> and growing fidelity by which a man goes on accepting the
> truths of God, penetrating them as deeply as he may. Too often
> the loss of faith is the loss of this fidelity, the grown man
> ignoring what growth of every kind implies—not abandon-
> ment of what has gone before but its development within new
> and larger limits. That is why repeated acts of faith . . .
> generously made with mind enlightened and will engaged, are
> of the essence of Christian life.[1]

". . . The loss of this fidelity, the grown man ignoring
what growth of every kind implies . . ."; one could hardly
find a better diagnosis of the *malaise* which paralyzes so
many men and women and causes them to break faith with
the Catholic Church in middle life, if not earlier.

For those of us who were very young children when the
second Flood, in the shape of World War One, broke upon
the world, the difficulties in the way of healthy development
of faith were fairly formidable. We were born, and spent

[1] "Four Words for Advent," by Illtyd Evans, O. P.; *The Tablet*,
December 5th, 1953.

47

our first impressionable years, in one world; we grew to adolescence and maturity in a totally different world. Had the difference been recognized at the time and our education adapted to it, much suffering would have been avoided; but in most cases the necessity for stronger weapons to meet a greater combat was not realized, with the consequence that our upbringing bore no real relation to the life which was to confront us when we left school. Our parents and teachers cannot be blamed: they assumed that traditional standards of morality, ethics and culture were to be our heritage, as they had been the heritage of our forefathers. With regard to the true state of affairs in the post-Armistice world they had not—they could not have—a clue. It is good to remind ourselves of this, because there is a whining note which rasps through much intelligent Catholic literature today, particularly fiction and autobiography. Catholic writers (too many of whom are lapsed or uneasy Catholics) are apt implicitly to protest, "I have sinned exceedingly through my parents' fault, my school's fault, through everyone else's most grievous fault . . . " We have sinned, of course, through no fault but our own; and if we are uneasy in our faith or if we have lapsed, it is because we have neglected grace.

The difficulties, however, were real enough: those in authority, by and large, acted on the fallacy that ignorance was innocence; they were apt to envisage discipline as routine imposed by authoritarianism, which precluded the essential leaven of *self*-discipline; the axiom that children are seen but not heard was widely accepted, which meant in practice that questions were not encouraged, so that in the sphere of religion many a child's practice was no more than formalism. For many of us, home surroundings were more Victorian than Georgian or even Edwardian (there is no doubt that the Victorian age lingered long after its time, like old scent, more stuffy than fragrant). This meant that

48

the majority of girls were not encouraged to think for themselves and whole fields of knowledge were automatically out of bounds. Our minds were semi-starved and therefore stunted, and when we became women we had not yet put away the things of childhood.

School background was even less conducive to realism. The teaching in convent schools was almost entirely relegated to the nuns, and it tended to be haphazard and dilatory. Religious instruction was confined to learning the Catechism and Gospels by heart. We were not educated to the liturgy and, outside of daily Mass, which was compulsory, devotional practices were the order of the day. A typical instance of these winks at me across the years. During the month of June we were encouraged to foster devotion to the Sacred Heart, and to this end a series of suggestions were pinned daily on the green baize noticeboard in the main corridor, above the cricket fixtures and the results of the arithmetic tests. One such admonition was: "For the love of Our Lord, I will be extra kind to the girl I most dislike—just for today." Some of us were embarrassingly popular—"just for today." Those children who are naturally ingenuous and uncomplex may thrive on this type of thing; others, too generously endowed with sharp-sightedness, develop an early cynicism.

Yes, the approach to the Faith was made through emotion rather than reason, and there is no doubt that the religious training in convent schools of that era was dominated more by heart than head: but the heart is not to be despised, it is by no means to be despised. Our Lady, whom we invoke as Seat of Wisdom, kept God's words and "pondered them in her heart," and this ideal fusion of intelligence and affection is found in the Catechism definition of prayer as "the raising up of the mind and heart to God." Our minds may have been undeveloped, but everything in the atmosphere of prayer which surrounded us induced to the turning of the heart to God, so that not one of us, looking back to the convents of our childhood, can fail to recognize the bond of love—albeit an inarticulate and as yet unproven love—which was forged between us and Him during those formative years. The red lamp that glowed before the statue of the Sacred Heart was in essentials no jack-o'-lantern of transient emotionalism: it was an abiding symbol. The bond was forged, and for those of us who can now say with gratitude, "I am *still* a Catholic," it has proved unbreakable, thin though it may have worn at times.

That, for many of us who are now in our forties, was the background. We were happy at home and at school: who could know that that sheltered, taken-for-granted security was a hothouse atmosphere which would lay us open to the harshest disillusionment in later life? It was indeed a case of "from quiet homes and first beginnings, out to the undiscovered ends . . . "

The obvious repercussion of our lack of education was maladjustment in every direction. As members of the Church Militant our generation left school ill-equipped for modern warfare. All too soon we were in the thick of it, and we suffered, and suffered badly, from that unequal development of heart and head. Those of us who had to earn our own livelihood probably felt the shock most keenly. There is little chivalry in the competitive world and, apart from the commercial aspect, we were up against the full force of what had been obscurely, and to us rather intriguingly, referred to during our schooldays as "*the* World." "The World," to our adventurous, romantic-minded, callow selves, was at first sight absolutely fascinating, and crammed with intelligent, charming people. A large part of the fascination was due to the fact that these new and most intelligent and experienced friends held values which were the reverse of those taught us by the nuns. Materialism is easy to detect when it betrays itself in obvious ways, in the worship of money, possessions and power as ends in themselves; it is not so easy for the untrained mind to withstand its more subtle manifestations. Our new friends positively throve on breaking all the old school rules: pleasure for them came long before duty, freedom of thought was—as they expressed it—"unshackled by dogma"; what we had been taught to venerate as purity they dismissed as prudishness (and this label is not always misplaced!). The whole notation of their eventful, colourful lives was pitched in a different key —and how beguiling was the tune they played! Against their sophistries we had no doctrinal training, against their allurements we had precious little armour of deliberate self-discipline, in the face of their obvious worldly-wisdom we felt horribly dowdy and dull.

It was then that we realized the weak spots in our education, and with the realization came the first humiliating initiation into self-knowledge—we were brought face to face with the unpalatable truth that "a man's enemies are of his own household"; so much in ourselves was ready to respond with disconcerting eagerness to the temptations from without, whether these presented themselves on the intellectual or emotional plane or both. In this first encounter with life one tended to throw out the baby with the bath: devotional practices were no bulwark, was dogma any more substantial? Given the concrete choice—an opportunity for happiness involving the sacrifice of what to a Catholic are ultimate values—would the *facts* of the Faith, now unglamourized by the *feeling for* the Faith, which had bolstered up our adolescence, prove of sufficient weight to tip the balance? Those of us who were fortunate decided that they had: but the struggle might have been less painful had our intellectual grasp of the issue been more profound.

51

With the survival of the first round, the first stumbling-block loomed large: there seemed little worth living for. When one is young, abstract truth seems very abstract indeed when it entails the forfeit of a warm, tangible human happiness. To us, almost totally unlearned in the things of God, the religion for which we had paid this price seemed a bleak, constricting affair of obligational routine. In our blindness we could not know that the first fumbling exercise of faith in the dark had wrought the beginnings of a transformation, that the stumbling-block was a stepping-stone.

Deprivation is one of the greatest and deepest channels of God's grace, since He Himself fills the void which He has permitted or ordained. To be forced to give up something for the sake of a principle leads one naturally enough to a closer examination of the source of the principle which has entailed this difficult decision. At this point our generation were in for a searching trial. We had learned our Catechism unquestioningly; now, with several years of adult life behind us, we returned to it with more receptive minds. The effect was devastating: not only was it like reading it for the first time, but the depths upon depths concealed in the simple questions and answers opened like chasms at our feet: what had been a comfortable classroom primer suddenly revealed itself as an apocalyptic vision. And we had actually accepted all that that vision entailed, by the fact of our Baptism we were committed to all it entailed!

Conversion, especially for those who have complacently counted themselves among the initiated, is not comfortable: it is the first stage in the process of being turned upside down. This crushing realization of what the Catholic Church demands of her children had the effect of throwing many of us temporarily off our balance. From carefree, thoughtless acceptance we were plunged into agonies of apprehension: stumbling-block number two hurtled into our paths with overwhelming violence. We had not been trained to test our reactions in the steady light of reason, and against the "fear that walks by night" we had no protection. For some time we became thoroughly neurotic on the subject of religion: devoid as we were of any sense of proportion, the letter of the law extinguished the spirit.

No one who has not been through this particular form of mental torture can gauge its intensity. Those of us who were fortunate survived, but many at this point fell away. There is no spiritual disease for which the Church of Christ does not hold the remedy: as Christ Incarnate healed the whole of the wounded human race, so in His Mystical Body He continues the selfsame labour of love. "All power is given to Me in heaven and on earth," He said after the resurrection, and to His disciples, "In My name you shall cast out devils." Only in the Church of Christ is this authority to be found; and this particular devil is cast out not by prayer and fasting, but by prayer and obedience. For the judgment that is distorted and obscured there is the assurance of Him Who said, "He who heareth you, heareth Me." It is not easy to submit one's judgment, and a diseased mind submits less easily than one which is healthy, since lunatics, in their own opinion, are the only sane people in a world of madmen. Only if and when subjective phobias, misconceptions and obsessions are surmounted by an act of confidence in that authority, can this stumbling-block become a foothold. "The fear of the Lord is the beginning of wisdom," but the love of the Lord is the fulfilling of the law, and absolute confidence is the first-fruit of love.

Once the fog of false fear had lifted, the horizon was infinitely enticing. Catholicism, we discovered, was not a dry formula to be learned by rote nor an impossible set of rules to trip one up, it was the most fascinating subject in the world. It demanded the whole of oneself: it was inexhaustible. In the first intoxication of this discovery, many of us lost our heads again (after all, they were new to the job; they had only been functioning, and that spasmodically, for half a dozen years at most). We were now fired with explorers' zeal to scale the heights: spiritual *nouveaux riches,* we longed to scatter largesse. Only the best was good enough for God: He should have our very best. The mistake many of us made was forgivable: "the best" was the most costly. Nor did we glance at the elementary truism that the most expensive present is not always the most acceptable to the recipient: in God's service the most costly is not *necessarily* the best in His eyes. We were in love with our own ideas of generosity and, fearful perhaps of being like the rich young man who "turned away sorrowful, because his possessions were very great," we entirely forgot the equally cogent parable of another man who went forth to a battle that was not his instead of parleying for peace. Asceticism and renunciation, for the sake of asceticism and renunciation, became our idols. Headlong we crashed over stumbling-block number three: mistaking our path, relying unconsciously on our own strength, we failed—dismally, utterly.

This was the most crucial trial of all. It was the most crucial because it was apparently final: we had been tried—and found wanting. This was more than a stumbling-block: it was a tombstone.

Now each individual soul is a unique and irreplaceable part of God's design, a separate miracle of creation. The gift of life itself is the first and greatest vocation, since God the Creator called each one of us by a secret name when He summoned us out of nothing, by His word. To each one of us He has said, through the prophecy of Isaias, "I have redeemed thee and called thee by thy name: thou art Mine." For each one of us the way by which we attain to Him is unique and solitary: for each one of us there is but one guide.

The solution to this enigma, the answer to this vital problem which is the only *raison d'être* of our lives, was given by Christ to His first followers in simple language. He said, "*I am the way: no man cometh to the Father save through Me.*" It is the personal love of Christ, therefore, which is the "spiritual sense" that alone will indicate to each one the path by which he must travel, which will keep him to that path, which will reclaim him when he has wandered from it; and "this 'spiritual sense' will be possessed by an individual as a fruit of his spiritual life, according as the Mysteries of Christ are accomplished in his soul and he passes into the 'new man,' being 'converted to the Lord.' "[1]

At this point we return to St. Peter and to the tombstone. To those who have been given the grace of first conversion— i.e., the realization of what the Christian life really entails if it is to be lived "in spirit and in truth"—the first two stumbling-blocks are comparatively easy to surmount: the wreck of material happiness can, by the very cleanness and finality of its end, be a stimulus; the realization of one's inherent sinfulness in the sight of God's transcendent purity, after the initial shock, is seen as a wholesome purgative to complacency; but to suffer the wreck of one's spiritual hopes must either make or mar. Judas and St. Peter are the classic examples: both failed disastrously, but the one, hardening in pride, saw his sin blotting out God's mercy; the other, chastened in humility, saw Christ's love blotting out his sin. To the one it was the ultimate stumbling-block, to the other the final stepping-stone which led to an entirely new life on quite another plane. " . . . According as the Mysteries of Christ are accomplished in his soul and he passes into the 'new man' " . . . behind the tombstone, in the darkness of near-despair, can be made the blind act of faith by which the mystery of Christ's resurrection is accomplished in our souls.

[1] Dom Ralph Russell, O.S.B., *Downside Review,* September 1951.

The exact wording is important: our wills consent, the accomplishment of the mystery is His alone. Capsized, emptied of every vestige of illusion and self-sufficiency, we either succumb finally to despair or we surrender unconditionally to Christ.

"Thou *knowest* that I love Thee!" St. Peter's reproachful cry to the risen Christ, following as it did upon his thrice-repeated denial of the suffering Christ, might be mistaken for presumption, did we not know with what immediate response it was met and with what a reward it was crowned —"Another shall lead thee . . . Thereby signifying by what death he should glorify God."

"Death, the end of action, is sheer contemplation and passion. We do not manage to die; it is done for us."[1] In their context these words referred to physical death, but they are even more applicable to this crucial surrender which entails the death of self, the mystical death of love. "We do not manage to die; it is done for us." All that is required is an unconditional "Yes" to Christ, Who said, "If any man open to Me . . . I will come in to him." We have only to lay ourselves open, wide open, without a single reservation or preconceived idea, to the invasion of His soliciting love. *Tollite portas vestras et elevamini, et introibit Rex gloriae.* He will enter because it is His desire: it is what He came for: it was the meaning of His Incarnation. The course of His invasion may be swift or slow, but the outcome is certain—the crushing and slaying of self-love. This is true "contemplation and passion"; it is complete conversion. If, as Christ said, no one by thought can add to his stature one cubit, still less by self-consideration can one decrease one's stature one inch. Self-love cannot be exterminated by self-examination nor even by self-hatred: self dies only in self-

[1] Hans Urs von Balthasar, *Thérèse of Lisieux* (New York, Sheed & Ward, 1954).

56

forgetfulness, absorbed in the sight of the Beloved. "Thou hast shown me Thy ways and Thou shalt fill me with the joy of Thy countenance." It is "passion" because it is His action, not ours: it is beneath His hands, acquiescent, quiescent in the darkness, that one suffers the throes of that death which are the pangs of birth.

The reason then why any one of us can say, "I am still a Catholic" is very simple. It is because, each in our secret and solitary way, we have discovered the truth of His words, "*I* am the way." We have discovered through experience that faith is not simply an intellectual assent to a creed, but fidelity to a Person: it is that troth which is "the highest thing a man may keep," a troth beside which all other love troths are as shadows to the substance. The Catechism, the very Gospels themselves, can only teach us *about* God: it is life, the willed acceptance, however weak and wavering, of the Christian life, which teaches us God Himself, through the Christ-life: and the faintest glimmer of that personal knowledge is worth years upon years of painful trial and error, of frustration, bewilderment, failure, and the loss of anything or everything else. The smallest fragment of that vision makes everything worth-while. "God made me," says the Catechism, "to know Him, love Him and serve Him." Once the personal knowledge, in the framework of the general knowledge, is vouchsafed, the love is born—"I know Him in whom I have believed."

And the service? Here too the answer is simple. "Another shall lead thee by a way that thou wouldst not"; or, conversely, "Thy will be done on earth as it is in heaven." But what *is* God's will? Theology teaches that He is essentially simple: His will is Himself. The Christian life of grace is the "adoption" by which we are made the sons of God: we exist in the eyes of God the Father only insofar as we are incorporated with Christ. How this rebirth, this one-ing, this incorporation, is brought about, St. John tells us in the first verses of his Gospel: we are to be born "not of the flesh, nor of the will of man, but of God." The signified will of God therefore, embraced in its entirety, is the impelling creative force which forms Christ in us. "*I* am the way, the truth and the life," said Christ. The individual Christian life is His individual unfolding of Himself: Himself, in a thousand disguises of circumstances, events, human contacts, no less than in apparent contradictions, temporal and spiritual —Himself, in the everlasting trysting-place, the "Now" where eternity and time intersect.

But simple acquiescence is not sufficient, nor is resignation good enough. "One does not," remarked one of George Bernanos' characters, "speak of *resigning* oneself to being loved." "Thy kingdom come. Thy will be done on earth *as it is in heaven*"—a sentence we most of us say every day, a sentence which we have not perhaps thoroughly understood. Once we have grasped its full implications, we have discovered the source of an unquenchable fountain of joy. "The Kingdom of heaven is within," said Christ. Yes, heaven is not here or there, like a place on a map; heaven is not so much a place at all as it is—a Person.

Frederick Wilhelmsen

Frederick D. Wilhelmsen was born in 1923 in Detroit, of Danish and Swiss ancestry, studied at the University of Detroit, San Francisco and Notre Dame. He teaches Philosophy at the University of Santa Clara. His first book, Hilaire Belloc, No Alienated Man, *was published in 1953. He is married and has three children.*

God is trundled through the streets of England once again. The Mystery Plays of York are revived. In medieval times, God was seated high upon the top level of a triple stage: an old gentleman with a great beard carried about on a cart by the guildsmen of the city. Below him, Christ was lying in a manger, was dying on the Cross, and was rising from the tomb, and on the lowest stage— at the very bottom—"Sathanus the fiend" was roasting in hell.

This drama in York symbolizes the faith I have known in the Catholic Church. To domesticate the drama of creation and redemption, and thereby to throw into awesome relief the tragedy of the fall of man and the evil that thus entered into the universe, is to fix as by a sign those truths of the Faith that have gripped me most powerfully all my life. For me, creation has always been unique, local, and therefore domestic. All those philosophies beyond the Church that have exalted the cosmos at the expense of the

59

shrine seem not only lacking in truth, but failing in poetry and dignity. So too, our Redemption is wrought not through some system of ethical abstractions, but through a Divine Person. This answers a deep-rooted need of mine: loyalty. Outside the Catholic Church, where is there any suitable object of absolute loyalty? Could I be loyal to a man who lived long ago and preached a noble doctrine on the shores of the Sea of Galilee? For those of us who were born into the Church, this is not enough: we have the living Christ.

In the old days, the men of York dressed Christ as one of their own in the rough doublets of the country yeomanry. In the chivalric Book of Hours, Our Lady appeared as a young woman of the court. In so doing, the men of the Middle Ages proved themselves profoundly historical and profoundly Catholic. It is said everywhere that medieval man had a low sense of history; the judgment is Hegelian or Marxist, or both: in any case false. To be so full of the past that it is clothed in the garb of the present is not to miss history; it is rather to thrust history forward into the very courtyard of the present. But this truth merely prefigures the essence of history, which is Christ present forever in His Mystical Body.

Finally, to place Satan just a few feet under Our Lord on the same cart, as it is pulled down the narrow streets for all to gaze upon in wonder, is not only to remind man that he is involved in a "terrible aboriginal calamity," but also to teach him that what looks like a meaningless and absurd universe is not. Although things *are* what they seem to be, sin can make what is *not*, look as though it were. Appearances to the contrary, sin and evil are not the texture of the world, and therefore we must harden ourselves in hope.

The Catholic Church explains herself. She is an absolute,

relative to nothing but God. Even more, since the Church bears God within her bosom in the Sacrament of the Altar, by participation the Church supports the whole of His creation. Thus she harbours the beauty of this world, and in blessing all things as she does wherever her life is lived in its fullness, she sends them forth, enjoining them to be themselves and to lead the life prefigured for them in the Wisdom of God.

A born Catholic, aware that he is a member of a "chosen race, a royal priesthood, a holy nation, a special people," and asked why he finds himself within the Church, can only answer that he really does not know. God gives him the Faith, but why God gives it is among the inscrutable things. God desires his salvation, but why God does is hidden in the Divine Will, and although he can know sometimes what the Will of God is, he cannot know why He wills as He does. Still, as God creates each man separately and endows him with an existence that is his own and incommunicable, so too does the Church come to each man as to an individual person, filling needs that are his own, and giving vision to those private intimations of the truth he may have traced in the darkness of his reason. The man born into the Church, baptized into its membership as an infant, discovers frequently enough that some of the Catholic truths have always informed and given depth and substance to needs and judgments he is prone to think peculiarly his own. Or he may find he has not really understood some doctrine of the Faith until its cogency, struck home only after much living in the world, finally forced him to judge things and men to be as they actually are.

I see the things that are and need not be. I believe that what once was, must in some sense, now be. Nothing is really lost; history is contemporary with the present. Through all the years the Church has fulfilled this early

61

vision, and has confirmed this persistent belief: the mystery of being and the majesty of Christendom transfigured in the twin doctrines of the Creation and the Mystical Body. But there is a third Catholic doctrine that never meant much to me as a boy: the doctrine of sin and evil. As a child, I thought myself incorruptible, both morally and physically. Sin had only the vague outline of a reality within my mind. Now I know its monstrous tragedy. Evil thus seen has not dimmed my first wonder at the mystery of things; my early belief that the entire course of history is united in sharing the gift of existence is still intact; I still hold that being calls forth from man the pledge of loyalty both to the gift and to the Giver. This grasp of evil and imperfection locks with my affirmations on creation and history, and the three of them provide an approach to my own personal understanding of the Faith. Of course, no Catholic grounds his faith on his own speculations. The Church is an absolute, and is measured only by God.

To look at the universe and fail to see it as created by God is to judge it a world completely absurd. This is the only sane judgment that can be made by a man who will not affirm God.

Facing reality today, those thinking men who are not of the Catholic Church (and who are not influenced by her) usually react in one of two ways. Some accept an absurd world and try to live with it as best they can; these are the sceptics who have always known it was either Rome or disillusion, and who, like Santayana, have not been afraid of disillusion. Others are sceptical of God, but not of man; the civilized integrity of thoroughgoing scepticism is too exacting for them; they cannot bear to live without meaning; they place their faith in human perfectibility, and then they go on to introduce their own kind of order into the universe; they attempt to dissolve the absurdities in existence; they tidy up the mess. These last are the "secular humanists." They are numbered by the millions in the Western world today. This is their century and they know it.

I have a great sympathy for the first kind of man—the absolute sceptic—because he neither denies the mystery of things, nor does he wound an already bleeding universe. He does not add to the absurdities. For the second kind of man—the secular humanist—I confess no sympathy at all. To pretend to a sympathy I do not feel in order to gain an apologetic foothold in the secularist camp, would be to fall into a great lie. This kind of person irritates, and the irritation is rendered the more difficult to bear because the men in question wish to dissolve the absurdities inherent in existing reality, and they succeed only in adding to them.

It is time I defined my terms: by absurdity I do not mean tragedy in the strict sense of the term. The ancients knew well enough that tragedy is invested with a high nobility; there is a sombre meaning, a black intelligibility, running through all genuine tragedy, filling it with the dignity of drama. We can follow the tragic hero to his destruction, and although we suffer with him, our reason is satisfied; we know why he came to his end. This is not the case with absurdity. The absurd is the meaningless. Not only does this kind of evil wound, but it bewilders. We see no reason for it; it is a vacant stare upon the broken countenance of human existence. Absurdities are everywhere. Each man can make his own list. This is mine: the cynicism of the rich, the cheapness of love, the loss of innocence in children, the blindness of the learned, the scattering of the family, the suffering of the sick, the death of infants, and the carrying of coffins. Surveying this desolation of withered expectations—steadily, without panic—the sceptic must, and does, estimate the world senseless, a place empty, and altogether without hope. "Depart from hope all ye who enter here": thus Dante, inscribing the portals of Hell; thus the sceptic, pronouncing judgment on this world. "If Christ be not risen, our faith is in vain." Without Him risen, and without God creating, the world is as the sceptic declares it to be. The sceptic is in the Pauline tradition. He reminds us that we are ransomed men; men rescued from his own vision of existence. He is part of the furniture of the Faith.

But the sceptical breed is vanishing in our day. It is being replaced rapidly by men of the other sort: the "secular humanists," those men who, refusing to recognize sin and evil as part and parcel of the universe in its present fallen state, refusing to see the world as fundamentally absurd from every canon of "secular" reason, ignore or sentimentalize evils that are absolutely unredeemable, and view all the others as "problems" to be dissolved by themselves through techniques developed in their own minds, forged with their own hands, and exercised by their own wills. This philosophy parades under many names, but perhaps the "secular humanist" label is the most accurate of all; "humanist" because man is made the measure of all things, and "secular" because salvation is thought to be within the reach of the powers of nature as mastered by scientific and social action.

Like Milton's Adam and Eve, the secular humanists go forth into life with "the world all before them," preaching "the happy end." And this is the irony of their progress: they heal no wounds; they dissolve no absurdities; they rather add to them. The secularists think they can eliminate human suffering, and for every cripple they send forth whole in body, they admit to their temples a man sick in mind. For every border raid they put down, they loose upon humanity a war more hideous than the last. They extend the franchise, and they cheapen the citizenry. They broaden the base of education, and they lessen the product. They suppress superstition, and raise up a mob of cynics. Wisdom is nothing to them, and the Christian tradition—full as it is of chivalry and romance—is utterly beyond the pale of their narrow and mechanical comprehension. They pull down the moral law in the name of freedom, and set up a hundred prohibitions in its place. They preach life, and establish by law murder clinics for the unborn in Sweden. Addicted as they are to measuring and counting, they would quantify all existence, level away every distinction, destroy the memory of the past, and finally stifle the movement of the human heart to rise above the level of the collectivity.

Secular humanism is man's conferring divinity on himself, and is thus not only a violation of the First Commandment, but is also the crowning absurdity within the whole history of the human race, for what could be more ridiculous than man worshipping himself? Absurd, for when man begins to admire himself in a mirror his pride makes him less attractive than before. Meaningless, because the vaunted earthly paradise is not at hand, because suffering is still with us, because the universe still groans under evil, because men are not better than they were, because men are worse than they were.

I admire the realism of the pure sceptic in confronting the fact of human absurdity. I deplore the refusal of the secular humanist to look existence in the face; he is a latter-day Pollyanna, blithely dancing through a graveyard, gathering roses while he sings songs of the happy time.

To refuse to look at evil is to fall into secular humanism. To look once at evil is to see it as the sceptic sees it. To look twice is to see it as the Catholic sees it: as a wound, a laceration cutting away the edges of being, but leaving intact the central mystery—the truth that men and things are, and are good. Reality is not what it ought to be; all things falter, and nothing falters more than man. Unless he take to worshipping himself, any man who thinks at all must be outraged at his own paltriness; he becomes aware that the actuality is but a mask, hiding the face that should be his own. This is a discovery of lost perfection, for I could not be horrified unless there was a memory inscribed in my nature of what I was intended to be. When I survey the wreckage of the human soul, I hear music curling round the ruined city of man; I hear trumpets sounding through the recesses of the human heart, proclaiming dignity, a lost paradise, and the promise of an eternal fatherland.

The irony of human reality and human possibility, the disproportion between what we are and what we can be, is an evident fact of experience. Seen together they trace a cosmic tragedy. Tragedy, once again, is full of meaning, and the Church alone possesses that meaning. Lying at the origin of all literature is the story of a Golden Age, and lying in the centre of every human soul is the hope. But only the Church guarantees the story, and only she fulfills the hope, bringing, as she does, grace through Christ, reconciling all fallen things to God. Without the Faith, we would be doomed to discover the possibility of perfection and beatitude, without discovering any means for their fulfillment. But "what we cannot do by ourselves, we can do through our friends," says St. Thomas Aquinas. The Church offers the friendship of God through Christ our Brother in the flesh, and this friendship is not only the hope of the world to come, but is also the only hope for mankind within history. This last truth I do not take on the teaching authority of the Church; I take it on my own experience and on whatever judgment I may possess concerning the history of Western civilization.

St. Paul tells us that Faith is of things unseen, but I do not need Faith to know that I am not what I ought to be, that I am involved in sin along with the whole of mankind. I do not need Faith to teach me that wherever the Catholic Church is accepted in the fullness of her teaching, there will I find men fully human and themselves. To contrast the secularized world with the remnants of Catholic Christendom, is to come to know all the more, if not the final meaning of grace, then certainly its effect in history. "Faith is of things unseen": true enough, but "by their fruits ye shall know them." These fruits cause me to rejoice in the patrimony that is mine. They root me all the more firmly to this holy company, the Catholic Church.

What kind of man does the Church make? I do not mean what kind of man does the Church shelter; she shelters all men, and it is one of her glories that those rejected by the world can find friendship and hope only within her walls. But the full Catholic, the man made by the Church through and through—the fruit of the Faith—what is he like? He is the man who, finding himself in a finite universe, looks within his soul and discovers, not only a nature limited in its very substance, but a nature wounded by that "terrible aboriginal calamity." The first of his virtues is humility: the realist acceptance of finite perfection. The second of his virtues is loyalty: a firm cleaving to the reserves of reality at hand for the creation of a decent personal life, and a just social order. The Roman Catholic conserves whatever God has given him, whatever his ancestors have bequeathed him. A profound reverence for creation informs his mind, stamps itself on all his art, is translated into the way he wrestles with nature in the struggle for survival, colours his relationship with society and with the state, steadies him in success, and anneals him in adversity. He knows the meaning of contingency, and he treads gently upon being, lest he shatter that most absolute of gifts. He does not tinker with existence. He rather celebrates reality. The vine and the cup are not foreign to him: he knows the meaning of sacrifice: he knows mystery.

I wish to be united with such men; not simply with those who are walking around the crust of the globe at this moment, but with all of them—those dead, those living, and those still to come. This attitude toward history is neither Greek nor modern, but Roman.

To the Greeks, history was nothing but time, and human salvation was achieved only by a flight into the abstract order. For the Greek metaphysical mind the only things worth saving from history were ideals. But the salvation of ideals does not, in the words of Newman, "warm the desolation of my heart." Nor does a handful of ideals satisfy a man burying his dead. As for the modern conception of history, it has even less depth than the Greek. It is untouched by imagination, and is altogether pedestrian. Nothing so refreshes the man of today as to be told he has met the challenge of history by moving with the times. Mobilism has become, not only a sign of intelligence, but a mark of virtue, and an evidence of high moral probity. But there is no poetry in all this; nor is there courage; this is a trick relieving men of the duty of fighting the times when they are bad, and although the times are always more or less bad, today they are worse than ever before. The Roman view of history was something completely different. It was rooted in the fundamental human need for familial and corporate continuity. It was full of piety. Man was not looked upon as an isolated atom, drifting amorphously in the fluidity of time. Man counted for more than "the flies of a summer morning." The famous *pietas* united all men in one society.

To the old Roman at his best (and at his worst) the family is knit together by blood and a common land turned over by hands that have received their patrimony from a line of ancestors stretching back to the youth of the race. The dusk falls on the back of each man as he retreats down the road of time, but as he has received from the past, so has he given to the future, and as they lived in him, so shall he live in them. And this is promised him by the household gods, and even when he no longer believes in his gods he still keeps them, for they are the badge of his service and the pledge of his immortality.

But what was symbol to the pagan, is reality for the Catholic. The Mystical Body of Christ unites all ages into one company, and I can talk to Augustine, not as to a memory, but as to a man. The Incarnation did not destroy time, but raised it to an altogether new dimension. When St. Paul speaks of the "life of Christ" he usually does not mean the thirty-three years Our Lord spent on earth. He means, as Msgr. Knox has said, an "energy" poured out on the world, filling all times, and transcending each one of them, uniting together the whole course of mankind, making the Franks before Tours the companions of the heroes of the Alcazar. The Catholic holds his youth against an aging universe; he begins his eternity while still a wayfarer within a world that passes.

The Catholic sees reality at the centre, and the centre is Christ, and as Christ is He through whom all things are created, the Catholic sees creation. Very early in life, I was filled with the mystery of being. When quite young I got down to the meaning of contingency, without knowing the name. Although I am not what I ought to be, I exist, and I do not have to exist at all. I find myself in a world that reflects my own fragile hold on being. To say that the universe of things need not exist does not mean that the universe need not have ever existed. *It is to say that here and now it need not be.* There is nothing in it, absolutely nothing,

69

calling forth its existence. The head demands the arm, and the arm demands the hand, but neither of them demands being. Chesterton's line about the "impossible things that are" sums up this absolute mystery lying at the centre of reality. Things are impossible in themselves, and at first sight it seems far more reasonable that there should be nothing, rather than something. Yet nothing is not; things are, and all of them keep on doing something so utterly mysterious that it dizzies the intelligence, and rocks the imagination. Defying abstract formulation, even the poet falters when he attempts to express it. That which things keep on doing, is—being. As a dancer does an act of dancing, so do all things do an act of being, and why they should so act, no man knows. St. Thomas expresses this, of course, in terms of participation. Each thing that is, shares in an existence not its own by right.

To pierce thus into reality, to go below the surface, swarming as it is with sin and disease and evil, is to affirm this world to be as it is: not an accumulation of sense phenomena, not my "representation" as Schopenhauer declared, not a series of "problems" to be explored by secular humanists, not a vast cosmos of raw materials to be exploited by a machine—but as the heritage of existence: a barony held in fief for the Lord.

For we men are, in truth, vassals, and the claim we have on existence is borrowed, and thus we owe allegiance to the God who gives us being, and even to the being He gives us, since the being is God's being, although not the Being of God. Fealty, piety, loyalty, the swearing of allegiance, the pledging of swords, and the bending of the knee—these are the realities that are always playing out their chivalric drama in the back of my consciousness, and neither doctrine nor polity that fails to place them to the forefront can ever receive from me more than passing curiosity, or half-hearted

70

attention. The Church has come to me all these years preaching her awesome doctrine of the "I Am Who Am" and of
His terrible Love, and of His betrayal and death on a cross
of Wood, and of His Kingship over all men in his Body the
Church. This is my vision of existence. This answers.

Antonia White

Antonia White was born in 1899 and educated at the Convent of the Sacred Heart, Roehampton, and at St. Paul's Girls' School. She worked for many years in advertising agencies and as a free-lance journalist. Her first novel, Frost in May, *was published in 1933. Two other novels are* The Lost Traveller *(1950),* The Sugar House *(1950). A fourth novel* Beyond the Glass *will be published in the autumn of 1954, and a collection of short stories,* Strangers, *is coming out in the summer of 1954. Has also done a considerable amount of reviewing and critical articles for literary periodicals. During the war she worked in the B.B.C. and in P.I.D. of the Foreign Office (French section). She has recently translated several French books, including Colette's* La Chalte. *With her first translation, Maupassant's* Une Vie *(1949), she won the Denyse Clairouin prize. She has two daughters and one grandson.*

I cannot be called a "cradle Catholic" since I was not received into the Church till I was seven years old, after the conversion of both my parents. My first reaction when I was told that I too was to become a Roman Catholic was one of dismay. From the age of four, being an only—and possibly rather precocious—child I had been an omnivorous reader of everything from pious Victorian children's books to Scott and Dickens. And all of these, when they referred to Roman Catholics, did so with strong disapproval. Naturally I dared not mention that I already believed them to be so superstitious and idolatrous as not to be proper Christians at all, as well as being often extremely wicked. If my father, the best and cleverest man in the whole world whose word was law, said they were all right, the books must be wrong. But it was all very confusing.

Presumably because I had reached "the age of reason," I was instructed for several months before I was received, by the eminent Jesuit who had instructed my parents. I learnt eagerly and conscientiously. My father said it was true and that was all that mattered. If he had told me one day that he had decided that, after all, it wasn't true, I am sure I should have renounced everything Father Sidney Smith had taught me. As it was, I entered unquestioningly into a new world, at once fascinating and alarming.

I think the teaching of Catholic doctrine to children in those days laid more stress on God's retributive justice than on His mercy. There seemed so terribly many ways in which a Catholic could offend God. Though I realized it was a great privilege to be one, it was also a great responsibility, since one could not plead ignorance before the Judgment Seat. Sometimes I longed for the carefree days before I had acquired all this disturbing knowledge. Then I would be in a panic that I had committed a grave sin against Faith. I had learnt one could sin in thought as well as in word and deed. How could I be sure that I had not given "full consent" to such a wicked wish?

However, I did foresee one clear gain, one unclouded joy in becoming a Catholic: I should have Our Blessed Lady for my heavenly Mother. Everything I had heard about her had inspired me with complete confidence. I was received on the Feast of the Immaculate Conception, 1906. She laid her hand on me that day and she has never removed it, not even during the thirteen years when I ceased to be either a believing or a practising Catholic.

For the first two years after my reception I never met another Catholic child. I looked forward immensely to going to a school where I would be like everybody else. Ironically, it was not till I went as a boarder to a well-known convent that I felt the real misery of being "different." In this wildly unfamiliar atmosphere, a nine-year-old convert—and a middle-class one at that—was as conspicuous as a sparrow in a flock of canaries. However, I settled down in time, and, in many ways, was very happy.

I cannot be sufficiently grateful for certain aspects of that six years' training. Our spiritual and devotional education was admirable: religion was woven into the texture of our daily lives so that earth and heaven no longer seemed far apart but interpenetrating at every point. The best and deepest impression left on me was that of the teaching and the personality of Father Alban Goodier, S.J. (late Archbishop of Bombay), who was for some time our School Chaplain. His weekly sermons and his retreats struck a note of quiet depth, of what I can only call authenticity, that I had never heard before and have never quite caught again in any other preacher. I can see him now, a shy, soldierly man, fiddling with the red marker of his New Testament as he preached and talking like a reserved person forced to speak his most intimate thoughts aloud. He impressed me as someone for whom the love of God was such a living, absorbing reality that it was the very marrow of his being.

Our education, though biased by a good many suppressions and distortions of temporal fact in the supposed interest of eternal truth, was wider and more unified than the specialized exam-cramming at the secular school I went on to at fifteen. Our lessons were planned so that one subject dovetailed with and illuminated the others. We were given a sense of perspective and continuity in history and culture, unfolding in sequence from Greece to our own day. Within

74

the limits of strict censorship, any natural feeling we had for art and literature was encouraged, while music and languages were quite admirably taught. But there were other elements in our training which still seem to me far from admirable. I am talking of forty years ago, and I understand things are very different now both in this and other convent schools. What we most lacked in my day was any kind of freedom: freedom to dispose of even half an hour of our own time as we chose, freedom to read any book except those in the very restrictive school library (some, even of these, were censored and mutilated), freedom, above all, to express the faintest doubt or criticism or even to argue in our own defense or another's in manifest cases of injustice. The nuns were meant to be regarded as the direct representatives of God, as if we were nuns ourselves "under obedience." I cannot believe this is good either for teachers or pupils. They had the right to read our incoming or outgoing letters, even to our own parents, and to withhold them without telling us, if they disapproved of the contents. It was a peculiarly dangerous training for girls going out as a minority into the confusing maelstrom of values that followed the First World War. Without accusing the nuns of anything so vulgar as snobbery, I should say that they tended to identify Catholicism with a particular order of society. Though they had a tender regard for the poor, provided they "knew their place," they envisaged any menace to the privileges of the upper, particularly the landowning, class as something dangerously like heresy. It was inevitable that many of the girls who went out to "defend the Faith" could not distinguish between essentials and inessentials and regarded the mildest political or social innovations as a direct attack on the Church.

Moreover, this inflexible education often defeated its own ends. Freedom and justice were particularly intoxicating ideas to those who had chafed under a régime against which there was no appeal. Confronted with facts and opinions which had been suppressed or distorted, their very lack of training in impartial judgment or wholesome scepticism made them all the more uncritically receptive of other points of view, especially when presented by people of higher intellectual calibre than their former teachers.

I had been taught to regard those who did not accept the Catholic faith as either knaves or fools. Now I met people who were manifestly neither but who very definitely rejected it, some on rational and not a few on ethical grounds. It was a shock to find that so many sceptics and atheists had a far stronger moral sense than some Catholics, though they expected no eternal reward for their virtue. Moreover, they were as ready, if not readier, to make heavy personal sacrifices for their ideals. It was impossible not to be impressed by this detached love of the good for its own sake, by this freedom of spirit which was not always anxiously wondering about its own salvation and engaged in keeping a kind of profit-and-loss account with eternity.

Though inwardly assailed by a great many doubts and self-questionings, for the next twelve years after leaving the convent I remained outwardly a staunch Catholic, attempting to defend the Church against all comers, though the stock answers I had learnt often seemed as unsatisfactory to me as to my hearers. My belief in God was unshaken, even though the "rational" proofs of His existence which I had learnt did not convince my sceptical friends. But often it seemed to me that this huge edifice of dogmatism and legalism, this empire which so fiercely resented any loss of temporal or political power, was very far removed from Christ's simplicity. The heavy burdens it laid on people, its proud complacency, painfully suggested the behaviour of the scribes and Pharisees whom Christ Himself had condemned.

Sermons fulminated against the materialism of the age, but the Church in general seemed to be not only far from indifferent to wealth and property but imbued with a kind of spiritual materialism.

It would be impossible, apart from lack of space, to determine all the complex and overlapping causes which led to my loss of faith. All that I can say here is that I reached a stage where I was convinced it was intellectually dishonest to believe in God. It cost me quite a lot to renounce this belief which had been so natural to me from childhood, long before I was received into the Church. Along with a sense of freedom and certainly a good deal of pride in having "faced up to the truth," there was a sense of emptiness. It took me a long time to acclimatize myself to a universe in which man was the highest form of being and all values determined by the human mind and the human psyche. Yet there was an austere beauty in this world where everything acquired a peculiar intensity and poignancy precisely because all that was beautiful or true or good could only be perceived and enjoyed during the span of human life. The perception itself was the only reward, and this applied equally in the spheres of morality, philosophy, religion and art. In this "Santayan" view, the great religions of the world were marvellous creations of the human spirit; embodiments of its high, but unrealizable, aspirations. Their only flaw lay in their mistaking poetic for literal truth. And, for Santayana, the Catholic religion was the most splendid and complete embodiment of "poetic truth." His philosophy inevitably appealed to someone temperamentally allergic to a bleak rationalism of the Bertrand Russell type, and for whom art was beginning to appear the highest and purest of human activities. Civilizations and even religions perished, but the art they had engendered survived. Art was neither dogmatic nor aggressive: no one had ever been tortured or oppressed in its name; it neither lusted for power nor forced people to submit to its domination. The discipline it imposed was voluntary and the delight it gave was offered freely and unconditionally to all.

Yet thirteen years were to pass before I was able, for an ironically brief period, to see Catholicism as a work of art. I could not separate it in my mind from my first approach to it even as a small child, when I had accepted it on my father's word as "true" in the most brutally literal sense. Did the Church contain the truth or did she not? That had been the burning question for my father in the long period of mental struggle which I now knew had preceded his conversion. He had staked everything on his conviction that she did, thereby seriously damaging his career.

The idea of there being a truth which it was desperately important to know and accept was too obstinately ingrained in me to throw it off, however hard I tried. There were too many mysteries to which my mind restlessly demanded a key. If there were so much the highest human intelligence could neither understand nor explain, it seemed to me there must be some order of Being infinitely superior to man. It might not be the God in whom I had once believed, but I felt there must be a spiritual world which existed independently of matter. Even in the realm of art where I felt most naturally at home, it was significant that the greatest poetry and sculpture of East and West implied such a belief and was often inspired directly by it. Surely there must be a way of discovering some universal, valid source of truth and making contact with it? I followed other clues . . . Spinoza and Lao-Tse, Buddha and the Bhagavad-Ghita. Often I seemed to be on the brink of finding what I sought. Human beings differed so immensely in temperament and gifts: perhaps one must look for the path best suited to one's particular nature and follow that. The truth

must be one, but there might be many roads to it. Yet whichever way I turned, there was always the great inexplicable
figure of Christ which must either be fitted in or explained
away. Confronted with Buddha's "way" I could not forget
that Christ had said "I *am* the way." What great Master had
dared to speak with such authority . . . to declare that He
was not only the way, but the truth and the life? If He were
not what He claimed to be, He was the greatest impostor of
history. I tried reading the Gospels without preconceived
ideas, as if they were some astonishing, newly-discovered
document. Nothing about the puzzling yet sublime figure
they described suggested either a self-deceiver or one who
wished to deceive others. And there were features about
Him quite unlike the great Eastern spiritual teachers. He
was crucified. He said that He would draw all men to Himself, not merely those who had reached a certain stage of
spiritual development. There was a kind of violence about
Him, unlike the passive serenity of Buddha: He said He
came to bring not peace, but a sword. And His disciples, a
quarrelsome, cowardly set of men, were always misunderstanding His teaching. Instead of consciously achieving
spiritual enlightenment through successive stages, enlightenment suddenly descended on them after He had left them,
not as calm illumination but in the form of wind and fire
which induced not contemplative stillness but such frenzied
activity that people thought they were drunk. If Christ were
indeed the great Master, might not the Catholic Church
have distorted His teaching by trying to buttress it with
philosophy and elaborate theological propositions? He had
said Himself, "the letter killeth but the spirit giveth life."
Nowhere in the Gospels was there any appeal to reason,
only to faith. He had said we were to adore God not in
temples, but in spirit and in truth. Was there anywhere I
could find the essence of His teaching, freed from the accre-

tion of ritual, dogma, and legalism? For a short time, I was tempted to go back to my very earliest sources, to the "evangelism" which had so strongly tinged the books I had read and loved in my early childhood before I became a Catholic. I was attracted by the Methodists, but they oversimplified the gospel to the point of meagreness. I was deeply impressed by the Quaker mystic John Woolman. I came in contact with Quakers and was attracted by their total reliance on God and their selfless charity towards man. But nowhere could I find anything which offered a key to all the mysteries and paradoxes of human nature and the universe in which it found itself. If there were no key and this life were all I had, it was high time I stopped speculating what it was all about and got on with the business of living as fully as I could.

I have said above that Our Lady kept her hand on me during those thirteen years of restless wandering. They were years of moral and psychological confusion as well as mental. They included a period during which I was only saved from total breakdown by over three years of strict Freudian analysis. Yet, through all this time, my belief in Our Lady remained an odd, isolated fact which nothing could destroy.

Illogically, though I could question the divinity and even the existence of her Son, she continued to be a reality for me. Nothing could reduce her to a beautiful idea or an Archetype or a Mother-fantasy. Perhaps the oddest thing was that I no longer thought of her as *my* mother, to whom I rushed in every emergency as I had done in my Catholic days. Inexplicably, she remained in my consciousness as the Mother of God, even when I no longer believed in God. I found myself saying the Hail Mary often during those years, not as a petition but as a kind of "honouring" of this personage in whom reason forbade me to believe.

It was not till after my mother's death in 1939 (my father

80

had died ten years earlier) that I reached some sort of mental "adjustment." Analysis had done one great thing for me by showing that my attitude to the Catholic Church was deeply bound up with my attitude to my father, who, far more than my instructors, had been the "authority" on whose word I had accepted it as true. This "liberated" me enough to be able to return to my "Santayan" outlook, accepting the beauty and poetry of Catholic doctrine and ritual (and nowhere had I found anything comparable to it as a whole) but not its literal truth or its binding precepts. At last I could enjoy it without guilt or fear.

After my mother's funeral, her kind old Belgian parish priest approached me with the inevitable question: Was it not time I returned to my faith and had my children baptized? All I could say was that I no longer believed it to be true, but that, if ever I became convinced again that it was true, I hoped I would be honest enough to follow my conviction. By that time, a return would have meant the breaking-off of a personal relationship which meant much to me. He said: "My child, I long so intensely for your return that to obtain that grace, I would gladly have my life shortened by two years." Now I knew from my mother that this priest, though very holy, had a great fear of death. Such sincerity and generosity touched me but did not convert me.

At Christmas, the following year, I thought I would go to Midnight Mass, for the first time since I had given up my religion. I wanted to go simply for its beauty, as I might have gone to a performance of Verdi's *Requiem*.

It was 1940 and, as the blitz was on, Mass was no longer at midnight, and I had to go to the church to find out what time it was being celebrated. Several people were waiting their turn for Confession. Suddenly, as if some invisible person were pushing me, I found myself, quite against my will, taking my place in the line. I ordered my body to get up and walk out of the church; it simply refused to obey. When my turn came, I automatically went into the confessional. I have never felt more blankly ridiculous than I did when I heard the little grating noise as the priest drew back the curtain from the grille. Naturally I had made no preparation for Confession; the time of waiting had been taken up in insisting to myself that I had not the least intention of going. I could only mutter, "Father, I've no right to be here at all." He simply proceeded with the usual "How long is it since your last Confession?" When I said "Thirteen years" he showed more interest than surprise. I told him I had completely lapsed from faith and practice; that though there were times when I could just imagine practising again, I was as far as ever from believing. Was I willing to practise again in spite of all my doubts? I found myself saying "Yes." Then, much to my surprise, he heard my Confession (after a false start or two I found myself making it as naturally as in the old days), gave me absolution and told me I could go to Communion on Christmas Day. I came away in a queer state; happy, apprehensive, bewildered and amused at myself.

All the same, I did go to Communion on Christmas morning. It was a very blind, doubting Communion; memories of what it had once meant and questions as to what it could possibly mean now came up together like two photos on the same film. There was, of course, a sense of peace, relief and "home again."

Afterwards I returned to see that priest, as certain technical details in my case had to be cleared up with Westminster. He told me that the day I had been . . . I can only call it *impelled* into the confessional, he had been suddenly asked to take over that box, which was not his usual one. He had also been going through a difficult period about his vocation to that particular Order. In his own words; "I was on bad terms with God and I asked him for a sign. I said, 'If I am where you want me to be, send me a sinner for Christmas.'"

Both my parents were dead, but there was one person to whom my return would bring much joy. I wrote at once to the old Belgian priest, expecting a warm response by return. Weeks passed and I heard nothing. I was disappointed, even angry. Then one morning I had a letter from his housekeeper. The old priest had died, suddenly and unexpectedly, just before Christmas.

Another thirteen years has passed since that Christmas. Looking back, I see more and more how exquisitely typical of God's ways it was that I should not come back to the Church on a calm, reasoned decision of my own but be unceremoniously bundled in, through the back door as it were, in response to others' prayers and as a "sign" to a loyal servant of His who was in trouble. I had gone out to look for Truth . . . so honestly as I had thought, but, in fact, with so much unconscious mental and spiritual pride. Never once had it occurred to me that Truth might be looking for me. And, at the precise moment when I thought my struggles were over and I had achieved "balanced adjustment" and mental peace, He pounced on me. I am sure now that the pressure at the back of my neck, pushing me into that queue for Confession was, quite literally, that of Our Lady's hand.

But do not think that the immediate result was interior peace and light. The ensuing months were some of the darkest and most turbulent I have known. It was very easy for me to suspect, as so many of my friends did, that my return was due to psychological necessity. I was over forty now and my life had been a conspicuous muddle and failure. What more natural than that I should "compensate" for all my frustrations by "regressing" to the childish longing for security and find it in the very thing which *had* symbolized security in my childhood—the Catholic Church?

However, there were two factors that did not quite fit the picture. One was that it occurred at a moment when I was not only peculiarly calm in my mind but when my emotional life was happier than it had been for years. The other was that faith, after my first passive acceptance, far from giving me a sense of cosy security, produced every kind of violent disturbance. For now I had to re-learn all that I once thought I knew. And in those thirteen years "outside" I had learnt and thought and experienced much which I knew was valuable and had truth in it. All this had to be sorted out, to be assimilated to, or rejected from, the total view to which I was now committed. That process is still going on. That first grace had, as it were, to be accepted consciously, and that was a slow and painful process. I can only say that I had now to make a full choice, to arrive at a free acceptance of all that was offered, with mind, heart and will. And, for a long time, everything was very dark. There was no inner sense of light or certainty, no "consolation" in prayer. And, on the mental side, I could find no guide. I read much that I was recommended to read, but too often found that old note of specious reasoning, narrowness, smugness or sneering.

I stumbled on, "practising" as best I could but in acute mental discomfort, beginning to feel I was shut up in an airless room. And then God took pity on me and opened the window. I had never in the old days had any contact with the Dominicans. But, at the age of eleven, I had acquired a peculiar affection for St. Thomas Aquinas. I knew nothing about him except his prayers in the missal, which seemed to me the best prayers I had ever read because they asked so simply and directly for things one sincerely wanted to have. A little later, I found another one which I loved even more

84

. . . the one beginning "O God to whom belong all things. . ." I used it so much that there is a black thumb-mark on the page, and I loved it so much that I often found myself saying it almost unconsciously during my thirteen years out of the Church.

When I returned, I found St. Thomas Aquinas had become immensely important. Someone told me that a Dominican, Father Victor White, who was deeply interested in Jungian psychology, was lecturing on the *Summa*. Subsequently I attended many of his courses. From the very first lecture, an entirely new perspective opened up, a perspective deepened and illuminated by Father Richard Kehoe's amazing discourses on the Scriptures.

That was the beginning of a new understanding of the Church's teaching, of all the immensity that is summed up in Christ and communicated through the Church in such a way that there is no aspect of human life or thought that it does not include. What had seemed so rigid and exclusive and opaque gradually appeared as living and growing, extending backwards and forwards in time and including everything from the homeliest to the highest. The rock was not a solid, crushing stone but a living organism, the Mystical Body of Christ. The great paradoxes, the great mysteries remained, but faith, though it could not resolve or penetrate them, could accept them and even rejoice in them, since in eternity God would give us vision. Meanwhile, even on earth, He occasionally gives us glimpses of insight into them, if only enough to reveal the depth upon depth still hidden. And the smallest of such glimpses, whether into the meaning beyond meaning packed into the tight kernel of a great dogma, or into the marvellous ways of God with the human soul or with the intricate network of human relationships both within and without the visible Body (since Christ is Lord of the whole world and works in it like the leaven in

85

His parable), includes and transcends all other joys of mind, heart or imagination.

If I were asked to say what satisfies me more and more in the Catholic religion, it is the way in which it stresses the reality both of spirit and matter. Everything springs from the great central doctrine of the Incarnation with its infinite implications. It is dynamic, not static, for the revelation in and through Christ that God is Love is a revolutionary announcement that has no parallel in any other philosophy or religion. For, in the doctrine of the Trinity, we have an entirely new conception of God, not as single but as triune, so that there is an endless interplay of creative love between the three Divine Persons. Again, in Christ, we have the union, not the *fusion*, of the human and the divine nature in one Person. We are not progressively absorbed into higher and higher orders of being but retain our human identity, even our human body for eternity, transformed and redeemed, united to God but not identical with Him. Where the Buddhist aims more and more at the renunciation of all desire, one could almost say that Christianity is based on desire. Christ comes to us literally as food for the body as well as to satisfy the hunger of the soul. He is born in a manger in Bethlehem, which means, "The House of Bread." Adam fell because he ate the forbidden fruit of the tree of knowledge, but Christ raises us up by giving us the commanded fruit of the tree of life which is the tree of the cross.

To be once more living in the Church is something which, year by year, I realize more and more to be the greatest privilege a human being can have in this world. All my years of proud and restless wandering taught me at least that nothing else so well satisfies all the demands of human nature. Moreover, during that time a new leaven was working in the Church herself, for since my return I have found a very different "spirit" among Catholics. The narrowness and rigidity of outlook are disappearing; the laity are encouraged to understand and to penetrate as far as they can the great truths of faith, instead of passively accepting them as formulae, and the Church is once more manifesting herself in her true light as the Mystical Body of Christ, working as a living organism in the whole order of creation. The older I grow, the less I look for external "accommodations," or worry about the differences in individual Catholics who may be profoundly shocked by each other's ways of apprehending their religion. The communion between them at the deeper level where we are nourished by the same sacraments and united in this same mystical body is too profound to be broken by differences of temperament and approach. How profound that communion is, how rich the source of life—that life which Christ came that we should have more abundantly, not merely in eternity but here and now—is something no one can realize more literally than a person who for many years cut themselves off from it.

If I return to where I began—to Our Lady—it is because she is, as it were, the bulwark of this great central truth of the Incarnation. As someone has said, "When the Mother is lost, the Son is eventually lost too." God chooses her as the free instrument of the Incarnation as Eve was the free instrument of the Fall—that profound mystery of the "happy fault," the "truly necessary sin of Adam." Over and over again the great heresies, those partial "choices" which divided the seamless garment of the truth, struck at her. And it is significant that within the last hundred years the Church has proclaimed two dogmas which must have seemed strangely irrelevant to the outside world—the Immaculate Conception and the Assumption. There are even Catholics to whom the latter seemed, not of course irrelevant, but perhaps ill-timed, a possible stumbling-block to the union of Christendom. But to others it was a very special sign of

the Holy Spirit, so mysteriously and intimately connected
with Our Lady, working in the Church. Recently, I have
been wondering whether the proclamation of the Assumption is not so much an emphasis on Our Lady's glory as on
her creatureliness. Within the Church there can never be
such a thing as Mariolatry, since every glory of the Mother
is reflected from, and instantly reflected back to, the Son,
by her who is the mirror of justice. But, outside the Church,
in the new and subtle forms of gnosticism now abroad—a
gnosticism associated with various esoteric groups and not
entirely disassociated from some interpretations of Jung's
psychology—there is a definite tendency to exalt the universal great Mother figure into something which could
almost be called the embodiment of the feminine aspect of
God, or even the matrix of the Divine Substance. But the
Church has always insisted that Our Lady, though standing
in a unique relation to the Blessed Trinity, is not co-equal
with God. It is Our Lady's humility that is her greatest glory,
just because it reflects the supreme humility of Christ, who
chose to be born of one who, though holy and privileged
beyond all others, was still a creature.

I think we forget sometimes that the Immaculate Conception was a fearful responsibility as well as a tremendous
privilege. Our Lady was created, like Eve, with a perfect
human nature, and like Eve, she had to make a choice which
would affect the whole human race. Am I wrong in saying
that Our Lady, though she did not sin, *could* have sinned?
We hear so much of her sinlessness that perhaps we are apt
to think sin was *impossible* to her, as to her divine Son.
Surely she was sinless, apart from the miracle of her being
conceived without original sin, because of her complete
pliability to God's will and her prompt response to every
grace? And perhaps it is this very creatureliness which
makes her in such a special sense the "refuge of sinners." As

Christ mediates between God and man since He contains both natures, so she mediates between Christ and us, since she truly shares our nature, though not its disorders and, though not God, is truly the mother of God. For millions of lapsed Catholics, as for myself, her hand must have been the last of which we let go and the first to draw us back.

R. R. Stokes

The Rt. Hon. Richard Rapier Stokes, P.C., M. P. was born in 1897; was educated by the Benedictines at Downside, and went on to Trinity College, Cambridge. He served in the first World War (MC and bar, Croix de Guerre, Order of the Nile). He joined the Labour Party and has been M.P. for Ipswich since 1938. He was Minister of Works in 1950, Lord Privy Seal in 1951.

I am a Catholic in the first place because I was brought up as one by a devout father who intended to become a priest, found he had not got a vocation, then married and had nine children: and by an equally devout mother who became a Catholic shortly after her marriage. My early training at home was followed by nine years at Downside under a very exceptional headmaster, Dom Leander Ramsey, who consolidated the position!

Why I remain a Catholic is a little more complicated. After leaving school I did nearly three years in France as a fighting soldier. There, without any shadow of doubt, my faith carried me through and enabled me to survive without suffering any real fear, or shattering my belief in God and the goodness that is in everyone. Rather more; it convinced me that given a chance to show courage, cheerfulness and comradeship men do not fail. When hostilities ceased and I started civil life, then, and only then, did I realize that, whereas in war we all had a common aim, the cheerfulness

in battle and comradeship in arms disappeared in peace in
the struggle for peacetime existence. It seemed to me that,
with all my training, whilst there was nothing wrong with
my faith, there must be something pretty groggy with the
practical application of it which led men to be such heroes
and so self-sacrificing in war but allowed them to become
so selfish and grasping when danger had gone. To this I
will return later on in this short essay.

The fact of the matter is that any other alternative
to the Catholic faith, however strongly reasoned, neither
satisfies my intelligence nor contradicts my training. The
Faith I find absolutely satisfactory and, as Campion said,
"completely compelling to any who give it an indifferent and
quiet audience." The Christian revelation is the revelation
best known to man. Whereas other teachers have been either
human or deified after death, the Christian revelation was
made by God himself. His declaration "Thou art Peter and
upon this rock I will build My Church" can bear but one
interpretation—the intention to found a Church with direc-
tive authority, to guide, protect and help each one of His
own human creatures through life. From this I deduce that
there can be only one Church, for God would not—and in
fairness could not—leave it to chance for us to decide which
way to go as a result of His own revelation in order to save
our immortal souls.

To my mind human existence ceases to have any
meaning at all without religion, religion has no satisfactory
meaning without belief in an omniscient, all-powerful and
all-good God, and belief in God little meaning if any without
belief in life in the hereafter. It is in the nature of things
that man should have doubts and difficulties about all this,
but the revealed truth as taught by the Catholic Church
satisfies my doubts, and I recognize that my difficulties arise
from my own mean intelligence and human frailty. This is

where faith comes in: faith has to handle the difficulties and overcome the all-too-human solution that whatever suits me must be right—a view which indeed has so often within my own experience proved to be so hopelessly wrong! Human existence without faith becomes a pretty muddling affair. Man cannot get along without it: he needs it to guide him in his main aspiration to satisfy his own spiritual needs, which themselves are of his very nature. The fact that faith is a supernatural gift of God itself requires authority to back it up, and that authority I find in the Catholic Church.

There is no disagreement about there being a Christian Church, but there is so much fundamental difference between the Catholic Church and other Churches claiming to be Christian that it and the others cannot both be right. The truth is that the Catholic Church can substantiate a claim to continuity of authoritative direction which can be substantiated by no other Church, Christian or otherwise. What stronger proof of authority could be required by any reasonable thinking man?

I am often asked how my political endeavours fit in with my faith and belief in the Catholic Church. This can be answered quite simply. I believe that God first made the world and then, to serve His own purpose, created man, endowing him with the extraordinary gift of free will: that man's spirit is in God's own image and likeness, and that God meant man to enjoy all the wonderful things in nature and in so doing give glory to God in his daily life of his own free will. This applies to all of us, not to just a selected few. After loving God we are instructed to love our neighbour as ourselves, which means so to order our own lives that they do not militate against anyone else's enjoying God's purpose. Man was perfect when God made him, and the fall of Adam, out of pure selfishness, has caused all the trouble—and who will deny that selfishness is the most prominent of the human failings which today lead to human unhappiness? I believe that when God made the world He provided in nature enough for everybody, for you cannot at one and the same time believe in an all-good God and that there is not in the storehouse of nature enough for us all. It is a contradiction which no believing person can possibly accept.

I do not believe that God created man to struggle and starve and fight about scarcity, but that he meant him to increase and multiply and enjoy the fruits of the earth to the full. This being so, why is it that everyone has not got enough? It is blasphemy of the worst order to accept that poverty and war are of God's making and inevitable. They are brought about by man's selfishness and refusal to accept the right path. Believing that there is enough for everybody and that the world is under- not over-populated, why is it that more than half the people in the world live on an income calculated to be less than the equivalent of twenty-five pounds a year? The answer is that they have been denied access to the storehouse of nature. In his great encyclical *Rerum Novarum,* Leo XIII made the position clear when he wrote that man's needs do not die out but for ever recur, and that the means of satisfying those needs are to be found in the earth and its natural resources, provided by God for the purpose.[1] Nature is not niggardly—

[1] The full quotation is: "Man's needs do not die out, but for ever recur; although satisfied today, they demand fresh supplies for to-morrow. Nature accordingly must have given to man a source that is stable and remaining always with him from which he might look to draw continual supplies. And this stable condition of things he finds solely in the earth and its fruits."

He goes on to say: "For God has granted the earth to mankind in general, not in the sense that all without distinction can deal with it as they like, but rather that no part of it was assigned to any one in particular, and that the limits of private possession have been left to be fixed by man's own industry and by the laws of individual races."

93

God never meant that it should be. Quite apart from the Church's teaching, the evidence of our own eyes proves there is abundance for everybody if we will only manage our affairs right. It is on this fundamental point that I find no contradiction between my Faith and my political beliefs. The land and natural resources must be used in the best interest of all the people everywhere—as God's gift to the whole human race.

I said earlier on that after the First World War, in which all with whom I came in contact showed such heroism and selflessness, I was shocked by the selfishness displayed in the peacetime struggle for existence. In wartime we had a common single purpose: in peace it could best be described as smash and grab. The fact is that, faced with death, people behave differently, and if we are to achieve the fine ideals so constantly displayed in war we must tackle the problem of ensuring man's needs in peacetime just as they are provided for in war. I remember the Minister of War in 1939 reporting to the House of Commons that many of the conscripts, on joining up, could only be classed as C.3. physically, but that after a few months' good feeding they quickly became A.1.—"Fattening them for the slaughter," I interjected. I also remember the Prime Minister's speech in Edinburgh about 1942 when he declared that after three years of war the little boys in Glasgow were on the average three pounds heavier than they were in peace! What an outrageous thing to be able to say, but it was true. Therefore we need constantly to remember that faith alone will not save us, we must also have good works. This I conceive to mean that, whilst it is the duty of the priest to teach the Faith, it is the duty of the politician to clear out of the road those things which militate against its full practical performance. It is because I believe that enforced poverty and want, slums and degradation can be swept away if we *live*

94

God's will, so that all may live a happy life in reasonable abundance—not to be confused with excess—that I stand where I do in politics and consider that the path those who think like me seek to follow best conforms with Catholic teaching.

Quite recently I was talking to a well-known man in the Near East about the danger of Communist infiltration into that large area where poverty abounds in the midst of plenty. His reply was simple and direct: "We have no need for Communism; all the best things that are claimed for Communist materialism are provided for in our Moslem faith if people would only practise it!"

Just like my Moslem friend I look for the authority which, through my short space of life on this planet, will help me to love God first and my neighbour next. "Neighbours" are often pretty tiresome people! I'm not bound to like them but to love them, which means wish them the opportunity to fulfill God's purpose and put no obstruction to their so doing in the way. All this is bound up with the free choice we all have of doing right or wrong. When ill a wise man consults his doctor: when the pipes leak he calls in a plumber. Just as ignoring the doctor may lead to disaster and not calling in the plumber certainly to discomfort, so will the flouting of authority on spiritual matters lead to the choosing of the wrong road. However disagreeable—and even sometimes difficult to understand—the prescription of the Catholic Church may be, it has never let me down. It is for this reason and reasons other than those I have enumerated herein that I remain a Catholic and could be no other.

Jean Charlot

Jean Charlot was born in Paris in 1898, of French and Mexican ancestry, served as artillery lieutenant in first World War. He came to Mexico in 1921, played part as maker of murals in the artistic revolution, studied Mayan art with many Carnegie expeditions in Yucatan. He is named in James Lane's Masters in Modern Art *as one of the nine most prominent modern painters. He has painted murals in Atlanta, the University of Iowa and New Jersey. He is now teaching at the University of Hawaii. For Sheed and Ward he has written* Art from the Mayans to Disney *and* Art-Making from Mexico to China. *He married Zohmah Day in 1943. They have four children.*

I am an artist, liable to receive impressions, moods, ratiocinations, even stray spiritual impulses, mostly through a specialized channel of sensuous reactions —the stock-in-trade of the maker of Fine Arts. Also it has been my lot to experience the Church with its attribute of catholicity underlined: my traffic among its grand-plays and road-stands encompasses a substantial spherical segment of our globe. All in all, it is perhaps the spectacle displayed, the stage sets—naive, sumptuous, pompous or comical—the hazards of taste entailed in the visit to every church, or chapel or churchman, that bind me irretrievably to the militant Church.

96

This does not mean that along with this sensuous intercourse no flavour of spirituality intrudes. My usual ways of learning and my professional vocabulary as well remain banked within the limits of visual and tactile happenings, concerned mostly with an appreciation of colours, textures and forms. I lack means of expressing from where it is that the path branches away from the well-known sights towards the invisible and the untouchable. Perhaps, anyhow, as is my earnest hope, at the end of this superior road the eye will again come into its own. One reads, of course, in the lives of saints, of their visions. Such happenings, even though they would prove vocationally pat, have not been the lot of my small virtue. There remains the collective promise of unitive vision as the end, not to be disconnected from that other promise of the resurrection of the body, including both resurrected eyeballs. Up there, we may perhaps delight again in contrasts and affinities of colours, rhythms, lights and shapes. I suspect that, even while on this earth, the good painter El Greco could hardly keep his specialized painter's knowledge from intruding on his visions, as he coolly notes that "angels are like candle-flames, that look big at a distance but small as they come near."

As a corollary to my profession, after twenty years of working from the model and teaching life-class, in what unkindly souls would describe as a Peeping Tom career, I have seen more women stripped than even Casanova, and as many nude men as a shower attendant. I have come, in so doing, to the unoriginal conclusion that the body is more important than the clothes, and for me people have ceased to be heads sticking out of clothing, and recapture, clothed or clothesless, the quality of purity that nudity was at first meant to convey. Having lost for people their sense of shame, I am mildly impatient that some aim to keep it, and even glory in it. Decency seems indeed a transitory affair,

97

a mean compromise brought about by the original accident, to be dismissed in eternity. A jingle runs in my head that I wrote in my twenties about the sights that await us in Heaven, when

> *ayant délaissé l'oripeau,*
> *Le costume des bienheureux sera la peau.*

I should add that, when I chose art as my career, I eschewed other, more substantial, pursuits. The kind of art that I make and my doggedness in making it just so, hardly constitute a paying proposition. Money is needed indeed when one has a wife and four small children. What money has happened my way has come sidewise, as it were. It would be impertinent to mention holy poverty in connection with rather narrow circumstances, especially if these are perfectly cut to taste. We always had enough, even something left over daily expenses for an additional and ironical burden: to pay storage on paintings that I know must be preserved for posterity.

The point I want to make is that, given this personalized, ostracized pattern of life, religion can never be for me the prop that it is for the white-collar worker, or the aura that fringes the pate of the real estate man, or the social cement that binds together baptized joiners under the paradoxical patronage of Columbus, uncanonized saint who learned ineffably to be alone. For the same reason that I am to an extent unworldly, I fail to be impressed by the overlapping of Church and World. When a Church chums too closely with a government, neither better nor worse than another, or when a churchman carves for himself fame as a radio orator or a best-seller, I wonder which one of the two incompatible systems, or which of the two incompatible ethics, has been intruded upon by the other. An artist is expected to be a romantic. True to type, I probably romance when I believe catacombs to be fit places for the faithful to worship in, and lack indignation when Church dignitaries are thrown into jail. Rather it appears to me as if it were some kind of return to normalcy.

Born and raised in France, despite sundry exotic ancestors, I practised in my religion what was then the norm for a little Frenchman of circa 1905, dolled in Fauntleroy suits, who could hardly squeeze far enough to kiss an aunt through the pillowed hurdles of bosom, boas, and plumed hat. Mother's piety was always alive. As the world she had known and its pomps gradually left her, this piety deepened to a hue of valid mysticism, but that phase came later on, towards the end. Father was a freethinker and, when not busy at his office, dreamed of a global anarchy to come that would prove a freethinker's heaven on earth, *le Grand Soir*. Mother's sweet proddings churchwise and father's caustic, amused disapproval proved an unmatchable combination for devotion. I could thus simultaneously obey and rebel, be docile and choose a path of my own.

Here should come the recital of my conversion, or of what takes its place in the case of the born Catholic. Unlike plants, and perhaps animals, all buoyant or burdened with heredity, man has to accept or reject, once at least as an individual, the soil, or habitat, he grew in. Baptized when he was only a bawling baby, a Catholic will take a look at his ticket for Heaven, and weigh in terms of self, if not the implied destination, at least the pre-mapped itinerary. This happened to me so early in life that I remember with what pride, on that Sunday morning, I clung to the hand of my older cousin, subject to the draft, which would make him all of twenty years old. It was summer, so that the church was in the country, in Poissy, the same sturdy pile of quarried stones, more Romanesque than Gothic, where St. Louis of France with his mother Blanche had worshipped.

Kitty-corner from the church was the town square with its chestnut trees, and, as a bronze premonition of the pitfalls of my vocation, there rose in its centre a statue of Meissonier, glorious native son, his bifurcated, frizzled beard sweeping awry a square palette that, in turn, seemed to drip its load of pigment over the velvet pants of the artist.

Once in church we knelt sideways and close to the altar, following Mass through the open woodwork of the chancel. Casually the priest, preparatory to preaching, took off his chasuble and appeared in his white alb. Monsieur le Curé was neither beautiful nor thin. His skin, sweating off the summer heat, gleamed with the deep veinous red of a florid complexion. It was already through the eye that I thought, and this spectacle of the ecclesiastic in his nightshirt, as it seemed, bibulous with *vin ordinaire*, his pug nose tipped with a blue highlight, loomed unbearably grotesque. How could a Faith represented by such a symbol have any truth in it? I should get up and go, never to come back. Physically, the opposite happened. My muscles reacted in place of a distracted mind. My elbows digged a little deeper into the arm-rest of the *prie-dieu* and my knees into its cushion. As swiftly as the vision and revulsion had come, they went, and the matter of faith was settled, for some forty years to date, and, let us hope, for as long as Time.

The Parisian priests who taught us Catechism had lucid heads, good enough for the Sorbonne of St. Thomas, and, together with the grain of Gallicanism in their make-up, there was instilled in the boy a deep devotion for their priestly powers, and an independence towards them that amounted to comradeship, regardless of the difference in age. My single attempt at servility went unrewarded: as we passed our final examination on doctrine before First Communion, I was asked what I would do if, in a conversation, the Holy Father explained to me a point of doctrine. Well, I wished for a good grade and the Pope was the boss of my inquisitor; of course, in such a situation as described, I said, I should agree with the Holy Father. This proved an incorrect answer: I was coolly treated to the distinction between a private opinion and a proclamation *urbi et orbi*. It was the first, and probably the last, time that I ever fawned on the clergy.

As I grew up, the making of liturgical art became the common ground between my devotion and my vocation. In my teens I was already one of a group that called itself Guilde Notre-Dame, made up of sculptors, stained-glass makers, embroiderers, decorators. The workshop atmosphere and approach to aesthetics through crafts served me well later on when, a world war having elapsed, I found myself in Mexico as a member of another group, made up this time of fearful fellows who made the bourgeois cringe, and shook the walls they painted on. They had this in common with me and the pious French friends I had left behind, that they too were humble craftsmen, good at their trade, which is a kind of virtue.

My career as a French liturgical artist was cut short when, with the priest's approval and working from blue-prints he had furnished, I planned the mural decorations of a new church in a Paris suburb. Weeks later, my exultant note stating that the sketches were at last finished was coolly answered: there had been a change of plans and murals were out. This, the first of many heartaches that I came to experience in my career as a mural painter, was one of the factors that sent me to Mexico.

Before leaving France, I should mention the authors who helped me to a realization of my personal attitude in matters that it would be exaggerated to call philosophical: at most, this consisted in a sweeping out of sight, hardly

101

further than under the rug, of the film of dust that interfered with the focus one needs on the outside before action may begin. At my most adolescent, at my pimples stage, Joris Karl Huysmans fascinated me. His attitude was thoroughly artistic; he consistently rated long words over short ones; he disguised with a sauce of obscure adjectives the clear taste of clichés. It was not long before an aestheticism so thick repulsed the maker of art in me, the joiner of art, so rarely troubled by the mental scruples of the art appreciator.

Paul Claudel struck deeper. In his work, beauty mingled fearlessly with a kind of grossness that he himself sees as a link with farmer ancestors bent for a lifetime under a hod-load of dung. There was bigness in that grossness, and Claudel's *Processional* taught me a decisive lesson in mural composition, as generous and lasting as a visit to Assisi.

Léon Bloy furnished me with ready-made answers to problems outside art-matters that I had neither the ability nor the patience to tackle. I saw him as full of tenderness and pity. To this day, I understand his admirers, but not at all his apologists or his extenuators. Bloy believed in a world peopled by gruesome puppets. More often than not, his Guignol, with red hooked nose and carnal leer, and humps back and front, and much strident-mouthed nonsense, wears the black gown of the ecclesiastic or, fancier still, a bishop's mitre. It did not bother me any more than had the cathedrals' Last Judgments or Dances of Death, that were hardly ever more polite. At the heart of the matter there remains the fact that Bloy was in love with sanctity. Having told in his *Last Columns of the Church* of his disillusion with men whose profession should have been holiness, this Catholic Diogenes with his lantern sank to the chin in the sewers of Paris and haunted its bordellos in a ceaseless hunt for a living contemporary saint. He never thought of looking where we now know for a fact that a certified saint sat—during eleven years of that search—namely, on the throne of St. Peter.

I adopted Bloy's concept of society in all its crude black-and-white, home-made theology, as angular as were the block books and pilgrims' penny sheets of the Middle Ages. Bloy's flair as a puppeteer delighted the boy in me, who had sat in knee-pants only a while before at similar performances, in the open under the *frondages* of the Champs-Elysées. In Bloy's playlets, the rich man was always all evil and, doubly leaded by sin and by the weight of a massive gold coffin, his body at the Resurrection would sink plumb to hell. Contrariwise, his interlocutor, the poor man, was all holy, and his mangled remains at the end of time, from whatever garbage heap the rich man had ordered them thrown onto, would reunite and rise unhampered and white to glory. Getting very much into the spirit of the play, I too longed to see the camel squirm and wish he was a snake, forever trying and forever beaten at his sport of squeezing through the needle's eye. I remember laughing aloud at an ecclesiastical footnote in a New Testament, meant to comfort, pseudo-archeological and very nineteenth-century: it mentioned for a fact how, in biblical Jerusalem, one of the lesser outer gates was called "The Needle's Eye" because camel drivers feared this bottle-neck to fast caravan traffic.

My life in France was on the whole rational, national, obeying this often heard dictum that a Frenchman is a man who ignores geography. There were though, simultaneously, un-French elements at work. Russian, *sephardim*, Aztec ancestors, warmed my blood to adventure. In art, I accepted as part of my patrimony the monstrous chubby forms of Indian idols, the squatty masked heroes of Mexican cosmogony, without letting go a whit of those other models, Poussin's "Eliezer and Rebecca," and Ingres' "Apotheosis of Homer."

For those ingrown exotic elements, Mexico furnished an outlet. My first Mexican priest, seen at landing, at Mass in the cathedral of Vera-Cruz, happened to be a genuine *Indio verde,* and all through the Consecration I watched lovingly the nape of dark green skin between the fringes of white hair and the gold galloon of the Sunday vestments. I was at last to see alive and rooted in its own soil what I had apprehended in Paris only from fragments, pressed between the pages of manuscripts dry as herbariums, or embalmed in museums' glass cases. For a while, I would be nothing but eyes, taking in this new face of the Church. I can only hope that, as in the case of the juggler somersaulting his devotions before Our Lady, there was a certain prayerful residue in my looking, or else I must confess to total distraction.

In France the visage of the Church had been not unlike the art of Maurice Denis, like a maypole dance in May, or a provincial out-door procession of Corpus Christi: little boys in blue satin and little girls in pink organdy holding beribboned baskets filled with rose petals to strew on the passage of the Host. In Mexico, the climate of the Church was reminiscent of late Fall, red leaves decaying underfoot or heaped for burning. It also looked like the art of Zurbaran: a black battleground strewn with the guts of martyrs and of heretics.

United States Catholics, if they think at all of the Inquisition, profess it to be a sort of Guy Fawkes propped high by disputing Protestants to embarrass us. In Mexico, over two hundred manuscript volumes filed in the National Archives tell its detailed local story since the sixteenth century. The stench of human flesh roasted for religious reasons still hangs on the air. Indians came to the Church so readily because it mirrored features of their old faith. The burning of heretics, with whatever zeal it was pursued in colonial times, remained a petty affair compared to the rate of human sacrifice of the pagan past; twenty thousand slain in one day at the dedication of Mexico's main temple. The Church turned towards the Indians a terrifying face, one that France had not seen since the thirteenth century and the Albigenses. Indians recognized and liked what they saw. Barring the technicality of giving over the culprit to the secular arm, a gesture as swift as any sleight of hand, it was the Church that garbed the lapsed and the relapsed in yellow robes and conical clownish hats and saw them to the stake. In their turn, heretics did not mind overmuch, as no man will readily slight his own role as a menace to Church and State.

There is no modern unwillingness to go on with such fiery sport: when American Shriners innocently held their convention south of the Rio Grande, they were barred by popular wrath—that grew nearly to the size of an insurrection—from visiting the Basilica of Guadalupe, lest an Heaven-sent earthquake rip it in two.

In the nineteenth century, when the freethinkers came to power, they retaliated. By the 1920's it was the Catholic who had become the hunted and the killed. The persecution of the Church that I witnessed in Mexico makes gory reading, and made not a few true martyrs. So, why gloss over a past as brutal as was that present? Perhaps, instead of hiding the past, we should rekindle a feeling of horror in the presence of heresy. In a world become Caesar's own, today's active horror is confined to economic communism. There are no defenders of the antiquated dream of the Inquisitor, that of preserving Christendom whole, though it is the greater aim and immeasurably the purer passion.

The Mexican Church of today reminds me incongruously of these stores I have seen in mining ghost towns that are adobe shacks with false fronts. It is at an uneasy transitional stage, with a highly groomed group of priests trained in United States seminaries, ready to give Mexico the blessings of what they have learned North—one could say the latest models of spiritual plumbing. But it is still the body of low church men, the country priests, missionaries in their own tropics, fluent at Indian tongues and as poor as Indians, that ministers to the great bulk of souls. As did the sixteenth-century priests, and at a scarcely slackened pace, they butt full-force against a pagan world in which there is more than an overtone of Satanism. In each village, as a matter of fact, the priest's white magic is pitted against the magic of the witch. I can swear to these men's zeal and to their squalor. I cannot swear in all cases to their scholasticism, or their sobriety. I cannot swear to their grasp of the meaning of social justice: the priest who lives on a big plantation, mans the owner's private chapel, is accepted as little better than an overseer, the difference being that his job is to keep the workers in line with the Host, instead of with a whip. But what immeasurably compensates for the shortcomings born of living in a feudal order is the fact that no Mexican preacher will ever bore, ever fail to exalt or to edify. The public admission of the average United States priest that he too is a sinner seems made with a thin-lipped mental reservation. The length to which the Mexican priest will go to publicly prove that he is a sinner, his display of heart and organs and his tearful gesticulations, leave no doubt as to both his repentance and his frailty. Carried over by the redundancy of the Spanish language, fortified by the clipped sounds of the *nahuatl* tongue, the country priest is an instinctive mystic, apt at creating images as fragrant as those of a John of the Cross. He will work himself hoarse as he describes the beauties of the spiration within the Trinity; he will well nigh fall off his perch as the rope tightens around Judas's neck and his cursed innards spill over on the frightened congregation.

I also liked what I saw of the last sliver of aristocratic Spain embedded in the neck of the Mexican Church like a fire *banderilla* in the neck of a bull. I watched the impoverished Marques de . . . , impervious to twenty years of revolution, who walked, draped in his cloak of Knight of the Holy Sepulchre, to church and his reserved stall, practically upon the altar, every morning at six. There, with the nonchalance born of long usage of his lordly privileges, unmindful of the plebeian congregation, he fiddled with his missal, picked his teeth, plucked at his nose and ears, fell asleep and awoke with a start to receive Communion. Perhaps, all that time, he was dreaming of *palomino* horses and pedigreed bulls, for the old Marquis is also the king of *charros*.

When I left Mexico for the United States, my devotions had become a more or less integrated blend of three racial attitudes—French, Spanish and Indian—and I talked to God in a number of languages. My piety paralleled the mixed aesthetics of the image of Our Lady of Guadalupe, robed in tints so light and so dark of skin, dressed in the insignia of an Aztec princess, impressed by Heaven on a lowly palm mat, but with a clarity of statement worthy of a Poussin.

I was reluctant to add to my pious mixed hoard of churchly manners still another mode in another country. At first contact, the United States Church proved a riddle: the radical change of palette, to use a painter's term, puzzled me. Perhaps it was Anglo-Saxon cleanliness, the repeated scrubbing of white skins until they turn piggy-pink, that proved the tallest optical hurdle. I did not know then that most American priests are provided with microscopic salaries, under those of the meanest manual labourers, and that their outward emulation of the mannerisms of successful business men is but sheer mimetism. At first sight, I felt confronted by what seemed to be an army of salesmen in cassocks.

Merchandizing and packaging, two arts I had missed in my far-flung search for art, were met everywhere within the American Church, not unnaturally influenced by American business mores. To this day, despite much pulpit talk, I understand less about the mystery of duplex envelopes than I do about that of the Trinity. At a New York mission, I watched in awe how Dominican Fathers, inventing a kind of perpetual movement, sold us candles that were put upon the altar but not lighted, before being returned to the pile from which they were sold again, and this ad infinitum. Too many preachers will spill over the mute congregation that of which their hearts are full, usually disturbed dreams of a balanced parish ledger. I remember how, in a sermon on the multiplication of the fishes and loaves, the priest emphasized the fact that seven baskets of foodstuff were gathered after the crowd had eaten its fill: thus the point of the miracle was thrift. It was in the Coolidge era, and to me, so shortly removed from John of the Cross, something seemed amiss.

Catholic congregations, socked from above by the preacher and licked underfoot by the flames of hell, must appear to a publicity agent as the ideal captive audience, into which soap and deodorants and breakfast foods may be funnelled with only a token resistance. For the priest also, the temptation must be great to sell his lambs on something else besides doctrine and morals, at least to suggest a boy-cott, or a voting ticket, or the right kind of pressure on a Congressman. There is a frightening power in the agglutina-tion of personalities into a mob, be it a pious mob. I shrink even from such justifiable events as the "optional" oath of the Legion of Decency, now performed at Mass, once a year, with Prussian unanimity.

Another lesser stumbling-block, but one never far from my poor marching toes, is the matter of Irishness. Neither France nor Mexico had me prepared for the billing of Ireland as the star of Catholic nations. On arrival in New York, I was genuinely at a loss when a monsignor, lifting his voice and his arms to a jellied pitch of fake emotion, mentioned without naming it a certain little green island known as the navel of the world and its beacon of peace. I knew Manhattan to be an island, but it hardly could be called green.

I learned to mend my suspiciously foreign ways the hard way. Entering St. Patrick's one afternoon, I slid unobtrusively for prayer behind a column, closing my eyes to visual distractions. Not long after, I was rudely shaken to awareness by a beadle as tough as any bouncer: "No sleeping in church allowed." Despite this assault, I returned to St. Patrick's to pray at the shrine of the Little Flower and, finding the altar rail grill open, knelt close to her statue until another beadle, as manly mannered as the first, expelled me threateningly. Later on, as I mulled over the cause of his violence, I realized that I had also been kneeling near the money-box.

"Cleanliness is next to Godliness"; this counsel of mediocrity and similar proverbs from hell jar when they intrude on the thinking of a Church that offers for our veneration Job in his filth and Benedict Joseph Labre the lousy. Attempts at sanitary holy water distributors, dripping one germless drop of the sacramental in the palm of each of the faithful, have failed, but perhaps not for long. The public kissing of relics and of Christ's wounds on good Friday is accompanied by the queer rite of scrubbing the reliquary or crucifix clean after each of the faithful has piously polluted it. Our Lord Himself did not shy from mixing His Sacred

Spit with dust and using the resulting mud to cure the dumb and the blind. The Mexican priest, at a baptism, uses his own saliva for a sacramental purpose with the abandon of a tobacco-chewing hillbilly. Here we know better. "Spit is a horrid word"; though this cigar-selling slogan is hardly part of Holy Scripture, we let it influence the form of the sacrament: the original rite of "Ephpheta" has here become optional.

Now that the initial shock is over, I recognize many admirable traits of the American Church. It was only Spanish prejudice, modelling its code of ethics after that of the cadaverous hidalgos of El Greco, that made me find fault with a Church for being in the pink of its physical condition. It also took me a while to unravel, from under the maze of practical endeavours proper to the parish priest, more than one unborn contemplative. I truly love the simplicity and common sense with which American monastic orders have streamlined monasticism without hurting its essence. Standards of social and racial justice heroically upheld in the face of prejudice have dispelled my early fear of a clerical bourgeoisie. It is logical that the United States Church, unburdened with the glorious ancient architectures of its European sisters, should be first to link itself again, on a large scale, with the live art of living artists. I trust that when the seminarians I know have grown to positions of authority, they will roundly shed overboard from the ship of St. Peter its Satanic cargo of plaster junk, saints à la mode, polychromed in all flavours of ice cream.

I now live in Hawaii. Missionaries sent to the islands could take but small comfort in the only recorded precedent to their task, that of St. Anthony the Hermit baptizing an Egyptian centaur. After all, is not the Great God Pan, in his extrovert animality, an equally likely convert, and a much

more eligible one, than the close-lipped Mammon that reigns
in less luxuriant climates?

Hawaiians revel in a physicality that clothes somehow
fail to divert, hide or sublimate. In the islands, beauty and
bulk have ever been synonymous and enormous fatness a
privilege of royalty. Within this bulk is paradoxically embedded Hogarth's own spiral of Beauty, a serpentine law
that mocks other, thinner, bodies which wear, hanging from
their centre of gravity, a sense of weight as straight as the
drop of a plumbline. The Hawaiian female may be shapeless
in terms of a sculptural form and quite unlike the stable
beauty of a marble Venus, but so is the swimming octopus.
Arms that seem as boneless and untiring in their motion as
tentacles taper delicately towards the agitated feelers of
ever swaying fingers. Hawaiian bodies are most alive at the
hips. For Hawaiians, the seat of noble sentiments is not the
heart but the intestines. To prove that he is, as we say, of
good heart, a man will not put his hand to the cage of the
ribs, but heartily slap his belly, thus proclaiming that he is
of *na'au ao,* a man with intestines made of light: he will
refer to a schemer as a *na'au po,* one whose intestines are
compounded of darkness. Thus it is fitting that history and
religion be perpetuated by the motions of the hula, or belly
dance. When the ladies of a sodality close in around the Holy
Sacrament and march in procession, fearlessly clothed in
Van Gogh yellow, how the gingerbread bodies sway, hard
put not to reproduce the dancing prayer of King David
before the Arch. In Mexico, Rome wisely allows ancient
rites to mingle with Christian ones: squadrons of men
masked as devils will dance their devotion before the altar.
In Hawaii, there is no need and no desire for masks, as it is
the body as such, and not as a symbol, that is a prayer in
motion. Even though the full-blown hula is not performed in
church it is an expected ingredient of church bazaars, and

111

some of the best were danced by a girl who soon after became a Trappistine. I hope that, as St. Theresa of Avila kept her Sisters well provided with tambourines for the times when their Spanish feet itched for a dance, Trappistines will see their way to making allowance for the hula, or their Hawaiian sister may feel rusty when her turn comes to dance it again in Heaven.

In Hawaii also I experienced, though this time vicariously, the feel of the Church in China. My friendship with Dr. John C. H. Wu, then on the faculty of the University, made me witness a present identical with that past in which St. Jerome, minus the mythical lion, minus the authority of future Councils that would call his work blessed, braving even the expressed wrath of God and his threatened chastisements, laboured doggedly to bind together forever his two heritages, pagan literature and Christian thought. John Wu's translation of the Bible will doubtless become the Vulgate of China. Besides being the Oriental Jerome, Wu wishes also to emulate St. Thomas, who baptized Aristotle posthumously. It is John's prideful boast that he will drag by the hair into the company of the Blessed his own thought-fathers, Buddha and Lao-Tse. Even though these two shaped to their resemblance, however diluted, the major part of the earth, John wishes for them a superior glory, that of patriarchs who, thirsting for truth, met face to face on this earth the Unitive Vision.

This pageant of the Church that I relate as I saw it will seem to some perhaps too much like a pageant: a parade, colourful and motley, seen from a sidewalk where the spectator stands and cranes his neck, entranced but lacking the urge to join and take part. Perhaps I have stressed the role of the eye unduly. There is a still deeper contact with the Church wherein all geographical and racial dissimilarities become reconciled, a common denominator or nucleus that binds together laymen and clerics all around the earth. This closest contact is again not particularly metaphysical but the tested exercise of another sense than vision. At those scattered moments in which I stop gaping at the show and mean business, the work of the eye is replaced by tactile experience. Physically the eye closes, while the finger-tips, tongue and skin make contact with the Church at its border in the sacraments. All the pomp, colour and rhythms of the liturgy do not match in efficiency the sacramental contact, from the dipping of the hand in holy water to the taste and texture of the Host at the palate, to, let us hope, the final massaging of feet and hands, ears and lids with the holy chrism of Extreme Unction. Sensuous to the last, my special field of devotion leans towards the physical matter without which sacramentals and sacraments could not happen. The one optional service that I rarely fail to attend is that of Holy Saturday, where fire and water and candle wax receive their blessing. Twenty years of teaching life-class have taught me that people are also matter, organic matter powerfully invaded by the Spirit, as are these other forms of matter on that Saturday morning. There is for me no deeper incentive to meditation than the fact that human bodies are pledged to resurrection together with the exercise of their senses. Perhaps Heaven, unlike the fluffy floating of clouds trans-pierced by light rays depicted in pious images, will surpass in its concreteness even this concrete world of today that it has been my vocation to observe and to paint.

Noël Sullivan

Noël Sullivan *lives at Carmel on the Monterey Peninsula. Mentions fifty years interest in music. He has been for fifteen years organist and choirmaster at the Carmel Mission Church. He has long been interested in race relations.*

Sixty-three years ago, on Christmas Day, I was born into a home that was deeply Catholic. My mother's character represented what (I have come to realize) was a peak of spiritual evolution in the framework of the Church. She was both gentle and strong, just and compassionate. In loyalty, she never faltered, and her generosity was directed by a self-discipline which gave balance and moderation to whatever she did. God's poor and His Church were automatically remembered with an unostentatious munificence whenever she indulged herself in what might have been called a luxury. My father, too, was possessed of a fervent faith, informed by a strong sense of historical backgrounds. From their Irish forbears, both my parents had inherited faith as a gift purchased at the price of persecution through earlier generations, and to this treasure given them at baptism, they each remained steadfastly devoted until death.

When I try to recall my very early consciousness of religion, a scene comes vividly to my mind. I could not have been more than five years old at the time. We were spending the summer in the country, and after I was ready for bed one evening, I was brought to the dining room, where the family had gathered. It was probably the Fourth of July, because I can still see myself standing on a chair, and in answer to the question *what was I,* articulated by one of the grown-ups, who expected a patriotic reply, I replied that I was "a little Catholic." No one had prompted me to say this, and the surprise and amusement of my elders gave me a sharp realization that I had made a significant declaration of allegiance.

Throughout my childhood, I was constantly surrounded by the evidence and influence of religious belief, always expressing itself in exalted forms. I saw no hypocrisy. I was never scandalized. Our Lady, the angels, the saints, the souls in purgatory, were familiars in our nursery. I had early, and without morbidity, a sense of death—its potential imminence, its absolute inevitability—and my first glimpse of the panorama of history down the ages came through the Advent practice of my dear old nurse, who, during the month of December, piously recited four thousand Aves, in commemoration of the forty centuries that man had waited between the creation of the world and the birth of Christ!

What education I received was in Catholic schools. Religion always interested me more than anything else, and objective discussions of all that was related to it made up a definite part of our family life. Three visits to Europe with my parents before I was twenty gave me a further picture of the Church in its unity, apostolicity, holiness, and universality. Two Easter seasons in Rome, pilgrimages to many of the great shrines, and audiences with the saintly Pontiffs, Leo XIII and Pius X, seemed to have completed the foundation work for a Catholic leverage on my entire life.

Almost every Catholic, I am certain, has found himself countless times over the years reliving, in relation to the

Church, the role of the "prodigal son," who, having claimed his inheritance, squanders it in a foreign land, from whence he returns in wretchedness and hunger to implore the unfailing forgiveness of his progenitor—but for me, the parable of "the sower" has also had a specific personal warning, which will sound until the hour of my death: the seed being the Word of God that I had been taught from the days of my earliest youth. What of the actual *soil* on which it had fallen? The Evangelist gives a detailed account of four categories and interprets the parallel in the heart of man . . .

Just after I became of age, my mother died, and I went abroad to live. I was there when the first World War began. Here, in a world different from anything I had anticipated, began the real test of the ground on which the seed of the Word of God was to fall. Would it be too shallow, too rocky, too arid, to give substance to the embryonic life—or would the weeds and thistles (of sensationalism and worldliness) smother the growing grain, frustrating the ultimate fruition implicit in the design of the Sower—Whose "will is our sanctification"? . . .

Undoubtedly, each age has had its staggering problems, but I doubt that the plight of the Catholic, with childhood memories dating back to the eighteen-nineties, confronting the world situation in and after nineteen-fourteen, has had many parallels. At a given moment, he, a perhaps unconscious Victorian, aware of the unfolding blessings of the Industrial Revolution, secure in the conventionality and reserve of the era, looks forward to uninterrupted peace and constructive prosperity—but the years that immediately followed brought every other type of experience. Treaties were violated, countries invaded and plundered, life and property destroyed, the aesthetic treasures of the world needlessly reduced to ruins—and some ironically articulate

116

protagonists of religious faith only opined: Why blame Christianity? It has never been tried.

Growing out of this bewilderment, there was a great surge of social consciousness. Liberal thought emphasized that almost all our evils stemmed from the *status quo*— monarchy, privilege, the exploitation of the masses—and machinery was set to work to remedy the abuses of power. November 11, 1918, dawned on a world made "safe for democracy," or so at least some of us were naive enough to believe.

In the quarter of a century that preceded the outbreak of World War II, practically every aspect of life changed incredibly. Revolution, which some had assumed was exclusively synonymous with Russian Bolshevism, asserted itself in every field, on every level of activity and thought. The very proportions of the planet were suddenly diminished through radio and aviation. Facilitated communication and transportation, accessible to everyone, brought home even to those incapable of an elementary grasp of physical science, an intimation, at least, of the implications of Einstein's concept of relativity. This discovery, in turn, had a strong influence in the realm of morality. All standards of conduct were re-appraised with more and more daring, under the microscope of psychiatry and psychoanalysis. Imperceptibly, the sense of sin vanished from the public conscience, for right and wrong could only be decided pragmatically.

To most of these attitudes and trends, secular educational institutions (entrusted with the direction of so large a percentage of the impressionable youth of the land) gave full assent and encouragement, and for those beyond reach of those formative influences, the written word—mass published—in conjunction with all agencies of entertainment, did everything in its power to "debunk" in the minds of young and old the convictions that had been accepted as moorings for many generations. Nietzschean thought, which its author regarded as "a plough to the mind," permeated the mental processes of sophisticates, and the belief, among the rising generation, that the "only real Christian had died on the cross," seemed to express a very generalized feeling regarding the influence of Christ's teaching after two thousand years. Even the theism articulated by Washington and Jefferson as part of the foundation and structure of our national life had ceased to be emphasized as a background or reference for conduct.

So much for the world-picture through the twenties and thirties of this century, calls-to-arms of religious spokesmen notwithstanding. And all this time, on the soil of the world hardened by scepticism, heartlessness, and greed, the Eternal Sower let fall the seed of His Word.

During the first two decades of my life, which was a very sheltered one, I was surrounded almost exclusively by those who shared and practised the faith of my parents, but once I was free to explore the world, my social contacts extended themselves, and "sheep from other folds" became my close friends. Were I to group them alphabetically, a long list would start with Adventists, Anglicans, Anarchists, Astrologists, ending with Unitarians and Yogi—Jews, Buddhists, Christian Scientists, Presbyterians, Quakers, Bahais, Theosophists, Communists, etc., filling the gap between. There were many with no religious affiliation whatever, some who described themselves as agnostic, and others, scientifically enlightened adherents to the concept of a mechanistic universe, who were articulately atheistic. Out of these groups, some had strong convictions, others were searching and bewildered, but very few had minds closed by prejudicial commitment, and almost all seemed to me, potentially at least, to belong to the *Soul of the Church*, following, in other words, what light they had and abiding by the dictates of their conscience. Courage, aspiration, honesty, unselfishness, dependability, characterized their lives, and even though their idiom was religiously foreign, the evidence they gave of love of God, through solicitude for their neighbour, commended itself to me, a Catholic, a beneficiary of sacramental grace, as a phenomenon to be pondered and scrutinized. Their creeds, their doubts, their rejections, became my familiars, and in sympathy, I have often experienced a partial identification.

Why, then, am I today a Catholic, claiming membership in the Mystical Body of Christ, which is the Church of my adherence, not to be confused with aspects of the structure represented by individuals and factions, who seem to me so often misguided and inept? All my life the unanswerable *problem of pain*—limitless in scope and time—has haunted and tortured me; while during the years of my so-called maturity, the paralyzing philosophy of determinism insistently presented itself as a tempting panacea.

In the sixteenth chapter of St. Matthew's Gospel, a scene is described and a conversation recorded: "Who do you say that I am?" Our Lord asks St. Peter; and the unqualified endorsement of his reply, "Thou art the Christ, the Son of the living God," with which He placed irrevocably the keys of His kingdom into the hands of the humble fisherman, seems to me to highlight as well as to dissipate the dilemma of Christian faith. For if without Jesus Christ, true God and true Man, the universe is *unthinkable,* then He must be sought and accepted on the rock, against which He has promised the gates of hell will never prevail.

A thoughtful theologian has said that what most strikingly differentiates Catholics from their separated brethren is that these last celebrate the *memory* of the world's Redeemer, whereas Catholics proclaim *the living* Christ.

It was this statement that turned my attention to the

119

liturgy, and for the stimulation and support of faith, it commends itself to me as something almost indispensable. For many "practical" Catholics, this aspect of religion remains an almost closed book, or else something taken for granted. One can have as much or little as he chooses, and though a tremendous effort has been made, during the last fifty years, to bring the faithful into close touch with this phase of our spiritual inheritance, there is an enormous work still to be done in most parishes, schools, and colleges before the true significance of the liturgical year is recognized by all communicants. How many of us realize, for instance, that in the course of the four ever-recurring seasons, reflected through the Mass and the Divine Office—stated in terms of sublime literature—enacted through ennobling ritual, the life of Christ is constantly relived? Advent (a time of penance) leads to the birthday of Our Lord. His infancy, His boyhood, His first miracles, the episodes of His early ministry, are commemorated in the weeks that precede Lent, when the shadow of His forthcoming Passion falls upon the world. On Palm Sunday, He is seen triumphantly entering Jerusalem, and the branches blessed and carried on that occasion, to the sound of glad hosannas, will be reduced to ashes and placed on the foreheads of the faithful the next Ash Wednesday, with the words: "Remember, man, that dust thou art." At the Last Supper, on Maundy Thursday, we behold Him actually fulfilling the promise "to remain with us all days," but out of deference for the impending tragedy of Good Friday, the joy of this festivity is postponed until the celebration of Corpus Christi, later in the year. Easter is followed by the Ascension, then Pentecost. The great events in the life of the Blessed Virgin Mary—her birth, the Annunciation, the Visitation, her maternity, her Dolors, her Assumption—are each associated with a special day, as are the feasts of the Apostles, the martyrs, and the saints, who have found in and through the Church, down the centuries, their way to God. There are vigils for each of the great festivities so that a pattern of balance is maintained, as between the darkness and the light of our universe.

Without being placed, strictly speaking, in the framework of the liturgy, Catholic observance has set aside certain months of the year under special dedication. What could be more indicated than to regard May—supernal in character—as nature's particular tribute to the Queen of Heaven? Or that June, the month of effulgence (when sunlight and flowers, at least in that part of the world where Catholicism is most strongly represented, are suggestive of inexhaustible munificence), should invite us in a special manner to worship the infinitely compassionate and sacred Heart of Christ? Then in autumn, the season described by Keats as being of "mists and mellow fruitfulness," we are offered for emphasized honour the holy Rosary, which retraces, one by one, the mysteries—joyful, sorrowful, glorious —of the united lives of Our Lord and His Mother. No devotion in Christendom is more widespread than this telling of the beads, and in the wreath of roses which they represent, both practically and symbolically, saints and scholars, illiterates and worldlings, every type of human being identifies itself with the petition: "Pray for us sinners now and at the hour of our death."

The mention of the word death reveals another aspect of the question, why I am a Catholic. What else, I might ask, is there under the sun which stands between us and the confrontation of the inevitable experience of life? For whether it is our own end or the death of loved ones, the Church alone can say: "Fear not."

The month of November, during which the ancients celebrated the feast of the setting sun, has been set aside

for the commemoration of departed souls, and through the
Catholic doctrine of the Communion of Saints, we are
taught that we can still be of assistance, through our suff-
rages and remembrance, to those detained in purgatory.

There is one last and very personal reply to the question
which motivated these pages. Many years ago, a small community of Carmelite nuns made a foundation in San Francisco, and after the first Mass in their chapel there,
Archbishop Reardon, in welcoming them to his diocese,
congratulated his flock on the blessing of their presence.
"Ask them," he said, "to make you dear to God." And these
are words I have never forgotten. As part of the pattern of
prayer and expiation for the entire world, contemplative
religious fulfill a great function in the Church. They "care"
for souls. This is their *caritas*. And having my own sister in
their midst, I have been the unworthy beneficiary of such
indescribable protection that I may still presume to say:
penitently, trustingly, and gratefully, I hope to die in the
embrace of Holy Mother Church.

Maisie Ward

Maisie Ward was born in 1889 in the Isle of Wight, daughter of Wilfrid Ward and Josephine Hope-Scott. During the first World War she nursed in the Italian Hospital in London. She was one of the earliest members of the Catholic Evidence Guild and has been speaking on their street-corner platforms in England and America for thirty-four years. In 1926 she married Frank Sheed; two children and the firm of Sheed & Ward are a result of their union. She has written The Wilfrid Wards and The Transition, Insurrection versus Resurrection, Gilbert Keith Chesterton, Splendour of the Rosary, Young Mr. Newman *and* Return to Chesterton.

When I was young an essay about why one was still a Catholic would have been wholly unthinkable. *Of course* we were still Catholics—every one of us who had received at the font the gift of faith, had been educated in a Catholic home and school, prayed and received the sacraments. Our friends outside the True Fold might have difficulties—not so we. Or if by chance there was some slight matter that troubled us—say, for instance, the problem of pain or the existence of hell—we were reminded with great heartiness how Newman had said, "Ten thousand difficulties do not make one doubt." The way to deal with difficulties was the same as the way to deal with temptations against purity—banish them instantly, make acts of faith. Faith,

123

which is after all an act of the intellect, was treated as wholly a matter of the will—it seemed as though the value of the virtue became greater, the harder it was made for the mind. No cradle Catholic, only a convert, could tell the history of his mind, for only a convert had a history.

But people did leave the Church, and what were we to think of them? Cardinal Manning had asked, when told of a priest's apostasy, "Is it Punch or Judy?" and this feeble jest was repeated with great admiration. The loss of faith was (we were told) the result of sin: impurity, drunkenness, or supremely pride. It was "inexcusable," argued the manuals of moral theology, so the good Catholic who might have tried to be charitable in other matters could here let himself go in condemnation.

If such was the intellectual atmosphere of English Catholicism in my youth, it was very far from being the atmosphere in my own home. My father and mother were two of the most utterly honest people I have ever known, and their faith was far too profound and too enlightened for them to fear the confronting of difficulties. Also they were soaked in Newman, and I smile when I think of the contrast between the use commonly made of his "ten thousand difficulties" and what it became replaced in its context. The two things, J.H.N. continues, "are incommensurable," and he adds that many of the truths that he would find it most impossible to doubt are also those which are most encompassed by difficulties—the first of these being the very existence of God himself.

I

My mother taught us doctrine as small children, and I remember with especial vividness our first day at the convent where, after a change of residence, our education was to be continued. A very young postulant, who definitely knew

124

less than I did, was set to teach doctrine to the "little ones." She told them a story of a child who lost her temper at the age of three, committed a murder at the age of thirty, and went straight to hell. The story was not well received at home, and my mother thereafter continued herself to teach us our religion, sending us to school half an hour late, after the doctrine period. This was not well received at school: there were four of us, one in each class, and the climax was reached when at the first diocesan examination we each came out top in our respective classes. When the examiner realized we were all Wards he appeared embarrassed—but he had already given his verdict.

The nun in charge, with "head bloody but unbowed," bestowed certain medals that had been promised to the most proficient on other pupils and told all the children that the examiner had "favoured" us because he had been at school with my father.

Judging by other people's experience, this incident might have shaken my faith in the Church: all it did in fact was to deepen my faith in my mother and fill me with the unfathomable contempt, that only a child can have, for the nun. It was not a good educational atmosphere. Later, at my second convent, the teaching was excellent.

I doubt whether the *very* young are often affected by religious difficulties: it is after leaving school and meeting the problems of life that knowledge of the Faith bears fruit and lack of that knowledge often spells disaster. And, too, the utter absence of the constructive work today made possible by the Lay Apostolate was a very grievous thing in my own youth. I spent several years beating about vainly in search of some vocational work. I lived for short periods at an East End Settlement, Mile End, where I met one of the most striking personalities I have ever known.

Sibyl Smyth Piggott—known to us all as Eliza—had in

125

girlhood cared for nothing but hunting. The loss of one eye daunted her not at all: she went on hunting. Once during an off season she visited Mile End, supposedly, like myself, for a short period. Only Eliza stayed for life, taking at first one month's holiday to hunt in, later giving up even this. Bit by bit her small capital was used up, placing orphans in homes, succouring the misery around her. She gave herself with her money—the most loving, humorous, simple self. Everyone adored her, everyone laughed at her. Her strongest suit in all the work she tirelessly did was teaching doctrine to half-witted children who, she often said, showed that they knew God when they appeared to know nothing else. It was her great joy to prepare them for their First Communion.

Curiously enough, here at Mile End, where women would tell you of their husbands producing by drunken kicks the premature birth of a child, where suffering and sin were very nakedly before one's eyes, the Faith seemed daylight clear—I fancy it was, with me at least, Eliza out of whose eyes it shone, although our parish priest, Father Doherty, also awakened my deep admiration.

Nor in my own case could I ever have been anything except a Catholic. But there were times when I could, but for my home surroundings, have slipped into being nothing at all. And in this matter I bow to the manuals which say one is inexcusable—for inexcusable I most certainly should have been, indeed was.

While my parents gave me intellectual foundations that were to stand me in good stead, I think they both lacked the educational mind that could have helped me to do worthwhile work in the years that followed school. I wanted to go to Oxford but was persuaded to give up the idea. I was happy for a short time as my father's secretary, but my mother thought he worked me too hard and the thing was dropped. I disliked being presented at Court and taken to dances, but a sort of uneasy worldliness was growing on me.

And then there were the heavenly delights of foreign travel: Brittany, Normandy, Switzerland, Italy, across Europe to Constantinople, Italy again, Italy always. Little *pensioni,* gay with flowers (full board, wine included, at 5 lire), pictures, churches, Ruskin teaching one to love Giotto, Browning giving one eyes for the full moon, "lamping Samminiato," learning a little Italian, climbing up to Fiesole, discovering all the things everyone else knew which yet came upon me with the freshness of a May morning—a thing which also is not a new discovery.

I think, although I went to Mass and prayed in the churches, it was at this time that my real spiritual danger had begun. This was such a fascinating world, so various and delightful one could never exhaust it. And little by little it swallowed up all my energies: creation pushed the Creator into the background. My prayers were becoming "lip service," distractions swept in unheeded, life stretched ahead and there was so much to do and see and feel here that the hereafter must be left to care for itself. "Life might last— one can but try."

This was one mood; another very frequent one was that of a profound and nameless depression which I never analyzed. Deep down I believe I knew that my life just then was pretty worthless.

When war broke out in 1914, I totally lacked spiritual reserves. I was feverishly patriotic, madly determined to nurse soldiers and full of scorn for all my old friends who had not instantly enlisted or found war jobs. I must have been quite intolerable.

I worked in a hospital till I broke down. My prayers got fewer and fewer. We were on duty 7 a.m. to 8 p.m. (two hours off), and the only chance for Mass was to get up at 5. I decided I'd "had it," and Sunday alone now saw me "fulfilling my obligation."

How wise the Church is in this matter of obligation. But for this minimum command, how many would abandon all pretence of "keeping holy the Sabbath" and even of the natural duty of adoring their creator. Apart from Sunday Mass I prayed by now hardly at all.

In the middle of the war my father died. Beside his death-bed, faith seemed visibly to pass into sight, and we were all left for the moment uplifted and fortified. But these moments cannot endure, and other elements were warring within me, briefly swallowed up by the glory of this death.

An eccentric uncle, dying a little earlier, had left part of the family property to every bishop of England and to four main Catholic charities. My father's position as residuary legatee seemed a mere farce, and he had undertaken a lawsuit which ended after his death in a compromise. Hurling myself into all these matters I suddenly realized with the full force of my imagination that I might waste my life totally, like an old aunt of ours whose really powerful mind had run to seed in dreams of past family grandeur and a possible resurgence. Worse than that, a miasma now enveloped my faith: it all seemed utterly unreal. A dull, cold, dark hospital did not obscure the supernatural with the radiance of Florence by moonlight, but it shut it out far more totally. Delight had passed, and I had not used it to discover God, who was behind it.

I had a moment of near despair, but I happened to open my New Testament, and my eye fell on the words, "The creature was made subject to vanity not willingly but by reason of Him who made it subject to hope." That night I really prayed.

Whether it be through one's own fault or quite blame-lessly that mist and fog cover the spiritual world, it is then that spectres loom through the fog, that difficulties appear quite indistinguishable from doubts. And it is then that the Catholic mind is most needed to rally to the will's support.

These "dead" periods have not been rare in my life; probably they are common enough with many Catholics. After all, the material world is so plain and obvious, and we are living in a society which stresses the material and whose very spirituality is what Gilson called Maeterlinck's, "of the earth, earthy." How many books does one read, plays and pictures watch, programmes listen to, in which God, the soul, eternity are even adverted to: how often are we shown any vision of life which sees it as longer than three score years and ten? For Gerard Manley Hopkins Our Lady was like the air we breathe: but the lungs of most of us are filled with a mixture of psychology and physical science and the fumes of pleasure or pain in daily living.

And then there are the obvious stones of scandal which reinforce this atmosphere. How can a good God let men die in agony, permit war when peace was promised on the first Christmas; how, above all, can He allow hell? Where is the soul to be found in the idiot child or in the dying old man whose outlook appears in no way different from an animal's? If the Church is God's Church, why the awful scandals in its history, why has it not transformed the world; why, wherever it is triumphant, has the world appeared to transform it?

These and many other questions surge through the mind, or form pictures in the vacant imagination which are much more terrible than any train of actual reasoning. At moments certainly one imagines that all is lost, when mind and will are in fact not greatly affected.

II

In many respects my experience after the foundation of the Catholic Evidence Guild in 1919 resembled that of a convert to the Church. Well as my mother and the nuns in my second convent had taught me, the gaps at that date in my religious knowledge were incredible. And the study which I now undertook had precisely the effect described to me by a convert as "lifting shutters in my mind." Catholic theology is the intellectual formation and expression of a reality—the most real of all realities. And what was now happening to me has been described by Mr. Belloc as the recognition of reality.

Another element was added by the almost daily contact with a street-corner audience. For the Catholic Evidence Guild is a society that exists to teach the Faith out-of-doors. In parks and at street corners a platform is set up, surmounted by a crucifix. The meeting opens with the Our Father, Hail Mary, Gloria and invocation of the Holy Ghost: it closes with the Apostles' Creed. Each speaker gives a brief lecture on some one doctrine and then invites questions from the crowd. Although we are eager that priests should speak for us, the C.E.G. is primarily a lay society. A rigorous training indoors prepares us theologically and technically for our work, but *above all* we learn from the crowd. The needs and the cravings of the men and women we meet, their "beginnings and surmises," are an invitation to us to assist them in arriving at the fullness of Catholic truth. But they are also an invitation to us to deepen our own knowledge and become capable of building a bridge from our mind to theirs.

Chesterton somewhere answers the man who asks an explanation of the crazy conditions on which alone the prince can enter the magic palace by saying, "If it comes to that, explain the palace." And my husband, once told by a heckler that *he* could make a better world than God had, entreated him there and then to make a rabbit, "just to establish confidence."

This was the direction in which my mind at first moved. The half feeling I had of the plausibleness of a naturalist view of life dissolved when I really encountered people who held it. For their whole position was a negative one and no attempt was made by Communist, secularist or mere anti-Catholic to explain the universe: they could see only the blots on a paper covered with a writing they did not attempt to read. And presently I found myself trying, with Browning, to enter into the minds of men who were endeavouring to limit life to what was here and now. With Browning, too, I recognized their failure:

> Just when we're safest, there's a sunset touch,
> A fancy from a flower-bell, someone's death,
> A chorus-ending from Euripides,—
> And that's enough for fifty hopes and fears
> As old and new at once as Nature's self,
> To rap and knock and enter in our soul,
> Take hands and dance there, a fantastic ring,
> Round the ancient idol, on his base again,
> The grand Perhaps!

From the age of twelve I had been a passionate Browningite, and it was with his help that I began to work out an idea which the Hyde Park crowds constantly confirmed: how hard it is to remain consistently an unbeliever, how hard, once you admit God, to keep Christ out; how almost impossible to look at Our Lord and deny His supreme claim. This too Browning, with the eagle's feather of the poet to wing his arrow, had expressed far better than any

131

apologist known to me. No mere catalogue of miracles and prophecy, but Christ's claim to

> Fill up, make one with His each soul He loves,
>
> His claim to be
>> Groom for each bride! Can a mere man do this?
>> Call Christ then the illimitable God
>> Or lost . . .

Seeing Our Lord as "The Way, the Truth, the Life," Browning faced, too, the fact that as we walk that way it often seems, like some mountain track, to disappear before our feet. Yet looking from below we see it stretch "from base to brow, clear unmistakable." And he asks:

>> What if the breaks themselves should prove at last
>> The most consummate of contrivances
>> To train a man's eye, teach him what is faith?

But must I part company with this tremendous fellow, this Browning, when it came to thinking about the Catholic Church? For the other side of "Bishop Blougram" was its sneering picture of Wiseman, and the same pen that gave us "A Death in the Desert" and "Saul" had written that very ugly "Soliloquy in a Spanish Cloister" and "Holy Cross Day." No, surely it was but fair to apply to Browning the same test as one applied to the universe: the positive versus the negative: read the writing instead of searching out the blots.

And after all were there not blots enough on the Church's own copy-book, was the "Spanish Cloister" an impossible picture, had not Browning *seen* the oddities in worship he describes in "Up at a Villa—Down in the City"? The Catholics who solemnly warned me against Browning had the same mentality as the unbeliever who saw only the blots on creation, or the anti-Catholic who saw only the scandals in the Church's history. To reach any reality you have to pierce through a sort of cloud of unknowing which conceals and sometimes distorts it. This cloud around the Church Browning never fully dispersed, though at moments he pierced it. For consider that when one searches for a supreme expression in literature of the moment of the Consecration at Mass it is found in Browning:

> Earth breaks up, time drops away,
> In flows Heaven, with its new day
> Of endless life, when He who trod,
> Very Man and very God
> This earth in weakness, shame and pain,
> Dying the death whose signs remain
> Up yonder on the accursed tree,—
> Shall come again, no more to be
> Of captivity the thrall,
> But the one God, All in all,
> King of kings, Lord of lords,
> As His servant John received the words,
> "I died, and live for evermore!"

The first line of the next stanza has always seemed to me supremely sad: "Yet I was left outside the door." Can any of us, lacking the poet's tongue, give witness of what it is we have found inside?

III

Reading even a little of the perpetual argument as to how the ills of today are to be met, I was struck by the fact that every remedy offered seemed to have about it the smell of death or dissolution. Not enough houses: limit your families. Too many sick old people: euthanasia. Unhappy marriages: dissolve them. Communist menace: bigger and better bombs. There is a sort of fearful kinship, too, between the mentality that will take fine agricultural land and turn it into playing fields, and that which will divert the marriage act from the giving of new life into a sterile search for enjoyment. Almost all the books, too, which have deservedly won high fame of late are cries of despair over the destruction of beauty and the perishing of freedom.

Starting one day to fly the Atlantic, I seized on a couple of books for companionship. One was *The New Yorker* collection of short stories, the other a medieval anthology. We came down at Gander in Newfoundland, and one of those weary waits in the airport began, punctuated by raucous singing from a party that had preceded ours and had already had several hours to get drunk in. I opened each of my books in turn and took alternate bites at them. (There was nothing else to eat until one of our passengers discovered and broached a large tin of biscuits. But there was, or had been, plenty to drink, as we who were sober found to our continuing cost.)

After a while I began to try to analyze the effect and the quality of my two books. As a work of art *The New Yorker* collection won in every respect. It was slickly and competently written, most of the stories were well constructed, nor was wit lacking. The medieval anthology was, most of it, hardly literature at all, and utterly diverse in its subjects and its quality. There was an account of how a servant should prepare his lord's bath; there was a letter to a parent from his son's schoolmaster; a scolding from a bishop directed at clergy who clearly were highly reprehensible, a dissertation by St. Thomas proving that life on this earth could never bring perfect happiness. But the medieval world had given birth to something unknown to the world of *The New Yorker*, and I began to ask myself why I was reading this book with such delight, why I had wearied so soon of the other. The answer came clearly and suddenly: the modern book, like

134

the modern world, lacked vitality; the medieval book, like the medieval world, was bubbling with it. This was a book of bits and pieces, but the skill of its selectors lay in the fact that it really did present a cross section of a vital and vigorous society.

Rightly enough Raymond Preston, leading us to a study of Chaucer, chose for his illustrations the glory of Gothic cathedrals, the loveliness of medieval illumination, the music of its singing. For with all the blots upon it and despite its battles and its plagues, the world of the Middle Ages was a world of hope, and was creative.

Beauty encompassed men, and the conviction of eternity enabled them to accept, often with energy and with delight, that matter of daily living which has become so burdensome to their descendants. The very monks who had abandoned the world had not despaired of it, and they wove into their missals and breviaries pictures of men and women tilling and spinning, hunting, hawking, dancing. This world and the world to come was one composite picture, and the spirit of God breathed over it, despite the sins of men and despite the devil—most realistically pictured in his successful or abortive attempts to carry off their souls. Living became a high adventure, and I believe if I had to choose on that social level alone I should be a Catholic. For the Church which gave this zest to life is the one society left today in which that zest may still be found. She is needed to restore the Natural.

But of course it all goes far deeper. These elements of vitality and beauty in medieval life are only by-products of that life of the spirit which the Church still pours forth upon her children in an age in which the world in general has turned aside from her.

An immense weakness in my youth had been the stereotyped and pietistic treatment of the supreme expression of

135

God's Church—the saints. The chapters on "The Saint's humility," "The Saint's charity," etc., could have been neatly clipped from one biography and inserted in another without discovery—more especially as he was usually called, not by that name of his own that is written in heaven, but simply (and I thought nauseatingly) "the Servant of God." The personality and variety of the saints was a chief discovery when Father Martindale, Henry Ghéon and others, began to tell of them. I fancy that any one of the saints studied closely would be enough, the rich variety of them far more than enough, to bring realization of a power in the Church not to be found elsewhere to produce something greater than a superman and certainly more lovable.

When St. Basil rebuked a Roman proconsul in the name of the people, the man exclaimed, "I have never been spoken to like this before." St. Basil answered, "You have never before met a Christian bishop." In the great bishops of that age—Ambrose, Augustine, Basil and the rest—the authority of sanctity is seen shaping a new world in the midst of chaos and dissolution, creating social services on immense scale, supplying for the failure of the civil authorities, making of the Church so stable a thing that Roman culture, laws and literature were kept safe right through the horrors of barbarian invasion to emerge, baptized and Christianized, into the light of the Middle Ages.

Nor was it only the bishops—though it was always the saints—who led this extraordinary movement. The hermits who fled from the cities were, by their prayers, the great example and powerhouse of the new people of God, they and the martyrs who died triumphant. And though Anthony kept fleeing into deeper solitude and Simeon died alone on his pillar, the solitary hermit more commonly turned into the monk of a monastery, who copied manuscripts and conquered the barren soil, making it fruitful. From St. Jerome and St. Paula's twin monastery at Bethlehem, whence the Vulgate came to us, to St. Hilda's at Whitby, which was the cradle of English literature; from St. Patrick, himself building six hundred churches and making of each a centre of a new civilization, to the glorious Benedictine abbeys that spread throughout Europe; wherever you look, you see a saint or many saints, and you ask what sanctity means. You see these monasteries, these places of creative life and culture destroyed by fire and sword, as wave after wave of barbarians sweep across the land. And you see that a saint endures all things, dies loving not only God but the men who slay him, or lives on (as St. Patrick did) to convert his persecutors and turn many of them into saints also.

For this is a stream that never dries, and cannot, in the Church's life. Christians grow cold, and the saint emerges from the fire of God's love, which consumes him totally, to bring back to them that warmth of love. "He was a burning and a shining light," said Christ of John the Baptist. That glowing heart of love, which melts snow and ice and beats so fast it all but breaks, is seen in saint after saint: in Francis and in Catherine marked with the wounds of Christ, in Philip and in Theresa, and more hiddenly but perhaps most profoundly in John of the Cross. Like runners across country, one of these athletes of Christ seems briefly passing to hand his torch to another, so that the light never grows dim.

Thus in that terrible moment of the Reformation, when Thomas More stood against Henry for the supernatural authority of the Church, when he held in his keeping the great tradition of Christian charity and Christian humanism, it was the monks of the Charterhouse going to their death upon whom he looked from the window of his cell and from whom he drew strength and inspiration.

Thomas More lost the battle, and England began to die with his death. But meanwhile the great saints of Spain were

137

pushing forward: Ignatius, Francis, Peter Claver, and Theresa were obeying the command of multiplication that is spiritual as well as physical. New worlds were opening. First Francis de Sales and then Vincent de Paul were faced with a task amid decadent French Catholics not unlike that of the early bishops in a pagan world. And presently a poor beggar full of lice was praying and expiating from shrine to shrine of Europe. The beggar's name was Benedict Joseph Labre.

Which was the greater, which the more important to the Church's life, this poor beggar or the Curé d'Ars, who as a little boy had seen him passing by, and it may well be had caught even in childhood a spark from that living flame? This is a question to which, if there be an answer, God only knows it. But I doubt if there is one. And indeed it is only partly true to say that each saint catches light from another: "He that is strong-hearted," wrote More in his prison as he meditated on Christ's agony, "may find a thousand glorious valiant martyrs whose example he may right joyously follow. But thou now, O timorous and weak, silly sheep, think it sufficient for thee only to walk after Me which am thy Shepherd and Governor and so instruct thyself and put thy trust in Me."

To write of More brings to mind the third great intellectual influence of my life. After Newman and Browning came Chesterton—in the long run the greatest influence of them all, especially because I could watch over the years his vision of the Church as it grew clearer. One thing he had seen as early as when he described in *Orthodoxy* the outward splendour and inward asceticism of Thomas à Becket. He had seen that the saint grows only in the Church and draws his strength from that divine source. And he expressed it perfectly much later when he wrote *ubi Petrus, ibi Franciscus*. The chief religion of authority is also the chief religion of the spirit in one very special sense. The urge of mysticism is widespread, but is often either stifled or driven into wild and dangerous fanaticism apart from the means appointed by God for its balanced development. The saints are richly various, but inside the Church they cannot escape a certain reference to the centre, which is the very thing that makes them saints, not fanatics or mere reformers. I have seen enough of these two types at street corners to rejoice that the Acts of the Apostles mentions the Church so often, as well as the Holy Ghost Who is the love of God working through a visible society. And indeed the sheer contact, at this same street corner, with men in their thousands would, I fancy, keep in the Church any sane Catholic. For their need of her is so obvious, their lack so pitiful.

Clare Luce compares the saints to a mosaic of Christ that is growing gradually into the completeness of His portrait. But this portrait is a living likeness; it is His Mystical Body, through which He does today the work He did on earth through His natural body. Thus to try to determine the relative greatness of the saints is as futile as it would be "if the ear should say, because I am not the eye, I am not of the body . . . . If the whole body were the eye, where would be the hearing?"

IV

Only the general ignorance of St. Paul's epistles can account for an omission even stranger than that of our neglect of the human individuality of the saints. This was the complete blank in our theological teaching concerning that supernatural relationship between the saints and ourselves, ourselves and one another, the saints, ourselves, and Christ Our Lord, which makes up the stupendous doctrine of the Mystical Body. We believed and daily repeated our belief in the Communion of Saints. But of the deepest

139

meaning of that communion, I certainly was unaware for nearly the first half of my life.

This doctrine, revealed to St. Paul when Christ said to him, "Saul, Saul, why persecutest thou *Me?*" gives us in its twofold aspect the whole secret of living. Christ is in us as He pours into His body His divine vitality; we are in Christ as the cells of that body, receiving their life through their identification with it. We are closer to Christ by grace than even His mother by nature. "Behold," He said, pointing to His disciples, "my mother and my brethren." But Mary's nearness to Him was not merely natural, she alone was *full* of grace, she "bore Him in her soul before she bore Him in her body." We can never fathom all that that nearness means, but we can draw nearer to Him through her help.

The first teaching of this doctrine was so tremendous in its effect that, in a world as torn and rent by enmities and divisions as is the world of today, St. Paul was able to exclaim: "there is now neither Gentile nor Jew, circumcision nor uncircumcision, Barbarian nor Scythian, bond nor free. But Christ is all and in all" (Col. iii. 11).

Talking to people who lived through the blitz in London, one touches a depth of regret, almost of nostalgia, for the charity and unity brought by patriotism during that moment of England's supreme danger. Why, they ask, half bewildered, did it die so suddenly? Why is patriotism not enough? Surely because humanity itself is not enough. When Saul the persecutor was stricken down to rise up as Paul the Apostle, God's command to Ananias to seek him out ended with the words "for behold he prayeth." Christianity has been defined as the union of man with God in Christ, and it is only in Christ that man can also be united with his fellow man, only in Christ that he can achieve the fullness of his humanity.

"Man was made," Caryll Houselander reminds us, "to

140

be caught up into the immensity of the Life of God, of the Blessed Trinity, the Life which is the cause of all other life and power. In God man's individuality is not swamped and submerged, but it is marvellously released from its limitations, set free in the infinite life of Love and borne along on its eternal torrents of beauty."

Saints, known and unknown, are those men and women who have wholly "put on" this divine humanity, and the life of the race is given by St. Paul its termination when each one of the "well-beloved people that shall be saved" has taken the place meant for him from all eternity in Christ. "Until we all meet into the unity of faith, and of the knowledge of the Son of God, unto a perfect man, unto the measure of the age of the fulness of Christ" (Eph. iv. 13).

The increasing momentum of the Lay Apostolate has brought with it a fuller development of the other aspect of this doctrine: the relation of Christ's Mystical Body with the outside world. Slowly we realize our immense responsibility. God, becoming incarnate, worked through a human nature. He used that nature to heal and to bless, He gave pardon through His human lips, He gave Himself with His human hands. In that human nature He suffered and died for the world. When, at the Ascension, that human nature left the earth, God incarnate continued to act, through a multitude of human beings. We, His Church, are the Incarnation continued.

Like Our Lady visiting St. Elizabeth, we have to carry Christ to others. Like St. Elizabeth welcoming Mary, we have to discover Christ in others. Layman as well as priest must be the channel of Christ's redeeming power, and if I am not the living cell God meant me to be, He will create another soul to fill my place.

"This is the secret," writes Caryll Houselander, "of man's capacity to fulfill his human nature through love, to atone

141

for guilt by his suffering, to experience joy in a world that
is overburdened by sorrow. He has been given back the
life of Christ—Christ's mind to adore with, Christ's love to
love with, Christ's sacrifice to atone with."

Everyone, I suppose, as life draws on, feels within him
powers he has not developed and now cannot develop,
things still to be done that he can never hope to accomplish.
I doubt if it be true, as is often said, that feelings grow less
keen in age. It is rather that we learn how little we can do, in
time, with desires that belong to eternity.

> " . . . only I discern
> Infinite passion and the pain
> Of finite hearts that yearn."

In youth the possibilities of life itself appear infinite. It
is the old who hear within them an echo to Caryll Houselander's saying, "Sanctity is the only cure for the vast unhappiness of our universal failure as human beings."

Yet there is at least one half-hour of every day which
we begin by approaching God as the joy of our youth, when
the promise seems fulfilled that that youth shall be "renewed
as the eagle's." "So little time" is often now the burden of
our thoughts, but at Mass that burden falls from our shoulders. The words come new every morning, though we have
heard them many thousands of times. Imagine any poem or
play that could thus be repeated and never stale. Those
prayers cover every human need: in them we ask pardon of
God and our fellows, in them we adore and love and thank
"through Him and in Him and by Him." We are brought
into the closest companionship with our fellow Christians
on earth—and in heaven with apostles and martyrs, con-
fessors and virgins, all the angels and the Queen of angels.
Our minds and hearts are enlarged to the measure of this

companionship; understanding and strength pour into us for the day we are about to live.

What would I not give that that daily immense experience might be allowed to me and all Christians in the fullest and richest fashion, when our tongues could sing or speak the words of life, *"Gloria in excelsis Deo," "Credo in unum Deum," "Suscipiat Dominus sacrificium,"* when we might actually voice our answer to the *Sursum Corda—"Habemus ad Dominum."*

In nothing was the lack of a Catholic mind more manifest in my youth than in our attitude towards the Mass. "You think of it," I was once unkindly told, "only as machinery for producing Communion." There is no better way for bringing understanding of the Action of Mass, of what is happening at the altar, than for the priest to dialogue the words with the people as he stands facing them at one of those low and narrow altars that in France are now so often placed in the centre of the church. Lacking this, we can still learn more, day by day, of what we are doing, and how to do it, during those thirty minutes when we are truly bearing our part in offering a worthy sacrifice to God, when the measure of our littleness is enlarged not merely to that of saint or apostle but to Christ Himself, truly present as priest and victim, re-presenting to the Father the one sacrifice of Calvary in which man and God are made one in Christ.

Communion, though not all of Mass, is an integral part of it, and it was logical enough that the daily coming of Christ to such a multitude of Christians should have led to a more ardent study of the Mass and of the whole liturgy. And now groups of laymen, reciting the Divine Office, are daily thanking God for his unspeakable gift and preparing themselves for its daily renewal. Nor is it merely fanciful when many French priests today translate the words (whose meaning no scholar will vouch for) *Ite, missa est* into the

143

simple French *Allez, c'est votre mission*. It is indeed our mission to make known to the world the unspeakable gift we have received.

Mass and the Real Presence are today, as they were when Christ first gave them to man, an immense stumbling-block to Jew and Gentile alike. It is at that point chiefly that men turn back and walk no more with Him. It is supremely because of this gift that the Catholic exclaims, "Lord, to whom shall we go? Thou hast the words of eternal life."

Hugh Stott Taylor

Hugh Stott Taylor *was born in 1890 at St. Helens, Lancs., an island of Catholicism where he had a "one in three" chance of being born a Catholic; married Elizabeth Sawyer in 1919 who was born at Preston, Lancs., with a similar probability of being born a Catholic. Educated at Liverpool, Stockholm and Hanover 1906–1914. Came to Princeton as Instructor in 1914 for one year and remained there ever since. Served the Munitions Inventions Department 1917–1919 in London, World War I, and the Manhattan District Project, at the request of the British Government, from 1940 to 1945. After World War II he was appointed Dean of the Graduate School in Princeton 1945 and relinquished the Chairmanship of the Department of Chemistry after 25 years in 1951.*

"For I, that had much rather have men not philosophers than not Christians, should be much better content to see you ignore the mysteries of nature than deny the author of it." *Robert Boyle*

In one of the upper rooms in the Wren Building of the College of William and Mary in Williamsburg, Virginia, there hangs on the wall a portrait of Robert Boyle. The attendant who shows you through this historic, and original, building of the early English settlement, and of the second oldest college of the United States, will tell you that it is a portrait of the man who discovered Boyle's

145

Law, that volume and pressure of gases vary inversely one to the other. If you press your curiosity as to the presence of that particular portrait in that particularly beautiful setting, your curiosity will be richly rewarded. You will discover that the College of William and Mary, and incidentally Harvard College also, were the recipients of benefactions from the Honorable Robert Boyle. He bequeathed a portion of his estate to these two educational institutions in Virginia and Massachusetts, ordaining that these funds should be used for the education of the American Indians and for their instruction in the Christian faith, with the hope that they might engage in missionary activity among their fellows on the North American continent. Out of the Boyle bequest, the College of William and Mary erected Brasserton House, which derives its name from the estate which furnished Boyle with the income thus expended. The attendant in the Wren Building will tell you that Brasserton House was reserved in part for the Indian scholars, and he further avers that there is no evidence that any Indian so educated ever became a Christian missionary.

Your curiosity will have brought you to the definite conclusion that, at least in the case of one very eminent man, in the earliest years of the modern era of science, in the seventeenth century, a dedication both to "divine science" and to the science of nature, natural philosophy, was possible and achieved. Boyle wrote a book entitled *The Excellence of Theology, Compared with Natural Philosophy;* another was entitled *The Christian Virtuoso,* designed to show "that there is no inconsistence between a man's being an industrious virtuoso, and a good Christian." If you seek further you will find that such was the temper of the age in which Boyle lived. Science, natural philosophy, was a single aspect of the total humanistic intellectual life of which "divine science" was an essential, harmonious element. It

146

is my present contention that this is not an old-fashioned attitude to life which the advances of modern science and modern knowledge have all changed. Indeed, I will go further and assert that it must become a new-fashioned attitude to life which society as a whole must re-acquire if it is to attain once more to health, satisfaction and salvation.

Harmony between sacred and profane science in a single modern physical setting is to be found in Castel Gondolfo, the Papal villa on the outskirts of Rome to which the Pope may now repair, a refuge from the summer heat of the Holy City. If you are especially privileged, you may be ushered through numerous antechambers into the august, yet very paternal presence of His Holiness, there to pay him homage, listen to his kindly counsel and advice. That is the normal limit of the visit to Castel Gondolfo, and one leaves the villa behind with the Swiss Guard on sentry duty at the gate on the village square as the car returns you to the city. To a few there comes the extra pleasure of stepping out of the antechambers of the Papacy into the extreme modernity of an astrophysics laboratory. Here, under a single roof, therefore, are all the paraphernalia for a world-wide supervision of the members of the Catholic Church and, by contrast, but not at all incongruously, the spectroscopes and telescopes, the densitometers, the electronic equipment necessary for an intensive scientific exploration of the extra-terrestial universe.

In the terminology of the late nineteenth century a great deal both of heredity and environment entered into my make-up. At that time, Freud and the subconscious had not attained to their primacy in the construction of the individual. It is a significant element in the heredity that both my grandfathers were converts to Catholicism. From that derives an intensity of devotion to Catholic thought and

147

action which was characteristic of both my parents. My mother had been given a college education such as was available to young women in England in the 1870's at a training college in preparation for the teaching of Catholic children in the primary elementary schools of the time. A dedication to the Catholic faith and a passionate devotion to the education of her own children and to her children's children, at any cost or sacrifice, were the lasting results of that early college training. My father shared the same dedication to religion but lacked the formal educational process that was hers. Probably the chance of a job in the chemical laboratory of a factory in industrial Lancashire was the determining element in his ultimate pursuit of a career in applied science. Certain it is that, at a very early stage in that career, in spite of the lack of formal training in science, he was making significant contributions to technology. He himself always recognized the empirical nature of his knowledge. It was accumulated in the hard school of experience. Later in life he was frequently surprised by the possession of scientific knowledge by his sons which came by training rather than by experience. On such occasions he was wont to question the processes of scientific thought or reasoning by which a conclusion was reached which he knew to be right from his own factual experience. His rich experience was coupled with a sound research instinct, ever ready to test a new formula, a novel procedure. He was, I believe, the first to administer oxygen from a cylinder to a workman overcome by carbon monoxide gas in a gas-producer plant. I know, from personal experience, that he was able by sight to determine the right heat for a pot of melting glass, for I was present when he reproved the workman for heating the glass "metal" too hot, even though the pyrometers recorded the correct temperature. "The pyrometers are wrong," he said, and subsequent tests proved that he was

148

right. I remember the first occasion that I accompanied him up Fifth Avenue, New York, in 1915. I was astonished at the length of time during which he observed some of the department store displays. Enquiry revealed that what he actually was observing was the quality of the polishing of the large plate-glass windows. To his trained eye the quality was not the best—to me they were just "polished plate."

As boys we never had the privilege of the basement in our home for "stinks" or other activities, for it was already the laboratory in which my father tried out some of his extra-curricular ideas. There is no doubt that my own interest in science derives heavily from that heredity and environment. What was further characteristic of my father was that there was an entire harmony between his life as an experienced scientist and his life as a faithful Catholic. And both of my parents would, had they known of it, have answered an enquiry of their children with the statement of Robert Boyle: "I should be much better content to see you ignore the mysteries of nature than deny the author of it." Not knowing it, they probably fell back on the answer in the catechism: "What doth it profit a man . . . ?" We were brought up in a parish served by Jesuit fathers, always known, yesterday and today, as Lowe House Parish, never by its name, "St. Mary's." Penal laws and regulations possibly determined its name. It was in Lancashire, where islands of Catholic faith had persisted undefeated from Reformation times to the present. Doubtless my parents had often heard that St. Ignatius had finally gained the adherence of St. Francis Xavier by prolonged repetition of the "What doth it profit" quotation. My parents in turn used it oftentimes in their admonitions to us.

With that heredity and environment I was sent to a convent school where boys were permitted to remain until they reached the "dangerous age of eight." We boys of the late 1890's were lucky, in that permission had been granted to lower the age at which the First Holy Communion could be received. The good nuns lavished especial care on our preparation for the Sacrament and then thrust us out into a wicked world. A year or so followed in a sort of intermediate school which the Jesuit Fathers were attempting to establish. Ecclesiastical disapproval ended the experiment, and so the boys passed on to the local Catholic elementary school. At eleven years of age, with the aid of a "town scholarship," I passed to the local secondary school, Cowley Grammar School. That was the year of transition from a definitely Catholic to a secular environment. As event succeeded event, from secondary school to university, from university to post-graduate research in foreign lands, to an appointment to the faculty of a private university in the U.S.A., the secular environment continued. Only at long intervals and for brief periods was it possible to return to the Catholic educational environment of the earliest years.

From the formative influences of home and school life, we passed, light-hearted and gay, to "bright college years." We were budding scientists rapidly initiated into the mysteries and the satisfactions of scientific research. We were the children of the new scientific age, imbued with all that confident optimism and belief in progress that the rapid nineteenth-century scientific development had bred. The new century was still young, and the prospect was for "magic casements opening wide" to still greater achievements that science would secure. "Science culturing man's animal poverty, leisuring his toil." Before the fateful shot at Sarajevo we had been witnesses of the international organization of science. Mendeleef, architect of the atomic classification, had come from Russia to the halls of science in England; we had spent *"wanderjahre"* in Stockholm, Helsingfors, St. Petersburg, heard Arrhenius discuss not only

150

his science but also his travels east to the Caspian, west as far as Berkeley, to tell of ions and the meteorites, the long migrations of eels from the Sargasso Sea to the Mediterranean, back again to breed; and the scientific basis therefor. Haber had told us in his shining new laboratory in the Kaiser Wilhelm Institute in Berlin-Dahlem how Malthus could be defeated as nitrogen was drawn from the air and "fixed" to fashion new fertilizers. In Hanover, Bodenstein and his students had studied the first two chain-reactions, one initiated by the new particles of light, the photons, the other under the impact of the swift alpha-particles from radium emanation. The latter research was completed one week before World War I broke out in Belgium.

The war to make the world "safe for democracy" ended abruptly in the closing months of 1918, and everyone hurried back to resume the paths of normalcy. There were, it is true, some ominous undertones from the four long years of warfare. There was poison gas at Ypres, and Zeppelins bombing defenseless cities of England, and the flight of German planes in perfect formation over London in bright sunlight on the first Saturday of August, 1918. There was nothing, however, which a Geneva Convention could not repair for a brave new world. Though Moseley, who had completed what Mendeleef had begun, had fallen victim at Gallipoli to the "random shot of a Turkish sniper," there were still many scientists left to carry on the work of discovery and progress. Aston showed us how many of our "elements" were really mixtures of two or more isotopes; and Rutherford taught us that by using swift alpha-particles as bullets, even the hard core of atoms might be reached, the fortress of the nucleus penetrated. They helped restore our faith in progress, scientific progress. Empires might perish, the map of the world might change, but science would go on and upward. Economic pressures would yield to the onward march of scientific discovery. Through minor and major depressions, as the free world yielded successive areas to totalitarian force in Communist-, Fascist- and Nazi-dominated lands, science in the main pursued "the even tenor of its way"; electrons and protons were joined by deuterons, while the cyclotron made possible nuclear bullets with speeds little short of the velocity of light. At the moment when Hitler set forth to conquer the world, Hahn had revealed that the nuclei of uranium could undergo fission so that cataclysmic chain reactions were well within the reaches of advancing science.

In scale of years World War II exceeded its predecessor by but fifty percent. In scale of destructive energy the excess was many orders of magnitude. A dozen airplanes over London in 1918 had changed to a thousand bombers over Berlin in one dark night, and these in their turn had yielded to one single bomber in bright sunshine over Hiroshima in 1945, with all the destructive potential of one thousand bombers over Berlin in 1944. At first only scientists were aware of the dread thing that had come to pass. Then, startled, the world came to an equal realization.

It is quite normal among the scientists to devise a way of life in which dedication to the pursuit of knowledge through sense-perceptions with appropriate experimental and mathematical analyses can bring sufficient intellectual satisfaction. There appears to be little or no need to add to such effort that contemplation which many intellectuals find so essential to tasks of scholarship. With the scientist this is all the more true if he is engaged in a rapidly developing phase of science where new techniques, new machines, and especially new hypotheses, are yielding a rich harvest to the worker. The scientist can rationalize the specialist effort which he pursues by insistence on the new yield of truth, scientific truth, that is being obtained. The Catholic scientist yielding to such impulse is none the less performing some measure of service to Catholic life and thought. Subconsciously, while serving science, he hails "each discovery as a striking manifestation of the wisdom and grandeur of the Creator." Pius XII assured him in his letter to Pax Romana, the international movement of Catholic students and intellectuals assembled in Amsterdam in 1950, that a real service to the Church can be rendered by those Catholics "who have won respect as experts in their work and for their uprightness of character." He indicates that action and testimony of this kind in one's own professional domain provide a necessary help to the Church stemming from the research or the particular culture. The data of competent and reliable technical knowledge are required today by Catholic theologians, and these must look to the sons of the Church for such data. He assures us that we take our share in the work of the Redemption in the measure with which we establish ourselves "at the very core of the intellectual movement of today." In a commentary on this theme at the Assembly of Pax Romana in Toronto in August 1952, a special commission of Catholic intellectuals summarized the position in these words:

> The presence of Christians in the world of pure thought is of itself apostolic even though contemplative truth is not involved or employed. It is the heart of the Christian intellectual which must be apostolic; his thought, if it is truly radiant, bears witness by its intrinsic quality.

It is a characteristic of modern experimental science, especially so in the areas of the physical sciences, that new directions and advances increasingly come from the younger men. With science, education and research organized on an ever-expanding scale, it seems that the younger scientists venture more successfully than their elder brethren into the yet unknown. Thus it is that with increase of years the scientist passes from the activist period into one of contemplation, where the relevance of his intellectual pursuits to the world, to culture generally in its other disciplines, assumes an ever-growing significance in his thought and life. That normal process of evolution has been accelerated by the crises of our times. The economic dislocations of the decade before the war, the swift advent of the nuclear age with the discovery of nuclear fission in the laboratory and the consequent technological development accelerated by the urgencies of war, all these have contributed to an awareness among scientists, both young and old, of the problems that human pursuit of science produces. They have served to give a "terrible countenance" to the problem of science and values. They have served to make men, including scientists, fear. Accompanying the fear there is also some measure of hope, since the new tools, if they can be dedicated to the arts of peace, are not less in their potential than as instruments of war. Fear and hope, however, are not of themselves sufficient to make us truly wise. We need wisdom if we are to survive in happiness. We need a faith, as well for scientists as for their fellow men. "A society without any idea of itself and without any faith in itself, without any common faith," cannot resist disintegration.

In the discovery of that faith the Catholic scientist has an immense and initial advantage. Whatever have been his preoccupations, his intensity of effort in the domain of his science, he has always been acutely conscious that science is not sufficient, that ultimately man cannot live by scientific bread alone. Dedicated to the values in his own science, he has nevertheless been aware, oftentimes unconsciously, of the variety of value. His conformity to the Commandments of the Church will bring him constantly out of his own world of science into the realm of religious values.

154

Happily often, in search of relaxation from the stresses of his own intellectual effort, he will find it in art, or music or poetry, find in them contemplative joy complementary to his normal productive activity, coming thus to a realization that

> Art is the true and happy science of the soul exploring nature for spiritual influences, as doth physical science for comforting powers advancing so to a sure knowledge with like progress.[1]

He may, with so many others of his fellow scientists today, turn his mind towards the existence of philosophical problems and recognize their central importance in the realm of culture and values. He will recognize the need for logic and for metaphysics to supplement his natural philosophy. He will recall how many of his own skills are dependent on the testimony of his fellow scientists, testimony, it is true, which, had he time, he could himself submit to the test of experiment, but which, in the majority of circumstances, he accepts on the assumption of the integrity of his scientific colleagues and their quality as witnesses. Thus, he will be disposed to examine with care all other forms of testimony and be prepared to accept such evidence in the historical record.

The scientist engaged not only in the research but also in the educational process must concede, upon contemplation, that in far too many instances in the modern techniques of specialization, the "trained" product, leaving the colleges and universities, is singularly unaware of the validity of other disciplines than his own in the quest for truth and wisdom. Among the science students he will be aware of a naive faith in the methods of the inductive sciences for the solution of all pressing human problems.

[1] R. Bridges, *Testament of Beauty* (New York, Oxford University Press, 1930), pp. 123–124.

By accident of opportunity, lavish and unique, my life in education and mature research has been spent, now for nearly forty years, in one of the private universities of the United States. The opportunity was lavish in the measure in which the facilities were made available for the conduct of research, unique in that, as a privately organized university, with firm accent on quality and no visions of numerical grandeur, it aimed to provide a high level of intellectual effort with a carefully selected group of students, undergraduate and graduate. It escapes, thus, some of the problems inherent in mass education at the university level. Originally the college was confessional (Presbyterian) but in process of time emerged as a lay university, loyal to the Christian tradition and inheritance, but with no confessional demands on its faculty. Professional competence rather than the particular "act of faith" is the criterion for acceptance in the ranks of its faculty. How it was possible to attain to a position of responsibility in such an organization with fidelity to the ideals of the Catholic faith constitutes the final sector of the present enquiry. Some sense of mission is essential to supplement the professional activity if interior satisfaction and peace is to be secured.

It ought to be recognized that, in the modern educational centres, outside the frankly confessional schools and colleges, the growing menace of secularism, or even frank paganism, is most to be feared. We must, however, recognize that to the extent that we, convinced Christians, withdraw from the effort, to that extent we abandon the secular colleges to the secularists. Wherever the "liberty of the act of faith" is conceded, whether in the university or the state, there devolves upon Catholics the duty to take their place in the organization and conduct of all affairs on the secular plane. Segregation in such circumstances might well become a sin of omission. Participation cannot be postponed until that ideal day, which, being ideal, must be recognized as remote and far from practical reality, when all men shall confess "one faith, one baptism." It is an unattainable ideal in the staffing of many Catholic colleges and universities. Why must we withdraw from centres where it cannot obtain?

The Catholic intellectual placed in the neutralist environment of much of the modern educational society has to formulate a philosophy of life in such an environment. If he is a realist, he must recognize that he cannot wait for a religious unity which cannot be expected in any near future. He will recognize that while some may essay the advent of such a unity by a more and more penetrating analysis of religious concepts, the great majority must address themselves to the practical problems of adjustment to a pluralist society which will undoubtedly persist for a very long time.

Maritain has addressed himself to this problem of unity in a pluralist society.[1] "A genuine democracy cannot impose on its citizens or demand from them . . . any philosophic or religious creed." This was possible, he states, during what he has termed the "sacral" period of our civilization, when "communion in the Christian faith was a prerequisite for the constitution of the body politic." He emphasizes that good fellowship must not be sought in any compromise of doctrine nor in a discovery of a common minimum of identity of doctrine. Rather is it to be sought in a friendship which possesses natural and also supernatural bases, the latter involving a love for God and God's love for men. From such a friendship there develops love of neighbour and a desire for co-operation with one's neighbour for the good of the temporal society. In a society of free men Maritain finds a

[1] See J. W. Evans, *Thought*, Vol. xxvi, p. 585 (1951–52) in a review of *Man and the State* by Jacques Maritain (Chicago, The University of Chicago Press, 1951). Pp. x, 219. Especially Chapter 5. See also Jacques Maritain, *The Range of Reason*, Chaps. 12 and 13 (New York, Chas. Scribner's Sons, 1952), pp. xii, 226.

basic community of doctrine in the "fundamental agreement between minds and wills on the bases of life in common . . . capable of defending and promoting its own conception of social and political life; *it must bear within itself a common human creed, the creed of freedom.*"

As Christopher Dawson has so eloquently insisted, the foundations of the culture and of the freedom of modern Western civilization are basically pluralistic. Against that civilization is ranged an absolutism that operates in a monolithic framework in which every freedom, all individuality, must conform to state decree. Within the confines of Western civilization there are some who would increasingly impose uniformity of educational opportunity and standards on its citizens. The free, private university is the principal bulwark opposing this levelling tendency in mass education. There the Catholic scientist can collaborate with the humanist in the preservation and maintenance of freedom, based upon the inalienable rights and dignity of the human person. *E pluribus unum.* Out of the many and their diversity, a unity must be welded, not in slavish conformity but in voluntary co-operation.

"Have you Catholics," asked two French professors of history,[1] "made a persevering and collective effort to 'save' this public secular institution, and make it, not Christian, but open to Christianity? You have been a great deal more preoccupied with safeguarding, in the face of this secular institution, a secular institution of a confessional character; in this way you have undoubtedly saved Christian souls, especially weak souls, but you are losing the public mind . . . A realistic religious policy does not only consider the risk which would follow the loss of confessional institutions,

[1] J. Vialatoux and A. Latreille, *Christianity and Laity,* translated from the French by H. Blair and J. E. Cuneen, *Cross Currents,* Vol. ii, pp. 15–36, New York, N. Y., 1952.

but also the risk which comes from absence in secular institutions."

By virtue of a "magnificent failure" English Catholic students and professors were allowed, in the nineteenth century, to return to the ancient Catholic centres of learning, now the secular universities of Oxford and Cambridge. What they have contributed to the spread of the Catholic Faith in England is now writ large in English letters, is heard throughout the whole land. They are a brilliant company, Benson and Knox, Plater, Martindale and D'Arcy, Hugh Pope, Dawson, Evelyn Waugh, Graham Greene, and so many others. What have they not done to save these secular institutions and to restore the ancient faith in England? There is need for like effort in the United States.

In a discussion[1] conducted by the Catholic Commission for Intellectual and Cultural Affairs at New Rochelle, N.Y., in 1948, Father John Courtney Murray called attention to a statement of Bernard Iddings Bell that "the core of any problem having to do with American higher education, including the problem of religion, will be found not in the colleges but in the universities and, within the universities themselves, not in their undergraduate sections but among the research scholars in the graduate and professional schools." Father Murray added that "there are probably no more than half a dozen centres of learning in the United States that are essentially determinant of a whole intellectual drift." He went on to plead for the "presence of missionaries" in these centres "on the only title which admits to presence—ability, learning, scholarly achievement . . . the basic thing would be alliance with the intrinsic purpose of the university—teaching, research, writing, direction of studies, conference; and then in and through this intellectual work, as itself an apostolic medium, the mediation of

[1] *Thought,* Vol. xxiv, pp. 41, 42, 1949.

Christian truth and the Christian spirit to the institution itself, in ways that only they could come upon who were actually about the work of mediation." There are many more than six university centres where such mediation would be welcomed.

By accident of fortunate circumstance, my journey through life led to a university that I deem to be one of those half dozen centres of learning and teaching in the United States, in which, as a scientist and as a Catholic, I might achieve that work of mediation. There are some, among my colleagues and friends, who wonder at the effort to combine a devotion to scientific research and teaching with a dedication to Catholic faith. Are they compatible? Does one supplement the other, or do they interfere? That they in no way interfere is a matter of personal conviction based upon forty years of empirical test. That they supplement one another is more difficult to demonstrate, although it seems to me profoundly true. We can, to repeat, hail "each discovery as a striking manifestation of the wisdom and grandeur of the Creator." And the work of the scientist demands those virtues of calm and detachment, of patience, devotion to accuracy and truth which are, after all, Christian virtues. Sir Henry Tizard has told us that, shortly after the Battle of Britain, a bishop of the Anglican Communion emphasized that science and Christianity were distinctive features of the civilization that arose in Europe and spread from that continent over the whole civilized world; that the principle of both is liberty, "the expression in unshackled freedom of the innate powers of the human spirit, the expression and vindication of individuality." As a Catholic, I am convinced that such freedom stems from Christ, who made us free.

Cecily Hastings

Cecily Hastings, *the youngest contributor to this book, was born at Kuala Lumpur, Malaya in 1924. She was educated, she says, by her family, various friends and the following institutions—an Anglican kindergarten, Ursuline and Benedictine convents, Rye St. Antony (a lay Catholic school), Somerville College, Oxford, the British Foreign Service (she was Vice-Consul in New York), the Outer Circle of Friendship House, the New York Gaelic Society and Young Christian Workers, the American Grail, the Westminster Catholic Evidence Guild, a Carmelite Convent. She works for Sheed and Ward and the English "Catholic Herald" and "Catholic Worker" and she has been an Evidence Guild speaker since 1948.*

It is a recurring surprise to me to discover every now and then, through some question or comment, that there are cradle Catholics who regard converts as in some way less the real thing than themselves: or, at any rate, converts who feel that some cradle Catholics so regard them. In practice it is impossible to give any satisfactory comparative account of the two. In theory the superiority would seem to be overwhelmingly on the other side. For one thing, the convert is the person who has learned the dogmatic content of the Faith when of an age to make something of the lesson. His knowledge of the Church's teaching does not consist, as does that of most

161

cradle Catholics, in hazy remembrances of inadequate school and home teaching, scrappily supplemented by such few sermons as do contain doctrine and not only disciplinary, moral and devotional exhortation. But what is more important, the convert is the person who has genuinely accepted the Church. He has not merely happened to find himself surrounded by her. He found the door and walked in.

For several years while I was growing up, I had a horrifying confidence that if I had been started outside the Church, I should almost certainly have found my way in, in a few years' time, by a process of simple observation and common-sense reasoning. I rather wished that things had been so. Not to be too hard on myself, I will say that I should really like to have made that free act of allegiance, considering it a gift (I did not realize then that it can be and has to be made by every cradle Catholic). But also, I should certainly have liked to have such a sure way of repudiating the irritating suggestion of non-Catholic friends that I was a Catholic simply because I was raised that way and had never thought things out for myself. I prided myself that I had thought it all out for myself. I professed a body of doctrines, to which I gave the label of the Catholic faith, which I was prepared to demonstrate to any challenger as logically water-tight and inevitably consequent upon universally admitted facts. In practice, of course, the label covered a considerable proportion of material heresy; nor was the sense which I gave to the word "demonstrate" one which was compatible with the nature of faith, revelation, or, above all, the thing revealed.

Roughly, I held that the existence of God was a fact that could be fitted into a straightforward logical proof; obviously one couldn't understand everything about God, so "mysteries" (meaning verbal contradictions) were no difficulty; obviously God was all-powerful, so miracles were no difficulty; Jesus Christ was God and man (in face of His claims He must have been either God, or a lunatic, or evil, and the last two were plainly impossible); and He was physically present in the Blessed Sacrament—He said so, and why not? Finally, truth must obviously be consistent and authoritative, so the only religious body in the world worth bothering with was the only one that was consistent and authoritative, i.e. the Catholic Church. That was that.

Apologetics (very elementary apologetics) without theology—without any sense of the implications of what I was asserting—was perhaps the trouble. Perhaps a good Catholic education (and I do mean a good one) adds up to that too often—training in devotion at one end, and at the other "how to answer," and mostly how to answer Protestants, at that. And a great gap where there should be a lively understanding of the staggering things implied in these assertions that are to be defended against all comers.

Anyway, I had learnt that one could "prove the existence of God" in five ways. I also thought that I knew the ways, or had known them once, in which I was mistaken. But that is a comparatively unimportant point beside the fact that I had not the slightest idea of what an earthquake I was speaking when I casually mentioned "the existence of God." It was, as far as I was concerned, an ordinary subject of discussion in which, by ordinary processes of reasoning, various premises led to a satisfactory conclusion. My idea of the matter was as far as it could be from any realization that not one of the terms used in the "proofs" I thought I knew how to handle were true of God in the same sense in which they were true of the things of my experience from which I drew my understanding of them. I had no idea that the words I threw around like "cause," "design" and "value" —and "existence"—could mean, once one was speaking of God, only something incomprehensibly different from what they meant in every other use of them. I might have said, as a form of words, that the Creator must of course be utterly different from creatures; but I certainly would not have been conscious that even saying *that* meant using the word "different" in a different sense from that which it bore in a statement about any other difference. There was not the slightest trace of an image in my mind of the bleak edge of human thought on which one must stand or kneel to affirm that the world is created; the "cliffs of fall Frightful, sheer, no-man-fathomed" on whose edge a rational man very rationally objects that to frame a question beginning "Why . . . ?" concerning the universe as a whole is making a meaningless misuse of the word.

In short, basing myself on what I thought was the Catholic position about proving the existence of God, I might have said then that I was a Catholic because the Church was a divinely instituted Rationalist Association. Time passed, and I discovered that this tidy little mental universe, with the conclusions to be drawn from it, which I had regarded as a considerable proportion of my "reason for being a Catholic," was an intolerable prison in which man, though he might disclaim it politely as a matter of form, was in fact the measure of all things, God included: and in which he consequently could not breathe. So this particular reason, in its original form, has as thoroughly as possible disappeared. I had subscribed to a body which, I thought, asserted a strict and all-embracing rationalism. I had now found both that I did not want to subscribe to such a body and that the Catholic Church was not one anyway. I had matched a false idea of the Church to a false idea of things in general: and so, when the two broke together, the break became the reason for being a Catholic—but in a new sense. For it was the living Church, listened to now a little better, that was found to be proclaiming the living and incomprehensible God; and it was that proclamation which smashed up the tidy little pseudo-world in which the pseudo-Church of my own invention had been asserting the provable existence of a God who fitted into the logical categories of finite experience. Something of what had formerly claimed my allegiance remained; it was still true that the Church was the stronghold of reason, that the denial of God was the suicide of thought. But these things had a meaning very different from that which I had given them in my mind before, now that they were only contingent echoes of the *mysterium tremendum.*

All this, of course, was not something that happened like a flash, but an extremely gradual process. It began, I think, with being taught the doctrine of the Trinity—clearly and analytically: the distinction of nature and person, the generation of the Word and the spiration of the Holy Spirit— in Friendship House Outer Circle in New York. The half-baked little rationalist found it all extremely satisfactory, but it was the end of her for all that. This simplified theological sorting out of the mysteries was the way, in the end, to the mystery. The Church had to seem to become very rationalistic indeed before the time came when it all turned over like an iceberg and the rationalism was no longer what it was all about. One might also put it this way: that the comfortable feeling of "Christianity not mysterious" could survive so long as one was anxious to assert the sovereignty of reason but not engaged in using the thing very much. Getting the mind working on the subject, as I was induced to do then, brings the cure for the comfortable feeling. Most of the work, indeed, was done for me, by all those friends in the Faith, priests and others, who are a large proportion of the reason why I am in fact still where I am, though there is hardly any mention of them here. I feel this is ungrateful, but it came out this way, and I believe they would all rather

I should put down something of what I received from them than that I should talk about them.

Nothing in the faith, of course, can remain the same once one knows, as distinct from merely saying, that one doesn't know what one means by God. Christ, my mind used to run, must of course be God, since He was neither mad nor bad and the evidence leaves no fourth alternative. So I still say, but it becomes a very different thing to say it when God-made-man no longer means: A logical abstraction (labelled infinite but as finite as any other logical abstraction) made man. "Why not?" would be a sufficient comment on this latter phenomenon. And it was that "Why not?" arising out of the total absence in me of any apprehension of the unspeakable mystery of God, combined with the natural evidence to whatever limited extent I knew it, which had constituted my conscious reason for accepting most of the mysteries of the Faith. If asked to comment on the scandal of the Cross, I should probably have spoken in terms of social scandal; the real scandal was none to me, seeing that I had not grasped what a shocking paradox I was being asked to believe. There were various reasons inclining me to believe these "mysteries," and none, as I understood them, was going to be such a two-edged sword as to make soul or spirit at all uncomfortable. This meant, of course, that they were not worth believing. The discovery that the Good News was such as to cut my rationalistic frame of mind into small pieces (after courteously satisfying it with a few verbal distinctions) was, simultaneously, the discovery that it *was* good news. The discovery that the distinction between substance and accidents was not the whole story about the Blessed Sacrament, and could never be more than an answer, given at their own level, to certain superficial questions, left the mystery as *the* Mystery of Faith; and it was not till then that I realized that I was being fed.

There are other doctrines of the Faith which would not have been so amenable to my rationalistic distorting glass. Perhaps fortunately, I knew nothing about them. In company with better Catholics than myself, I thought that whereas predestination was a horrid Calvinistic doctrine, free will was a nice Catholic one. Just as I approved of the Church in the erroneous belief that she asserted the absolute sovereignty of human reason, so I approved of her in the erroneous belief that she asserted the absolute sovereignty of human will, thus saving freedom and dignity from the clutches alike of the dreadful reformers who grimly asserted the absolute sovereignty of God and of the miserable determinists who denied God and their own freedom together. It was not till I was halfway cured that I began to realize that there was a Catholic doctrine of predestination: and even then it was a nasty shock. I had always been a happy Pelagian, with no semi- about it. One worked out one's own salvation, standing on one's own two feet: one was master of one's fate and captain of one's soul—anything else would be unfair. When this picture was broken up, did the passion for freedom which had been, in this matter, the "reason for being a Catholic" collapse too? By no means. It had been a poor apology for freedom in comparison with the freedom which is a moment-by-moment gift from the sovereign freedom of God. That kind of working out of one's own salvation was a miserable substitute for the reality, which is a love affair; in a love affair the distinction between choosing and being chosen becomes an impertinence. And I was learning that "freedom," "choice," "will" meant something different in relation to God from what they meant in relation to me; so that there could be no occupation more futile than trying to draw a common frontier between them—a line at which one gives way to the other, with their separate territories lying on either side of it. Again, the breaking up of the "reason" had turned out to be a stronger reason than the reason itself had been.

"Cultural Catholicism" went the same road. It gradually dissolved into too great a confusion to be a reason for being anything. In its extreme form it consists in deciding, on any and every ground from preference to principle, what things are to be deemed to contribute to the worthiness of human life, and then declaring that the Church has, in her actual temporal activity, been the patron and guardian of these things throughout her history. The chief objections to this attitude, as normally found in the concrete, are its lack of truth and its remoteness from genuinely Christian values. Thus delight is taken in a hazy image of the Church as the enthusiastic defender of all the Maypoles, graveyard dances, mummeries and junketings she ever did her level best to stamp out (on the basis of the occasional, touching, exceptional instance of an adoption and consecration of such). Or she is hailed, in defiance of all her doctors, legislators and spiritual writers from the beginning until now, as the great Tolerator and indeed Lover of drunkenness, cheating the customs, brawling, loud, hasty and casual behaviour in church, and working off one's good, healthy animal spirits in physical violence towards Protestants, Jews and heathens. There was a time when I regarded this sort of thing as a particularly authentic, as well as enjoyable, expression of the true spirit of Catholicism, and an excellent reason for preferring the Catholic to any other religion.

Turning to the rather more respectable forms of cultural Catholicism—"the Faith is Europe and Europe is the Faith"; the sort that makes the Church (in her actual temporal activity) the champion of "progress" by weaving a legend of a monastic Welfare State destroyed by Henry VIII; by remembering Nicholas I on torture and forgetting Innocent IV on the same subject; remembering Mendel and Pasteur

168

and creating a (highly unsuccessful) smoke-screen round Galileo; remembering St. Peter Claver and St. Vincent de Paul and forgetting the bottle dungeon in Castel Sant' Angelo and its replica at St. Andrews; remembering the Social Encyclicals and ignoring the existence of ecclesiastically owned slums; the sort that makes the actual, concrete, historical "Catholic thing" the great guardian of beauty and the wedding of sensuous experience to spiritual meaning by assuming that Quattrocento paintings were what they were *because of* being Catholic, whereas repository statuary is what it is *in spite of* being Catholic—the whole "heads I win, tails don't count" concoction is incapable of being anything whatever. Yet a kind of sleight of hand had once made it seem as if it could be a reason, and a strong one.

But falling through that floor again meant falling further into the Church, not out of her. There being (as far as I am concerned) no third alternative between the Church and secularism, the discovery that her history did not, in fact, present an edifying spectacle of the right things being steadily promoted by concerted Catholic action was no reason for leaving her. For leaving her would simply mean saying that since so many of her members and leaders, who asserted the unconditioned reality of these values of truth, justice, mercy and beauty, did not, apparently, mean what they said, I should make *their* apparent failure to believe in these things into a reason for not believing in them myself. The secularist alternative turned those values to meaningless abstractions: to embrace *that* would mean siding, on the deepest level, with every ecclesiastic who ever sent a prisoner to the bottle dungeon—merely for the sake of escaping the uncomfortable necessity of recognizing him as my fellow Catholic.

Obviously I must give some account for saying that,

as far as I personally am concerned, the only alternative to adherence to the Catholic Church, with all her Roman Congregations on her head, is acceptance of the assertion that there is nothing real except this physical-chemical-biological-psychological world, endlessly analyzable and in need of no explanation.

As to the alternatives provided by divisions amongst Christians: the points of disagreement between various forms of Christian opinion and the Catholic Church are, for me, decided by the fact that each such divergence has to be expressed, sooner or later, by the word "merely." I mean that wherever there is a choice between giving to some part of the Christian revelation either a more expansive, many-dimensioned, richly complex, open interpretation or, alternatively, a narrower, flatter, thinner, more restricted one, the former is always the Catholic one. The points of departure, all along the road from Unitarianism upwards, are marked by some rejection of the Catholic meaning whose expression involves a "merely." "When He said 'I and the Father are one,' He merely meant. . ."; "The rite of baptism is merely. . ."; "What He did at the Last Supper was merely. . ."; " 'I will give to thee the keys of the kingdom of heaven' merely means. . ." and so on and so on. And, as far as I am concerned, any sentence with "merely" in it, applied to divine revelation, is condemned by the presence of the word. Whatever else God's word to man might be, it would not be "merely" anything.

You can find plenty of comments by Catholics on various passages condemned by the same test: on certain sentences of the Sermon on the Mount, for instance, or on our Lord's words to his mother at Cana. But when a Catholic resorts to the word—say, in an effort to show that "resist not evil" is not to be interpreted as a condemnation of St. Joan of Arc—the mistake he has made is in not realizing that it is

170

in the interpretation which he rightly rejects that "merely" belongs. The point about the real meaning of such statements is not that they mean *less* than the interpretation falsely offered as "the plain, literal meaning." The real meaning—of, say, vowed virginity in contrast to self-castration, to take another such text, is something incomparably wilder, more revolutionary and more exacting than the "mere" meaning falsely understood. A slip into a "merely" by a Catholic commentator does not represent anything integral to the Catholic position; whereas such attenuation seems to be the very substance of the various rejections of it. There is not a "Protestant" value within the Christian whole—divine transcendence, human helplessness, spiritual freedom, universal priesthood, or anything else—which does not turn out, in the end, to be at its strongest, wildest and richest within the ponderous machinery of the Roman Church. Not, of course, that they can be found to be so in all or in most day-to-day, would-be expositions of the Church's mind. But when, at last, one manages to get at something centrally and authentically in the full stream of her tradition, that is what one discovers it to be. For example: one soon finds that the heckler who seems for a moment to be asserting the priesthood of all the faithful is in fact making a sterile denial of any priesthood whatever in the New Law. This would not, however, be much of a reason for remaining a Catholic if the only alternative to that sterile denial were the almost equally sterile assertion of clerical monopoly, duly authenticated by a nice choice of texts, which one is more likely than not to find, even today, being offered as "the answer." What simply leaves both of them unworthy of a second thought is the discovery, like the breaking of spring through a great freeze or a thunderstorm after drought, of what the Church really does say about priesthood, and how it energizes in different ways in every member of the mystical body of the High Priest. Again, one is left with very little inclination for sticking to one's rather wet berth in a corner of the scuppers of Peter's boat after listening to some ecclesiastical fascist pouring scorn over a Nonconformist's apparent assertion of spiritual freedom. What keeps one from jumping overboard (into unbelief, not Nonconformity) is not a blandly paternalist description of how nice it is for a Catholic to have a nice, cosy sense of security. It is the realization that the Nonconformist's assertion had gone up a blind alley: it asserted "freedom from," and "freedom from" is not freedom but a sense of well-being; which is not freedom any more than security is freedom. "Freedom from" means "freedom from any uncomfortable demands," which soon means "freedom from reality"; freedom from the truth which makes us free. The freedom which is the effect of truth is not "freedom from" but "freedom to." Its measure is that it includes even the freedom to choose to stay within earshot and order-shot of the ecclesiastical fascist, and apply even to him, in the teeth of all he may do to make the application apparently intolerable, the words "He that heareth you heareth me, and he that despiseth you despiseth me." Which is something like freedom. I do not mean that being a Catholic implies any particular degree of facility in the exercise of such freedom. But it does imply being put, for better or worse, in the situation which calls for such free choice.

But what about the questions surrounding Christianity as a whole? I must confess that the glaring mutual contradictions between the various loudly confident offers to explain away its fundamental News in terms of something else has become part of my personal apologetic. But it is not only a matter of mutual contradiction. Take the question often urged against the Catholic of how one can possibly remain in a Church which asserts as historical facts—and then

172

makes the whole extra-historical welfare of mankind depend on them—events whose close analogy is to be found in stories and rites current throughout humanity: how can one, runs the objection, accept this, seeing that it is universally agreed that these stories, etc., have no historical meaning and only, at best, a psychological significance—a beneficial effect on the personal and social life of those who participate in them ritually or imaginatively: (not such a poor best, when one comes to think of it—still, that is beside the point). This curious "comparative religionist" argument seems to be based on a breath-taking begging of the question roughly expressible as: "It can be safely assumed that myths and rites, intimately connected though they are with some deep pattern in human nature, do not, nevertheless, express any transcendent human need which was eventually to be met from outside humanity." Or, to put it the other way on: "If there were to be a divine intervention in human history, it could not possibly, in its outward operation, bear any analogy to the ways in which humanity has constantly expressed its need for such intervention; but the Christian Gospel does bear such an analogy; therefore the Christian Gospel cannot possibly be a divine intervention in history." A foolishly gratuitous assumption, even if it were not the case that the trial-and-error methods of scholarship applied during the last three quarters of a century to the Gospels have driven us back at last to the historical reality of the events recorded in them.[1] But those events—and the conclusions immediately drawn from them by those who experienced them—do bear their strong analogy to the comparative religionist's myths and rites; no question of that. Someone, then, in the first century was using historical events symboli-

[1] I mean, the events as a whole. Obviously no scholarship can provide that certainty in the absolute reliability of the Gospels which belongs to those who regard them as a divinely inspired record.

173

cally. If it were not history but late invention, there would be no difficulty: but the last half-century has explored that avenue and found it a blind alley—no good for a clear escape, though one can still lurk there at a pinch. Nor is the symbolism, familiar from humanity's myths, something tacked loosely to the events: it lies in the events themselves. Someone was speaking the ancient symbols in real historical facts. And who in this world is in a position to do that?

The comparative religionist argument points to the depth beneath, and strangely makes of the continuity of Catholic faith with the religions of mankind a reason for not being a Catholic. It would appear to be a better reason for not being a human being—to which indeed all the anti-Catholic arguments come at last, the "crimes of the Church" argument most clearly of all. But there is someone on the other side pointing to the height above, and telling me that there is a better way to the ultimate meaning of existence than this faith tied to the particularism of an acknowledged myth —real historical event or not: that these toys are all very well at a certain level, but real spiritual maturity involves recognizing them, at last, as illusions and schooling oneself to follow a higher path. Though it can take various forms, this summons is apt to be linked to recommendation of Buddhism, and for that reason I will try to explain why it also meets me as an inadequate and mistaken summons by reference to the invitation to Buddhist enlightenment broadcast on the Third Programme last January by Mr. G. P. Malalasekera. As with almost any such brief contact with Buddhism, Confucius, Judaism, even Islam, one of the reasons for not being greatly affected was the inevitable question: What is here being said that I do not already hold, but in the context of something more, here denied? That is always a first, and inadequate reaction; but this talk went

174

far enough to provide the elements of a real choice, of which I want to say something. I realize very well that I am out of my depth. As Mr. Malalasekera said, his twenty-minute talk could do very little, and the little I can gather from it and other sources is no qualification for making any contribution to the dialogue between Christianity and Buddhism (which, again, is only one form of this unbelieving spirituality) now being conducted by the competent. But some of it is directed at us, the incompetent. We are called upon to account for our cleaving to a saviour-myth rather than recognizing our saviour as a projection of spiritual resources which do not, in a state of true enlightenment, require any such mythical expression.

Well, then, that in which I find this higher religion wanting is precisely its rejection of the whole dimension of human life which has been and is expressed in myth and ritual: the reduction of this to other terms, dismissing it as an illusory formulation of something else: which amounts to an amputation of part of human nature. In practice, it means cutting oneself off from the mass of mankind, who do in fact seek their salvation in the forms which these sorts of higher cult of the self reject as invalid. Mr. Malalasekera began his talk by speaking of over 500,000,000 Buddhists. But in fact the religion—the "Way," at least—of which he then went on to speak is not the religion of any such mass of people. They do not live by the rejection of myth; they have re-invented myth. I, as a Christian, share, it seems to me, the religion of most of those 500,000,000 more truly than those who see and accept Buddhism as Mr. Malalasekera presented it. Mere numbers are no guide to truth; but the apparent inability of man in general to live without a saviour-god is a fact to be taken into consideration. Where the difference lies between me and these Buddhist brothers of mine is that in asserting that these salvific events really happened,

175

I am making a statement which is common ground even between me and those who deny that the events were salvific: I stand on this unique junction of the myth which all men obscurely desire—and I will not divorce myself from the rest by trying to destroy my desire for it—with an historical event as concrete as Mr. Malalasekera's broadcast. And it is that—the desire of the ages become an everyday reality—which is the sign both to the height above and to the depth beneath. This is why, for us, the creed really is the same for the theologian, the mystic, the "unspiritual" peasant, the child. However much more one may be able to say about it than another, their faith is in the same event in which the myths came true, issuing in the same day-to-day actions communicating with that event, in the same teacher divinely guaranteed by that one event, in the same social life, with its awkward demands and confusions, stemming from that one event. Of course, it comes to this: that I am a Catholic because "I believe . . . the third day He rose again from the dead." And however much I can say about historical evidence or psychological necessity, I also know that the creed is an act of grace. I can easily say why the comparative religionist's objections are no beginning of a proof that it did not happen. Less easily, but still without any dubiety, why the "higher reality" school give me no reason for wishing that it had not, or feeling that it does not matter one way or the other. But it is by grace that I believe that it simply did happen.

The most real question of all still remains.

No coincidence, delusion or deception would be too wild as an explanation of all other evidences, if once the denial could be made that there is anything not subject to the analyzable limits of this universe of sense-perception: if once the assertion is accepted that it is meaningless even to ask whether there is anything. "Is," indeed! Why the only mean-

176

ing we have available for the word is the meaning we
analyze out of our own experience; and we are at least
agreed, believers and atheists together, that it doesn't mean
that when we use it to say "God is." So how can I continue
to put the question? And it would make so many things so
much easier to stop putting it. But it would also mean
destroying the best of the experience out of which the meaning of what we say is to be analyzed. That is: if I
insist that the analysis must be total, and so reduce the
significance of everything I know to the limits of sense-
perception, then the statements worth making and the questions worth putting lose the meaning which gives them their
worth. They must be supposed to mean no more than
statements about bed and breakfast. But they do mean
more. Whatever else is true, it is true that you love me and
I love you. Whatever else is true, it is true that it is better
to listen to Bach than to listen to Hokey-Cokey. Whatever
else is true, it is true that it was better to die in Buchenwald
than to live at Berchtesgaden. And these are the things
which are left as meaning no more than "It would be nice
if it were a fine day tomorrow," if we remain fast in a refusal
to accept a meaning for what we say beyond the limits to
which we can analyze it in terms of sense-experience. There
is enough left of our experience which will not submit to that
analysis; enough to be the beginning of the bridge that must
stand out beyond the cliff's edge. We do not know on what
the other end is to rest: we do not know what we mean
beyond this point. We know we don't. But if we therefore
conclude that we mean nothing, we are going to have to
throw over the edge so much of what we supposed lies on
this side of it, that we shall have nothing left to live on. It
is all very well to complain—perfectly truly—that we have
no adequate terms in which to put the question. But unless
we put the question

> how shall the rivers run
> or the suitors persuade their loves
> or the erosion of the land cease?[1]

If we come to the point where we have to condemn ourselves to talking nonsense in order to avoid talking nonsense, then it is time to admit that reason demands its own transcendence and that we should say our prayers, after all.

Seeing these things as I do, in the name of what greater good, not part of her treasures, or under pressure from what intolerable thing in her, outweighing all the rest, could I leave the Church? There is no standard by which I can judge her and find her wanting, except those standards which are stated in their strongest and most absolute form as part of her teaching. The one accusation against her which really matters—not the frivolous, silly ones about bad popes, and so on—is concerned with her apparent disregard for the human person as a value in himself. This seems to me to be the underlying fault in those hateful things which appear as *characteristic* of the Catholic way of behaving. To anyone with any sense, the things done by Catholics which are, plainly and avowedly, done *in spite* of being Catholics are no kind of grounds for criticism of the Church. The difficulty arises over the things that seem to be done not in spite of but *because* of being Catholic. That tyrannical manipulation of other people's souls and lives, perpetrated in the name of the spiritual works of mercy, whose achievements are sometimes such as to draw from an observer the admiring comment that it would take a Catholic to do a thing like that. And—coming at last to the real scandal, the

---

[1] David Jones, *The Anathemata;* Sherthursdaye and Venus Day (London, Faber and Faber, 1952), p. 226.

unmistakable stone of stumbling to so many exiles from the fold, the misery of so many within it—the apparent pre-dilection of so many of the Church's leaders, generation after generation, for the employment of secular *rather than* spiritual means. It seems as though, when it comes down to a concrete choice, they actually *prefer* to act on men as a social lump by external, coercive means *rather than* to win their hearts to a free allegiance by the incalculable action of the spiritual forces of which the Church disposes. They positively seem to like governmentally guaranteed privileges *better* than freedom from the ambiguous demands which have to be met in return for them. They give the inescapable impression that so long as social pressure is driving the masses to Mass, they really don't mind whether or not each individual is resorting to it as a free act of worship—that they only fall back on offering it as a free act as a last, desperate remedy when the favourite weapon of social pressure is no longer available. Is it that you can count the results of secular action—whatever it is that you then mean by a "result"? You can organize and be sure of your good-looking statistics—only, what are they statistics of? You cannot count the results of working from within and below; you cannot be sure of ever seeing anything of them at all. Is that the reason for this queer preference, in practice, to be seen in Catholic policy? It is a riddle that I can only give up in despair.

I am aware of the protests: that the coercive method is not, even in practice, the Church's preference and first choice; that, on the contrary, she insists on the primacy of spiritual means—it is only that she will not refuse to employ temporal means also when these can be placed at the service of the spiritual. I will not argue the point; though I should like to comment that we see the picture from England, where the coercive approach is hardly available; but I will

not insist on the actual, provable predominance of the coercive approach. I only record it as an impression that is
apt to be received, and of which, speaking personally, I
cannot rid myself; and it is *my* impressions that matter if I
am trying to explain why *I* am still a Catholic. The difficulty
remains in any case: just *what* service are coercive means
supposed to be able to render to the working out of human
salvation—which is what the Church is here for?

I am supposed to be writing a statement of why I am
still a Catholic; that statement does not need to include such
an answer on this question of coercion as will satisfy anyone
except myself. For my statement only needs to include an
explanation of how I, who consider that the services which
can be rendered to the Church's real work by methods of
coercion are so limited as to be almost negligible, continue
to belong to the Church when I see those who must be
regarded as having the best right to represent her so often
resorting to those methods in apparent preference to any
others.

What is the objection to the policy of coercion? I am
using the word in a very wide sense, to include all sorts of
external pressure and suppression, however discreet and
lacking in the obvious horrors of torture and the stake. Why
not, then, apply external pressure, with or without govern-
mental help, to organize people into religious observance
and to ensure the public acceptance, at least, of revealed
truth? Because if such pressure is required to produce these
things they cease to be themselves, and are worthless. External religious observance under pressure is not a religious
act. Assent to a true formula under pressure is not assent to
the truth at all.

To avoid a possible misunderstanding, I must point out
that the word "pressure" as I am using it does not apply
either to ecclesiastical command or dogmatic definition. A

command is a summons to an act of free obedience. A definition is a summons to an act of free assent. If free obedience and assent are not forthcoming, then it may happen that pressure is brought to produce an external appearance of them. That is the thing I am deploring; but the command and definition themselves are no denial of freedom. The point of pressure is precisely to substitute some other thing in human nature—fear or social shame; things that *can* be manipulated from outside—as the mainspring of a given human action, instead of the will itself—because its free choice *cannot* be manipulated, but only approached in the dark in collaboration with the Holy Spirit. The difficulty arises when leaders of the Church appear, in their normal policy, to be perfectly content with the pseudo-obedience and pseudo-assent which can be induced by methods of pressure; to treat them as a satisfactory substitute for genuine obedience and acceptance, instead of as a species of blasphemy. And, since the pseudo-varieties are, in the short run, much easier to obtain, this amounts in practice to a predilection for them.

The common policy, then, of so many recurring representatives of the Church is to employ and wish to employ methods of producing an appearance of Catholic profession and observance which amount to an encroachment on the integrity of the human person as a free agent. Now, this is not an exclusively Catholic failing; surrender to it is simply human, to be found in oneself and all over history, not just Catholic history. But it has been sufficiently practised and, which is really the heart of the difficulty, sufficiently *defended in principle* by Catholics over the past seven hundred years to make itself felt as a particularly Catholic occupational disease. Then why (since this is what I am supposed to be writing about) am I still in the Church? Considering the personalist grounds on which I reject this habit of coercion,[1] where else could I be? Once again, I can see no reasonable stopping place between Catholicism and secularism. Then to whom can I go, when, on this particular matter of the unassailable integrity of the free human person, it is she who has the words of eternal life? The truth that it means something to say that a person is not a thing and is not to be manipulated from outside to the denial of his freedom is her truth. I can find no basis for it whatever in that universe of impersonal, inexplicable forces which has, by chance, produced something which dubs itself personality; the alternative to the created universe she preaches to me. It is by what she says that I can condemn the policy of which I speak—and she says it in voices of those very spokesmen of hers who, in practice, seem often to regard a large part of her service as consisting in a skillful and successful violation of persons. The alternatives are to remain in the Church where these things are and have been done, in every degree from murderous tyranny to well-intentioned short-sightedness, and assert with her, in her and through her that they are wrong; or to make them a reason for leaving her and simultaneously—I speak for myself—abandon any grounds for saying that they are wrong.

Living in her is not as comfortable as it used to be, after the collapse of all the old reasons for feeling at home in her (though each turned, as it collapsed, into a better reason for remaining, they are not such comfortable reasons). It is not at all comfortable to feel so hopelessly at odds with much of the official action of those who are truly in authority in her—worse, to see it as being at odds with her own deepest teaching; very far from comfortable to have to keep

[1] The habit itself is easy enough to understand as resulting from conclusions drawn from the divine source and guarantee of the Church's truth, and the eternal importance of it to every single person. Only, the action resulting from this conclusion seems to be flatly contradictory of precisely those two points.

one's brain constantly at work feeling and never forgetting the hard cutting edge of dogma—yet it is a truth of experience that each of those hard points, if allowed to go on biting, will open up at last a sudden, unlooked-for light and richness. But it is not comfortable. Nor to be offered, on paper, the riches of a liturgy which a combination of clerical indifference and late custom hardened into rubric makes, in practice, inaccessible. It is little comfort, even, to be fed on the sacraments and gathered into the sacrifice, when the Church, as well as the world, has, almost everywhere, reduced herself to a state in which the setting of those things is powerless to speak to the heart. Divine realities were confided to her ministry in a medium of symbolism answering to the deepest natural human needs. In the centuries of her life that medium of symbolism was first developed and enriched, then whittled away, or just allowed to shrivel up, almost to vanishing point—leaving the divine realities themselves indestructible, of course, but not remarkable for their accessibility to the hungry mind and heart. And to the majority of us, to whom the liturgical revival is still mainly something of which we receive news from others, that is the situation now: a bare skeleton of "validity" continues to operate in a desert of gestures whose meaning is all but forgotten. Nor is it comfortable to be told that one is a Catholic, of course, for the sake of being comfortable, so as to be let off having to think, and wrapped instead in beautiful ceremonies and sweet emotions. But the alternative is always the same: throw out the hard cutting edges of dogma because it isn't easy enough to make sense of them—and thereby make nonsense of the whole universe; lose patience with the Church's almost total failure to realize in practice the power of her own symbols—and so deny that there are such things as symbols; rebel against her habit of tyrannizing over the very human personality whose dignity

183

she asserts—and lose all grounds for asserting it against her. It is certainly not comfortable to stay on board; but the alternative doesn't even try to disguise itself as anything but spiritual suicide.

Harman Grisewood

Harman Joseph Grisewood *was born at Brobourne, Herts,
in 1906, was educated by the Benedictines at Ampleforth
and went on to Worcester College, Oxford. Since 1932 he
has been with the B.B.C., first as an announcer, then as
Controller of the Third Programme, now as Director of the
Spoken Word. In 1940 he married Margaret Clotilde Barley
and they have a daughter, Sabina. In 1949 he published a
small book* Broadcasting and Society.

"Why am I still a Catholic?" is not a question that
for me involves research into a number of possible
decisions. The short answer is because I am made that
way. Yet there is a long answer, and I have found it worth the
seeking though the long answer is but a wandering meditation upon the short one. A man may reckon his life according
to his encounters with circumstance and thus attempt to
ascribe his whole condition to the accidental element in
experience. But in the mazes of introspection he is likely
to find another factor of persistent importance, and this will
be an awareness of selfhood that cannot be dispelled even
by recourse to the most thoroughgoing deterministic theory.
Another man may take account of himself in terms of a
series of personal choices that contribute to a state of satisfaction or discontent, but he too will be forced to allow something in the audit that is neither in the category of willed
decision nor in that of mere environment. I have found the

185

root of my own attachment to Catholicism neither in circumstance nor in decision—though each contributes a support—but in a subsoil that underlies these and is stronger than both. These roots, because they pass out of sight through the layers of conscious experience, are not easy to demonstrate or explain.

Our vocabulary of causality and our habits of causal thought are set in modes of circumstantial or voluntaristic explanation. The appetitive or instinctual has its place in emotive statement; but its analysis is left to the scientist. It is not for us to interpret ourselves to ourselves in such terms. There is, it is true, a communicable appetitive language for the common desires of the senses; but where the attempt is made to comprise the higher faculties in an explanatory statement, then appetitive language is avoided and we proceed with the instruments of reasoned discourse to compose an intelligible causal chain of circumstance and will.

It is possible that the Greeks understood these distinctions more evenly than we. Aristotle and Plato used the word "pathos" in opposition to "dunamis" or "praxis" or "ethos." In our own day we are noticeably more at ease in our didactic explanations with the world of "dunamis" (power), "praxis" (doing) and "ethos" (habit). The world of "pathos" (undergoing or feeling) is for the poets or the fiction writers; it does not interpenetrate our schematized world as do these other orders of experience. It is allowed as an aesthetic or —rarely—as an ecstatic antithesis. But to Aristotle and Plato "pathos" seems simply another and no less familiar mode of experience and experimental communication. It may be the psychologists of the future will leave us such a language for the use of our Western World. Those will most avail themselves of it who must make an attempt to explain themselves as religious creatures.

186

There is much that can be said and has been said of the Catholic religion or of the Catholic state of mind in terms of praxis and ethos. But to answer the question "Why am I still a Catholic?" praxis and ethos are for me too external in reference. And yet there is no equivalent language of pathos. As the elucidation of the way I am made must involve the experiential, I hope the following section of personal narrative will be excused.

Stones fell harshly against the sordid brickwork. We hurried on past the disgraceful cottages to gain the safety of our own gates. To our astonishment we had suddenly realized the stones were meant for us—for me and my brothers and sister. I can remember my small brother's face gazing uncomprehendingly from his perambulator at the boys who threw them. "That's for your b—— Communion," they shouted. It was more interesting than frightening. I was seven.

These stones, and other demonstrations less tangible but no less hostile that followed, came as a surprise to the grown-ups in the family as well as to us children. We had moved to a part of England whose last acquaintance with the Catholic faith was during the painful controversies of the Reformation. This was explained to me by my father and vividly illustrated as we picked out some rough lead bullets that still stuck fast in an oak door of our new home. The house had offered stout resistance to the Puritan army when the Earl of Essex advanced upon Oxford and quartered his men in the district.

The atmosphere we lived in was late Victorian on the surface but seventeenth-century on the under-side. As we put to rights the Pre-Reformation chapel and opened it for Mass to the growingly tolerant village, we came to understand that we were moving through two hundred and fifty

187

years of history rather uncomfortably fast; and that these stones and imprecations which greeted our own—and to the throwers no less outrageous—act of defiance were not the onset of some new aggression but rather the mild reactions to a weakening impulse, which not so far off in the race-memory had expressed itself in gibbet and rack.

I remember my mother telling us that old Catholic families would understand this sort of behaviour more easily as they were part of the historic situation that gave rise to it. She added that it would be affected in us to speak of ourselves as "Cartholics." It would be proper to do so, she explained, if we were cousins to the Duke of Norfolk or if ours were an "old Cartholic family," but we were Catholics and it would be bad form by this detail of speech to seem otherwise.

Our Catholicism was Italianate. Its tradition in the family was no older than Tractarian Oxford where my grandfather had become a Puseyite and went "over to Rome" at the time of which Disraeli wrote in *Lothair*. He married an Italian. My grandmother's religious habits were effusive and lux-uriant. The sight of Gothic vestments troubled her as some dangerous deviationism from which she should protect herself and her children. She found little to content her in the English scene outside the Catholic circle of her husband's friends. Our family had led a sequestered life in conse-quence. And so it was that the yells of the Oxfordshire urchins were more of a shock to us than I fancy they would have been to others of our sort. But ours was a family of buoyant spirit and such incidents, which ceased after a few years, never afforded us cause for dejection or even dis-quiet. My father's typical response was to drive a large party to the neighbouring villages in what was called a waggon-ette, from which one of the Redemptorist Fathers, invited for the purpose, would explain the elements of Catholic

188

worship and offer to answer questions. Sometimes, bricks would be hurled instead of questions. Rosaries would then rattle against the sides of the waggonette and the horses would start off home at speed. But these forays I remember were carried through in an atmosphere of zestful pre-war good spirits. The return was more like that of a shooting-party or picnic than of a troupe of proselytizing Romanizers. I record these recollections not because the events are of much interest in themselves, but because the experience of them gave to my own Catholic life a context—an English context—which for me was important and which I could not have gained from the atmosphere of my grandmother's baroque chapel. The context was not at first corroborative of Catholic truth; it was merely engaging as a piquant experience.

The Catholic England at that time was small enough to explore pretty thoroughly. It offered the charm of a coherent and consecutive society. You were never a stranger in that society. Those you met for the first time seemed glad to see you; they knew about you in advance. They knew your friends or your relations. They talked to you about other people whom you would like to know or perhaps just knew, and about grown-ups of long ago who had known your grandfather. Everyone talked about everyone else—not in a whispering, gossipy way but to give news. News was important. News of the Meynells, of Mr. Belloc, of Lord Fitzalan, and of Cardinal Bourne. And as you grew older you were adding to the possibilities of the conversation by knowing more people and knowing more about the people. It was a fairly well defined world. The limits to it were set by being a Catholic and in knowing the Catholic circle. All this applied to England of course—it scarcely occurred to us to think of "abroad" in the same terms. Those who lived in Europe were first of all foreigners; it was nice to find

189

they were Catholics when you got there because it gave
you a feeling of bigness after the smallness of your own
English world.

We children were sorry for people who were not Catholics—not because they were outside the true faith—but
because they seemed to miss the enjoyment that our religion
afforded us. The chapel was for us a centre of festivity. We
enjoyed the alternation of solemnity and rejoicing and the
rich subtle variety of the liturgy. This place and what went
on there seemed easily in harmony with the other strenuous
pleasures of nursery or garden. The fact that it was the
centre of our home life was achieved without strain. It was
by turns grave and gay as was life itself. It irradiated our
play no less than everything else. I can remember well that
one of our most diverting pastimes was hearing through
the wire grilles of their hutches our tame rabbits' confessions in two tiny violet stoles.

This picture of childish happiness may mislead the
reader into thinking that we were nice children. In some
ways we were horrid. We were prone to scorn others who
had not our own cast of mind and habits. We thought that
anything that was not congenial to us was simply inferior.
We thought people who had sentimental holy pictures in
their prayer-books were "awful"; we thought people who
put their heads down too long in prayer were "awful". We
once stayed in a house where on fast days the toast was
weighed at table in little balances—we thought this was
"awful" too. The process of growing up and being educated
was, to a large extent, simply an encounter with what we
had regarded as the awful, the alien, and thus the merely
inferior; later came the attempt to acquire some sympathy
and respect for this strangers' world. The process was managed with the conventional pains and surprises.

It would be convenient for the effectiveness of this

190

recital if I could point to some moment of realization that the childish appreciation of religion had been replaced by an adult understanding. It would be too good to be true if what was perhaps a fortunate start thus continued by a process of steady development to a wide maturity of outlook and a deepening of insight. But my own memory provides nothing of the sort.

The encounter with the grown-up and educated world seemed to afford less and less delight. The influx of intellectual ideas left "incapsulated" the experiences of childhood and brought about what seems to me now a merely conventional disassociation. I took it for granted that the scenes of my own childhood were the most important experiential facts of existence; what I was told lay before me in futurity appeared impressive as described by grown-ups but less inviting. I say *scenes* of childhood because the impressions were concrete and defined as in Schumann's Kinderschenen; there was nothing Wordsworthian about them; we trailed no clouds of glory. But the new life of growing-up seemed like a task by comparison, engrossing at times and streaked with joys but not of the same unmixed texture of delight—that had gone altogether. It was like progressing through a valley that became steeper and more symmetrical, meaning echoing meaning from each sheer enclosure. One became acquainted with the formidable syntax of the moral scheme; with the language of retribution, of petition, of salvation. But the pattern of all this had little charm. I accepted what was said as part of growing older and as bound up with the prospect of ever increasingly having to do for oneself which seemed less and less agreeable.

I have been prompted to consider since what is the value of the intellectual scheme of the Catholic religion regarded as nourishment to oneself in one's brief earthly religious life. I am not thinking of the scheme itself in terms of truth or error but of the schematization considered subjectively as a private process and religiously as nutriment. I know that powerful intellects and those in whom the current of religious life flows strongly and who are conscious of this flow and of its strength seem in their written evidences to have suffered little from what I have sometimes felt in myself, through weakness no doubt, to be an erosion of a truly fertile religious life. I might have expected, and was encouraged by some to expect, that an acquaintance with the exposition of religion would itself be an attractive element. And, of course, exposition where it corresponds with the inclination of the mind has a charm for the mind and for the heart where there is alliance between the two, as there must be in a genuine truth-seeking and truth-holding. But there can be dangers for some in the supremacy and splendour of conceptual arrangements. It is a strong and well-balanced person in whom the attractions do not displace a less definable but more personal and commonly shared characteristic of religious insight. The corroborations I now value most are not those of heart separately nor of the mind separately. They are not proofs for the intellect nor promptings of the affection. They are certainties not arrived at by argument nor wholly by custom nor always wholly by consent. They are rather the assurances of an impulse that would test the validity of what is sought by what seems to be kindred and congenial. The reflections assisted by education and upbringing are confirmed by an appetitive sense.

Among the strongest intimations I experience that establish the Catholic truths are those received by listening to Wagner or reading Milton. These impressions draw me deep down into the non-Catholic mind. Or rather one should say the once-Catholic mind. They are true manifestations of the Christian West, and they testify by example more cogent than argument to the change that comes about through forsaking the old religion. They solicit a hidden choice. If I were to experience an *attrait* to the Wagnerian or Miltonic disposition, I should do so against the grain of my own Catholic-mindedness. What in fact takes place is a gratitude for the revulsion. I know by taste that I would not care to live in the disposition of mind that these typical manifestations create. This conclusion of the appetitive self has no relation to the art-value or art-pleasure of the works in question.

Our world has lived long in a state of religious dislocation and fracture. Men have grown up in valuable and rich cultural traditions, Calvinist or Lutheran, and these diverse religious cultures have bred habits and tastes markedly distinct from those of the old forms. I find myself strengthened by an acquaintance with these rather than distracted. I feel I should greatly miss the reinforcement they bring were I to live wholly in a world of Catholic practice. The contrast has become part of Catholic living.

When I am made peevish or indignant by some Roman extravagance or by some disagreeable institutional harshness, I need to be made aware by some tangible evidence of the rightness of the Catholic scheme. And this is commonly afforded not by Catholic witness but the reverse; by the example in conversation or reading of an outlook so estranged from the Catholic world that the repulsion from it rights one like a boat that might have capsized in rough water. It is not only repulsion that I experience; often, I see deeply-moving examples of piety and goodness. But one has to consider the style and mode of what is done and not merely the content. The content is like the usefulness or efficiency of an object. But the style and mode is important too as testimony of the culture in which the object

193

is an item. The style and mode of piety and goodness are a testimony of the institution and religious culture of which the human being is part. Sometimes I feel admiration for the content and repugnance for the style and mode. The repulsion is from some exclusiveness to my own scheme, which seems one of inclusion. From the something less to the something more; from some impoverishment to a richness; from something partial to what is complete. For these corroborations I am deeply indebted to the fissured diversity of our English world.

To some outside the Church the Catholic scheme seems an exclusive one. But I have not found the Catholic experience to be so. The Catholic experience seems to encourage a positive and explicit value to be set upon truth and goodness wherever it be found; and to encourage a delight in the seeking of it. A constant proximity and mingling with the non-Catholic, once-Catholic milieu allow some understanding of how the symmetrical façade of the Catholic scheme seems to manifest an exclusivism. The formulations of the Church and its uncompromising explanation of them are liable to give such an impression; this is necessary for the institution. Such are the characteristics of institutions—especially for those who do not live within them. An Aztec might gain such an impression of the British Parliament by a perusal of the Standing Orders. This belongs to the world of *praxis* and *dunamis*. But the witness of *pathos* is other.

It is commonplace that what brings men to the Church is the discovery that she is true. But what holds you to the Church is the continued experience of the truth. For some that experience is to a large degree intellectual; for many it is largely an experience that may perhaps be called moral. For some others—and these are nearest to me in relationship—the experience will seem to be of a congeries of faculties that I should call appetitive. The truth is tested in

194

the desire for truth—however fitful or wayward or feeble that desire may be. And this mode of experience will lead a man toward what can be ascertained by taste and appetite. It may be thought by some that to prefer the Catholic religion on grounds of taste is to offer too low and too terrestrial a reason for adherence to sublime truth. In offering this lower-scale reason I do not thereby reject the higher. One of the glories of the Catholic scheme is its power of condescension and inclusiveness, so that the stupid and weak are no less Catholic than the quick-witted and robust.

If this appetitive attachment be a valid Catholic way for some, it must make demands upon the universality of the Church which others may not find the need to call upon. I do not refer to the ubiquity of the Church but to a universality of another kind, to her inclusiveness. The Catholic temper is not prone to exclusivity in the fact-world of truth and goodness and beauty. She disposes men to an enlargement of the understanding, not to a narrowing. There is no tapering off in this world. The discernible conic structure is to eternity; and we now are in the thick base. The historic Catholic deposits endow the inheritor with freedom and not only with duty. The duty is to the whole world according to the creature's capacity and our freedom is to the exploration of it.

In speaking of historic Catholicism it is necessary to keep in mind a distinction. There is the official order and the private order; it is a cardinal error to confuse what is proper to each. The official order is regulatory, normative; the private order is exploratory. The one is collective, the other solitary; the one protects, guides, prescribes, the other is venturesome and questing. The natural environment of the one is illumination, of the other perplexity. The one is not afraid and needs no bravery, the other must proceed fearfully and can always do with encouragement.

So it is possible to talk of the authoritarianism of the former, of its inflexibility, of its infallibility; but these terms are scarcely applicable to the Catholic person living his life. He feels his mortality maybe more than others for whom it is not illumined so plainly. And the definitions with which he is furnished make the world more meaningful, not less. The anguish and the delights are heightened. Nothing is avoided. Nothing excluded. There is no stop or halt for the exercise of the Catholic temper. It must be extended to capacity. And this is always painfully greater than we like to imagine. If a man is not goaded by truth, then he is goaded by charity, and not only by charity of the affections but of the mind and the imagination. A religion that drives one thus seems to me apt for sluggish human kind. And these goads are most precise and yet most varied in the Catholic system.

There is I believe a vocational spur for some to participate in the world by realizing in themselves the detail of terrestrial transience. And this participation will vividly illustrate Catholic truth. There are those perhaps who will object that there is nothing distinctively Catholic in this sort of illustration. But for those who understand membership of the Church in the way I have attempted to describe, there can be no challenge to her, and there is no alternative. She is the religion of all cultures, yet deeply and tenderly understanding in each the things of place and of time. She is the religion of the violent and of the gentle; she is the religion for the dull, long stretches and for the great moments; for festivity and mourning; for the crowd and for the solitary. Hers is the religion of Hopkins' Jack Joke into immortal diamond. It is the drift of these reflections to suggest that much in this mode of apprehension is less a discovery of maturer years than a humble re-appraisal of what was a childish understanding.

196

Jane Wyatt

Jane Wyatt. *Born in Campgaw, New Jersey; educated Chapin School and Barnard College, New York. She has had an active career on the stage and screen, appearing in such pictures as "Lost Horizon," "Task Force," "Pitfall," and such plays as "Hope for the Best" and "The Autumn Garden." She is married to Edgar Bethune Ward and they have two sons.*

 "What dost thou ask of the Church of God?"
"Faith."
"What does faith bring to thee?"
"Life everlasting."

There is something very touching in the thought that these tremendous questions are asked us when, having recently entered the world, we are carried to the baptismal font where, as babies, we so solemnly agree to renounce Satan and all his pomps.

The Church never talks down to us at any time of our development. It has always been a source of surprise for me to discover, time and time again, that the "Penny Catechism" has not been softened or watered down for childish minds, but that the entire Catholic belief is there presented, stark and whole, for the six-year-old to learn. The Catechism also means precisely what it says. It may be naive of me to admit that, just as Santa Claus dematerialized and the stork flew out of the nursery, so I expected that the more ad-

197

vanced Catechism would offer some alterations in its answers for more adult minds. The Church indeed is always ready to feed us richer fare as we demand it, but the fact remains that the Penny Catechism teaches Truth, and Truth with no window dressings, for very little children.

It must be fairly easy for converts to say why they entered and why they remain in the Church. Obviously they have thought a great deal about it before they made any such vital decision, but to us, who renounced the pomps of Satan as infants, it's not so easy. I imagine a great many of us stay in the Church out of habit and fear of hell-fire. But I am sure the greater majority of us have never thought of leaving the Church, because the faith we so unwittingly asked for at our baptism has been granted us, and because at every turn of our lives the Church has not only come up to our expectations but exceeded them. I have no desire to be a martyr, but if I were put to the test to die or renounce my faith, I would die for Christ because there would simply be no other choice.

As I look back on my childhood I realize that I never had the typical Catholic upbringing. My mother is a Catholic but my father was not. Our home was a Catholic home because my mother made it one, but religion was not a warm, easy, contributing factor. This was due to my father's feeling about the Church. I suppose in a way this tended to strengthen our faith, but it also made us wary and a little secretive. Religion went underground. We had to be careful not to let Papa know we were going to receive Holy Communion, because he felt it was very bad for us to go out in the cold without breakfast. Although he liked fish, it annoyed him on Friday. During my adolescent years, my father, who had only partially recovered from a severe illness, became increasingly prejudiced. He had had a lawyer's training, was well versed in Catholic doctrine and had a

very good mind. This made it difficult for us children, because he would ask us a theological question and then
analyze our answers.

My sister and my brother and I went for a catechism
lesson once a week with a nun in a cloistered order. She was
a deeply spiritual person, but from our point of view she
seemed to have no connection with realities or the problems
of the world; yet as the years go by I have had many opportunities to remember her favourite quotation, "What does
it profit a man if he gain the whole world and suffer the
loss of his soul?"

We went to non-Catholic schools, and I am sure that I
never divulged to Mother Mary of St. Carthage how
shocked I was to find, at the age of thirteen, that although
the girls in my class were presumably Christians, their ideas
of God, and particularly of Christ, seemed very unchristian.
Several didn't even believe that Christ was God—only a
very, very good man. I remember how I suddenly found myself very hot and trembly and flushing bright red as I
declared that if I were not convinced that Christ is the Son
of God I would cease calling myself a Christian and become
a Jew. I realized that if Christ is not the Son of God, then
the whole of the New Testament would be a lie of which the
Catholic Church would be the continuation. When Edith
Stein, the outstanding German philosopher and convert,
told her mother of her determination to become a Carmelite
nun, the deeply religious Jewish mother cried out in despair,
"I don't want to say anything against him—he may have
been a very good man—but why did he have to make himself God?" What a heartbreaking speech and how terrible
its connotation, for no matter how good a man Christ might
have been, how could we accept His teaching even in part
if, like an inflated Roman Emperor, He had "made Himself
God"?

199

At thirteen, values tend to become black or white, but I still believe that if I were not certain that Christ is God, I would choose the Jewish religion before any other. "Spiritually we are Semites," said Pope Pius XII, using the present tense, and of course he is right. We are still Jews, but we have also been given the faith to see the promises of the Old Testament fulfilled.

Personally I have a very deep feeling of association with the Old Testament and find it easy to share its longings and searchings and the distant memory of a better time. I often imagine that I have listened to Jeremias; that I have wandered with Moses and was with Abraham in the Vale of Mambre. Thus I particularly appreciate the fact that while the Mass is being said every moment of every day in some part of the world, mention is being made of Abraham and Abel and Melchisedech, that mysterious figure in Genesis. Although Abraham and Abel and Melchisedech belong to such a far-distant past, they are still invoked and remembered by the priests who are their successors of four thousand years. It is this sense of continuity and the telescoping of time that is so wonderful in the Catholic Church. As the world shrinks with our onslaughts on time and space, the four thousand years which separate us from the splendours of Abraham seem very short.

After school, I went to a non-Catholic college, and until comparatively recently I have not had any Catholic friends. After two years of college, I went on the stage, and I have never felt that there was any antagonism between the Church and the theatre. On the contrary, they seem to go arm in arm. Certainly the greatest spectacles and the richest pageants take place in the Church. Even the fasts and penances of Lent are dramatic. They all add richness and warmth to the storehouse of emotions which is an actor's life. As a matter of fact, the teachings of the Church can be used by an actor in a very practical way. The Church teaches us to lose self to find oneself; to abhor lukewarm-ness, to try to attain a certain detachment while living in the noisy, busy world, and all these things are actually practised by an actor while he is studying a part. From the moment that he makes his first entrance on the stage as a fledgling, he must find a way to lose his self-consciousness; he must work to free his inner self from its agonizingly stiff, self-conscious body; he must continually aspire to a detach-ment which will permit him to discard the unneeded en-cumbrances of daily life and personal characteristics. Only in this way is he able to reflect, like a film negative, what he is exposed to in the part. He also becomes more vul-nerable to the author's ideas and to the playing of the other actors. And if God hates tepidity, so does an audience! Better be downright bad than lukewarm or tasteless. But it's this very vulnerability which makes the actor's life more open to pitfalls. After all, we actors do live in a world of unreality and emotion; of bitter disappointments or up-setting success. It's all so very personal—ME-ME-ME! Values so easily get twisted that it's not very difficult to begin believing the press notices, especially when they are ultra-favourable. But from the moment we Catholics start our Catechism we are taught that sin is sin. No matter how we dress it up and pretend to ourselves that in this instance it's different, as Catholics we have to face the fact that sin exists. It is this full consciousness of sin for which I've been very grateful: it X-rays hypocrisy and undermines the dream world of glamour. There is always a temptation to build oneself into a colourful personality who lives outside con-vention and accepted standards of morality. Living just by convention is a bore, but living for God is a challenge. I find that challenge best represented in the Church.

It was when I went on the stage that the catholicity of

the Church began to mean a great deal to me. I was meeting new people, different people, people with different incomes and different backgrounds. I was self-conscious about the set in which I had been raised. I resented cliques and class boundaries, and I was grateful, so very grateful, for the generous, selfless, classless hospitality of the Church and the comforting welcome of the Mass—the same Mass in whatever city I found myself.

Now that my sons have been to Catholic schools where religion is as natural as oxygen, and family life is a continuation of the Holy Family, now that my husband has joined us at the Communion rail, I know why my godparents asked, in my name as an infant, for faith.

J. G. Shaw

James G. Shaw *was born in London in 1909, moved to Scotland at the age of three, and came to Canada some twenty years ago. He is now one of the best known of Canada's journalists and literary critics. He is one of the founders of the Thomas More Institute for Adult Education in Montreal.*

One thing I like about the Catholic Church is how it has changed since I first knew it.

I remember it some forty years ago when it was narrow, closed-in and fenced all around so that all you could see was bars. But it was comfortable and safe. You lay on warm feathers with soft woolly blankets tucked around you. If in your folly you grew reckless and kicked off the blanket or stuck an inquisitive hand out through the bars, it put you firmly and gently back where you belonged, tucked you again into the warmth of the blanket and made soothing, mock-serious noises to tell you that, though it was displeased with your foolishness, it really did understand. If you grew restless, there were wavy blue ribbons and bright coloured things that made interesting sound-effects to distract your attention and keep you quiet.

This Church didn't give you much room, but it was just the right size for a cradle.

Then I remember soldiers marching home from World

War One and the world growing larger. The Church, too, had grown a bit. It was more things. It was Sisters and Brothers and Priests and Catechism and School and Mass. It was Confession, Communion and Confirmation.

It was, "Who made you?" "God made me." "Why did God make you?" "God made me to know Him, love Him and serve Him in this world and to be happy with Him forever in the next." There were a lot of other questions and answers and you knew them all by heart, word for word. But the others didn't really matter except for getting them right and coming first in the class. There wasn't much meaning to any of them except the first two that came back and back again in your mind. "Who made you?" "God made me." "Why did God make you?" "God made me to know Him, love Him and serve Him in this world and to be happy with Him forever in the next."

There was something fitting about the pointed personalness of the questions—the "you" coming from the vague outside, and the "me" being shot back into the outer darkness like a rarely released ray from the inner light no one ever saw but yourself.

That was the trouble with the Church in those days. It was part of the circle of goodness that hemmed you in. Your father, your mother, your teacher, the school, the Church. And the Church was the worst part of that conspiracy of the not-you. The others used it to close the circle. They even used the fact you were a Catholic to make you part of their planning against you.

Not that you ever felt they were bad. It was just that they didn't *know*. They didn't know you were going off as a cabin boy with Sir Ernest Shackleton on his next trip to the North Pole. They didn't know you would have gone up by yourself in a balloon and shot a flaming arrow into those zeppelins. They didn't know that if this had been the age of drummer boys, you would have waded ashore in the first ranks at the Dardanelles without breaking step or missing a beat. How could they know all this? But there they were, there the Catholic Church was, squeezing you and shaping you and making you into something you didn't want to be.

Not that it was bad to be a Catholic. It was wonderful and you were proud of it. Not about things like heaven and hell. They were like your father and your mother and your teacher and the priest. They were true, they were inevitable, but they weren't real. They didn't enter into your scheme of things. The pride came at other moments when being a Catholic joined itself to the real you.

Like when Edmund Campion showed visitors through the Tower of London under the noses of men who were searching for him all over England. Or when John Ogilvie rode smiling to his death through the streets of Glasgow.

And at the oddest incidental moments it would raise you to a cloud of the dreamy emotionalism that served you for personal ideals. You might be with hundreds of men and boys, standing together in church or at an out-door altar. You would listen to your loudest voice matching the thunder of theirs, oblivious of everything except the sound of marching men and you among them as you sang,

> Faith of our Fathers, living still
> In spite of dungeon, fire and sword.

That was the real stuff . . . that "dungeon, fire and sword"! As if such things could stop us! There was lots more of it, too, right down to the repeated last line,

> We will be true to thee till death,
> We will be true to thee till death.

That "true to thee till death" was exactly right. That's what we Catholics were like.

Then there were other times. During the month of May we had little shrines to Our Lady in every class-room and one out in the corridor. We would line up every day and sing together,

> Hail, Queen of Heaven, the ocean star,
> Guide of the wanderer, here below

How true! How real! That was exactly you. A "wanderer here below" out alone on the ocean with only a single star to guide you.

> Thrown on life's surge, we claim thy care
> Save us from peril and from woe.

There it was again. That peril and woe you were always walking through and nobody around you understood. But here was somebody who did understand. Somebody who would shine down on you and stay far away from you like a star while you fought your lonely dangerous battle; somebody whose care you could claim.

The Catholic faith, I must admit, wasn't very lovable in those days or very intelligent—stuffing minds by rote and feeding the emotions on the folk songs of a persecuted people.

But it grew up a bit more and took another step towards maturity somewhere between the two world wars. First it became lovable and then intelligent, very intelligent.

I remember a Catholic young man who fell in love with it during this time. It was around the end of the Flapper Era when pleasure was leaving a particularly unpleasant aftertaste in the mouth of the world. The Catholic faith

206

began to glow with an inward goodness that was most attractive exactly where the heavy presence of unloved desire most repelled.

It offered beauty that could be plucked flower by flower and increase with the plucking without ever losing its bloom. In place of disappointed attainment, and despair, it offered an infinite succession of possible achievement, and hope.

And it held out all its loveliness—this, perhaps, is where the young man was completely overwhelmed—it held out all its loveliness to *him*. He, personally and individually, was loved by Goodness and the demands of love were upon him.

He searched, like any lover, to know the beloved, to learn her desires and anticipate them, to know her wishes and make them his command, to study what he must do, what he must become, in order to make himself acceptable in her eyes. By being loved and loving he discovered anew the law of love-in-sacrifice, and by sacrifice he purified himself for love.

The young man was a stumbling lover. He was not always understanding, nor always bright in his lady's eyes. But he was ever quick to please according to his moment and, though sometimes out of grace, he was never for an instant out of love.

The Catholic Church was wonderful in those days and the discovery of its new brightness an unending pleasure. It was Hilaire Belloc striding lustily along the path to Rome. It was Chesterton hymning the heart of England and discovering he had sung the soul of Rome. It was both of them brawling boisterously with all comers in defense of the right God had given men to go gaily in the dark. It was Maurice Baring arriving at the River Styx and emptying his mind to shape an epitome of good taste in answer to Charon's question, "Have you anything to declare?" It was Gerard

Manley Hopkins and his grubs-in-amber offering a key to the meaning of all that thirty years of "modern" poetry had been trying to do. It was an altogether wonderful and exciting introduction to the beauty of belief.

But first love is rapture made to lift a man to heights from which he can find his level and settle down.

Again the Church changed. I remember it. There had been a depression. It had sobered the flappers, who were now mothers watching their sons grow up for another war. The Church turned to the young man and said: "This romanticism is all very well. But why? What is it all about? How do you know it is true? Can it possibly be? Just look around you. You are not the only one who can answer the first question with 'God made me.' All of them can, or else your own answer was not true. Was it? Is it? How do you know? Why? How?"

Yesterday's lover found himself in a new Church. The woman at his side had turned strangely demanding; but she was still beautiful and he was still in love.

The young Catholic man, if the truth must be told, met this change in the Church by ignoring it. He plunged into the new task his lady had set with all the old spirit of discovery and reaped at first the same fruit of fresh delight.

It was all so easy, so obvious. All the questions were drawn up in order, with all the answers set down. It was like doing geometry. You proved theorem one and theorem two followed. Then came theorem three and right on to the end of the book. There were a couple of *pontes asinorum*, but only asses got stuck at them. True, it took a little work, a little intelligence (said the young man) and a good teacher to help you over the rough spots. But there it all was—the meaning of all things in their ultimate causes—lined up in well-ordered, unassailable array. He could only pity people who could not have all this placed before them or who were too unconscionably impenetrable to receive its intensive and comprehensive revelation.

The young man knew, of course, that other people had reached other answers. Rejecting those was as simple as finding the truth. You just said,

> Anyone who says this, is wrong.
> Kant says this.
> Therefore Kant is wrong.

The young man was still in his first love. He was at the stage where nothing exists outside the lover and the loved. He could not possibly think *with* anyone. Everyone had to think with him. Objections were easy because he only noticed those he could see through eyes blinded with the light of love.

Perhaps something enigmatical about the smile of his lady—still beautiful and still beckoning—as she received his latest gift, made the young man realize that there really had been a change. This was no sweetheart waiting a wooer with another bouquet. It was a bride watching her man lay the foundation of a lasting home.

However it came about, the young man I remember suddenly awoke to the new demand. He straightway fell into the arms of his changed lady and in the falling seemed to have lost his bride forever.

He found, when he tried to think for himself, that he couldn't prove the existence of God. He was quite certain nobody else could prove it.

He went to the wise men who were his teachers. It may have been that they were not so wise but more probably this was merely the moment when the cataract grows full before the sight-restoring operation. The wise men pointed at the answers. The same answers that had been circling around the young man's head for weeks and weeks without meaning. They repeated them over and over, quietly at first and then with less patience. Wise men through the centuries, brilliant men, men of genius, had accepted these. Why weren't they good enough for the likes of him? It was sheer arrogant, egotistic presumption to reject them.

This the young man could not deny. But it was no help. Here again was that inevitable but unreal constricting circle of authoritative good coming from his boyhood to close in on him once more. He must not let it. He was a man now who had looked on the smile of Truth and must follow it. No one else could answer for him to his love but himself. He must break the circle or crawl back to his boyhood— which he could not do because his beloved was no longer there.

So he cried out in protest. What are your axioms? Who is your God? You begin with the unprovable and end with the unknowable! What good is the proud interlocking of your in-between structure? Why not admit it is the elaboration of a genius to defend from rational attack a truth you believe without being able to prove?

There were no answers. At least none that could in this moment ease the young man's doubt.

He went away to think things out. If there were no God, then what of "God made me"? What of the Truth-Beauty-Goodness that had thrilled him in his ideal, the Catholic Church? What of the love he had thought for ever? What of all the other people he had been presuming that God made?

In the last question he found his strange bewildered answer.

All right. There was no God. The whole beautiful dream he had known from his childhood, loved in his youth and taken for his bride, was without being. It was a projection of man's wishful thinking. Granted all this, it was still beautiful, it was still good—even if it was not true.

Its corporal and spiritual works of mercy still compassed all any man could do for his fellows—feed the hungry, give drink to the thirsty, visit the imprisoned, shelter the homeless, visit the sick, bury the dead, admonish the sinner, instruct the ignorant, counsel the doubtful, comfort the sorrowful, bear wrongs patiently, forgive injuries, pray for the living and the dead.

All history from the days of the apostles showed the Catholic Church doing these things in countless places and in myriad ways. It was doing them here and now all around him.

The young man had an unshakable conviction of the truth so many poets and philosophers had seen before and after John Donne, "no man is an island intire unto himself." He had lifted to its soundness in Ernest Hemingway's title "For Whom the Bell Tolls," and he had found its fundamental justification in St. Paul's teaching of the Mystical Body. It stayed with him now and rationalized a desired conclusion.

He would stay in the Catholic Church although he no longer believed in its God. Where else could he find such companionship in good? such guidance for direction, strength for accomplishment? How could he better use his one life?

For some months, the young man lived his sad, erroneous dichotomy. Then something—habit, if you will, or loneliness, but better the insistent need of his love—brought him to another and truly wise man. This man had a reputation for learning and had won academic degrees and some scientific distinction. But it was not in this capacity the young man visited him. He went to a friend who was also a priest. He went to a priest who remembered His Master standing outside that door without an outside knob, a priest who never violated the sanctuary of another's soul and a man who respected the struggles of another mind.

The young man wanted to tell his friend of the position he had taken. He knew he could talk frankly without danger of being told he was a fool or a knave or anything but the same friend of his friend. He knew he could walk into the room, find release in companionable talk, and walk out again without the added weight of unasked advice.

That is how it was. The eyes that met his outpouring of tumbled thought showed no shock, no disbelief, no dismay, nothing but genuine interest and friendly sympathy. The first words the priest spoke, in a voice that always seemed to carry a half-amused and half-bemused ring, were these: "Me, I have about half-a-dozen things I can prove to my own satisfaction. When doubts start boiling, I hold on to those and let the rest swirl around me."

The young man could have laughed out loud in sheer relief. Perhaps he did.

The talk went on, pouring intensely from one side and falling in gentle phrases from the other. It named the six things the priest had mentioned, it bartered comment on philosophy and philosophies, it spoke of God and goodness, of men and sin.

But the young man wasn't really with it. None of its detail mattered, he was carried away in its total flow.

That outside circle had broken. Or had there ever been a circle except in the darkness of his mental habit? He was free. He was an individual.

As the priest talked and he answered, his mind was racing off to meanings beyond the words. His heart was alive with love for a new Church. His eyes had been opened for the first time on the relationship between individual thinking and the common truth. He had a new world to look out on.

Plato and Aristotle fitted in together with Aquinas disapproving the Immaculate Conception and Duns Scotus proving it. Mahatma Ghandi was in the picture with Catherine of Siena. Percy Bysshe Shelley was one with Francis Thompson, William Langland with Rabbie Burns. Norman Thomas, Al Smith, and Herbert Hoover came into focus with Machiavelli, Robert Bellarmine, Thomas Jefferson, Demosthenes, Alexander the Great and Mayor Hague.

The Church certainly had changed. And I remember well that this Catholic man was more in love with it then than in his youth when he thought it was the only thing in the world.

This sort of settled, open-eyed love is an entirely different thing to carry around among your fellow men (and to live with) from the secret and sacred flame that makes the young lover self-conscious. The flame is still your own and still sacred. But the love is no longer secret and you don't particularly care who knows about it. Apprehension is gone, and with it sensitivity. What could not be spoken about before without at least the show of crossed swords, now becomes the subject of banter which skips across the surface expressing, in the inarticulate way men have, a shared knowledge of the depth that lies beneath.

Grown-up Catholicism is a lot like married love. Within himself a man makes adjustment from the romantic to the classical. Among his fellows he enjoys an easy, respectful and familiar recognition of his status. "Who was that Religion I saw you with last night?" "That was no Religion. That was my Church."

I know a man who had reached adulthood in his faith just before the dropping of the first atom bomb. The event registered on his mind, as did everything else, through the fine-screen of his Catholicism. He felt horror for men in the mass that such an act should have been possible. But he could not for the life of him understand the panic of individuals at the thought of an atom bomb dropping on their

213

own cities. Death for the individual, he knew, is the same, whether it come by tripping on the cellar stairs or in a communal holocaust. In the fact that men had devised a means of dealing it out more quickly to more people the man could see nothing more than one more argument for staying in the state of grace.

For this particular Catholic, the adjustment within himself was a gradual opening-up and rearranging process which, he hopes, will go on until he dies. It possibly started with understanding that there was a difference between failing to see God in a syllogism and denial of His existence. It grew to an insight into the sacredness of the individual person. This brought the man a new respect for the lives and the opinions of others, along with a new freedom for himself. It brought a flood of light to bear on the meaning of Charity and why it is "the greatest of these."

The man began to see clearly that he could only go to God or turn away from Him by an act of his own free will. The going-to-God was the only important thing, the only thing, he had to do with the sum total of his whole life and with every action in it. No one else, nothing else, could do it for him—not the priest, not the bishop, not the Church. He alone must do it. They, like the State and all its functions in their degree, were means placed at his hand to be used in submission to their due dignity but with no surrender of his own.

There was a corollary to the fact that the only thing he had to do was serve God. It was that the only place he could see God in this life was in his fellow man: ". . . when you did it to the least of these." So he knew that he must serve God where Christ had told him he could find him.

But his fellow man has also only one thing to do with his whole life. So the only way he could ultimately serve his fellow was by helping him perform the only act that is of any value either to himself or to God—an act of the love of God proceeding from his own free will.

If he brought a man to God in this way, he would be going to God himself, closing to its perfection the triangle of moral obligation—self . . . God . . . fellow man. Perhaps, the man thought, this is what lies behind the belief that no man goes to God alone.

Carrying this adult Catholicism among his fellow Catholics was not the easiest of the man's tasks. Some Catholics never grow up. Many stay in the cradle and keep their Catholicism an affair of the warm blanket, the wavy ribbon, the soothing noise and the bright rattle. Others, who sometimes rise to prominence in and out of the Church, remain good (or naughty) Catholic boys long after they have grown beyond that stage in everything except their Catholicism. They want to stay within the constricting circle of recognizable good, letting their presence in it serve as their response to God while they hold it off from the private world in which they really live. Some happy people, and there are saints among them as well as heretics and fools, never leave the romantic rapture in which no one exists but themselves and the object of their passion. From them, whether saints, heretics or fools, come the non-conformists who are thorns in the side of the Church's body politic. They serve, like His Majesty's Loyal Opposition, to keep the government good. They keep orthodoxy from hardening into a close-wrought, bejewelled globe whose elaboration becomes an end in itself and which grows to obscure or stifle the living flame it was fashioned to protect. Many pass through the several stages only to shrink from the fullness of the last and settle down to a compromise that feeds on a combination of them all. Most of us Catholics live too large a part of our lives somewhere in that compromise.

It took some time for our Catholic man to learn that the

Church was for all and not just for him. He had to recall his own discovery about the sacredness of the person. He had to remind himself that every individual is a concatenation of heredity, environment, hopes, desires, dreams, strengths and weaknesses that God alone knows. He had to learn that vocation was individual within the group, that each man can go to God only as himself.

Carrying his settled faith among non-Catholics, our grown-up Catholic found fresh reason every day to give thanks for the gift of Faith, new proof that it was a gift whose giving is a mystery. Wherever he found truth or goodness he recognized it as part of his own heritage and knew it would find itself at home in the Catholic Church. He could not conceive of anything good or beautiful or true that could not be found in the Catholic Church. He could find no natural explanation why so many people who were good, loved beauty and sought truth could not accept the Catholic Church. Faith, he knew, *must* be a gift and one often granted, within its mystery, under the process labelled Baptism of Desire.

When I said that the man did not know any reason why these people could not accept the Catholic Church, I was not telling the full truth. The man knew that he, being one with them and in possession of that faith, was to blame. He went to his bride the Church and told her so.

But that is altogether another story.

There is a limit to how far one can keep this sort of thing up without on the one hand invading the intimacies that make impossible a full answer to the question, "Why do you remain a Catholic?" or on the other, running away from the question altogether.

The fact is that, if taken as strictly personal, the question is an impertinence. It is a bit like asking, "Why do you keep on loving the same old wife?" (or wearing the same old face).

Catholicism is like that to the cradle Catholic. It is as much a part of him as breathing. More. He can do without breathing.

Catholic attitudes, Catholic people, Catholic customs, Catholic beliefs, all these one can talk about. A man may write about the things he likes or doesn't like about Catholicism. But about the thing itself as it lives in him personally, only he who has the words to strip his soul to the world and the will to do so dare speak.

For Catholicism is not a matter of arguments and answers, of people and places and things. It is a life of communion with God, directly and through one's fellow men. Without understanding of this, all else that may be said about it is superficial and mostly meaningless.

And who is strong enough to speak honestly of himself down in this innermost core of all his living—the place where his Catholicism either is or is not? Who will tell of sanctity refused? Who will speak the shame of rejecting good because perfection was out of reach? Who will admit he knows he must see God in his fellow man and at the same time detail the treatment he has given through his fellow man to God?

Not the present writer. If it be understood that I am shrinking from the edge of the spiritual truth which is the whole of Catholicism and staying on the level surface of polite discussion, I can tell some of the things I like about being a Catholic.

I honestly like everything about it, including the bad things because they make me feel better. I like its history and its geography. I like Catholicism's determination to stay alive for Christ and a Catholic's willingness to die for Him. I like the fact that the Catholic Church is as old as

Christianity, as young as the newest baby, as wide as the world with all its people, and as narrow as Christ.

I like the things it has taught me, one by one as I was ready for them, about itself. I like, for instance, that it has taught me to say this

> Man was not created to serve the State;
> Man was not created to serve the Church.
> Man was created to serve God.
> Church and State exist to serve man in serving
> God, a relationship exactly expressed in one of
> the Pope's titles, *Servus Servorum Dei.*

I like the fact that the Catholic Church, while holding the express purpose of expanding its membership to as many people as possible as soon as possible, ordains celibacy for the very people who would be most likely to give it good and abundant increase.

I like the fact that its symbol is a sign of contradiction. There is an underlying antinomy in things that teases the mind for ever. The ancient philosophers wrestled towards a central truth by juxtaposing the One and the Many, the Way Up and the Way Down. All men face the same complementary contradictions daily. The Catholic Church resolves them by acceptance and offers what explanation it may.

How can a priest hold God in his two hands every morning in the interval between shutting off an alarm clock and rushing over for ham and eggs and the start of his daily business? He does. How, as Charles Williams once asked, can there be room for works of supererogation in a religion that demands we give everything to God? There is. And there is explanation for both.

One of the most splendid contradictions is that the Catholic Church is—and must be—at once holy and universal. It demands holiness of its members. It will be content with nothing else. Yet—and this is the most consoling thing about the Church—it exists specifically for sinners. All its machinery is geared to them. Its graces are channeled for their easiest use. Its liturgy is written for them, its life spent for them, for them all its prayers are said.

Since the Church is for sinners, it is for everybody. It is universal in the human as well as in the geographical or the chronological application of the word. This universality joins not only good with bad, but also stupid with brilliant, cynical with naive, crude with refined, radical with conservative, the mob with the master, the precious with the plain. It *must* have room for them all. It must in its integrity be recognizable, understandable and lovable to each of them.

If it were a Church that only myself and my friends could understand and appreciate, it would not be the Church of Christ who died for all men.

The most humanly satisfying thing about the Catholic Church is that in its universality, it is hugely, crudely and magnificently just what it should be.

The Catholic Church not only fits the seven ages of the individual man, it answers the needs of all seven of them simultaneously, in the same man and in all men.

It also fits the seven ages of mankind which are perhaps represented around the world at this moment in time. The Brahmin scanning the Vedas, Buddha under the Peepul Tree, Lao-Tze with the Tao, Confucius with his Five King Canon, even Mahomet claiming the mantle of Christ, were all seeking the Catholic Church as much as Moses striving for a sight of the Promised Land. Had they seen it and known it for what it is, they would have found in it the fullness of that truth of knowing and of being they strove so hard to elaborate, fragment by fragment, for themselves.

And we cradle Catholics have it all handed to us gratuitously. What a terrifying thought!

Erik von Kuehnelt-Leddihn

Erik Ritter von Kuehnelt-Leddihn was born 1909 in Styria, Austria. He studied in Vienna and in Budapest. His career as a writer started when he became Vienna corre-spondent of the Spectator *at the age of 16. He has taught at several American universities and colleges and has published novels as well as books on sociological and po-litical subjects. Among his books are* Gates of Hell *(1933),* Moscow 1979 *(1946),* Liberty or Equality *(1952),* Black Banners *(1952). He is a spectacular linguist.*

Who, according to certain slightly romantic ex-pectations, would have a good chance of becoming a militant Catholic? The ones most likely to conform to the mental picture of a future devotee of Catholic Action, I think, would be an Irish lad from Co. Connemara with numerous brothers, uncles, sisters and aunts in religious orders; or, after a dramatic conversion, a bright young MVD agent, a scion of an agnostic Jewish family, or a New Eng-lander descending from three generations of Unitarian ministers, if not a Hindu Brahmin studying at Teachers' College, Columbia.

Original qualifications for any "militancy" I had very few, except, perhaps, the circumstance of having been born on July 31st, the feast of St. Ignatius. Apart from this happy coincidence my antecedents could not have been worse since

I am an Austrian, the product of a country which, according to official statistics, is "solidly Catholic," and never in the past had the privilege of a Protestant or Pagan suppression. What good can you expect from the Faith in such a nation? The Church in Austria to most impartial observers always seemed to be somewhat relaxed; our great ecclesiastic art is baroque; our priests appeared to be humble, urbane and accommodating; the ties between the higher clergy and the State were not inconsiderable. After all, the Habsburgs (more so than the papacy) were the prime movers of the Counter-Reformation, and without this dynasty's genius for organization and the zeal of great Saints it is hard to see what, humanly, would have saved the Catholic Church from becoming an Italo-Hibernian sect. The House of Austria, moreover, broke the power of the Grand Turk after the two sieges of Vienna and at the battle of Lepanto. To this co-operation between secular and spiritual forces my forebears and I owe the Faith. Without this intervention of Providence one wonders how many Americans today would have to answer the call of the muezzin from minarets; Islamic art would then not be restricted to the temples of the Shriners in the Middle West.

My family background might be evaluated at least as negatively as the cultural configuration of Austria. My two grandfathers were high-ranking civil servants of the Empire; my father, on the other hand, breaking with a tradition, was neither an officer nor a bureaucrat, but a scientist, and one of the pioneer researchers in radium and X-ray treatment. The damages done by the deadly rays undermined his health; it took him eleven years to die, but his unshakable Viennese humour never deserted him until the very bitter end. A half-practising Catholic during most of his life, he turned later with great fervour to the Church. My sister I always remember as profoundly religious. Her husband,

221

Baron Gottfried Engerth, who died in 1943 and so escaped the concentration camp, was a psychiatrist, brain surgeon and Vice-President of the Catholic Medical Guild. Of all men I ever knew he left the deepest impression on me; he was the perfect synthesis of saint, scholar and nobleman. He realized, no less than my father, that medicine is incapable of solving any of the fundamental problems of our existence.

Thus the Faith as a real force had entered our family by the late twenties. It created no conflicts but merely strengthened existing trends. The residues of nineteenth-century liberalism in our circles were never very effective but manifested themselves in a weak mixture of indifferentism, a certain moderate anti-clerical sentiment and a mild, rather benevolent scepticism. (Thus I could never convince my otherwise very pious grandmother—*nata* 1842, *obiit* 1942—that she ought to go to Mass every single Sunday, and my own dear mother is still unable to see the wisdom of frequent Communion.) Yet religion with us remained interwoven with a lot of purely parochial traditions and notions. Not that it was marred with anything as vulgar as nationalism masquerading as "patriotism"—according to Dr. Johnson the "refuge of scoundrels"—but it still was regarded as part and parcel of a genteel way of life beautifully at harmony with the local scene. Thus Catholicism with us was tied up and encumbered with a good deal of non-essential bywork, with the Habsburgs and the gorgeous Corpus Christi processions, with the whole subtly secularized magic of Christmas, with the baroque art of the Counter-Reformation, with a specifically Austrian sensual *joie de vivre* and the open air Masses celebrated at the various meetings of medal-bedecked war veterans.

One can see easily that this Catholicism was not nourished by its real sources; it was full of worldly aspects in the negative sense of the term, and it later roused my fiery antagonism. As an extenuating circumstance, though, one ought to remember that the collapse of 1918 had produced a stiffening of all these wrong alignments. The Church survived the catastrophe (which really *was* a catastrophe since we have now entered a period of endless "Wars of Austrian Succession"), but most of her psychological and some of her material props had fallen out from under her; the cherished monarchy had gone and with it four-fifths of the realm and its inhabitants. I doubt whether an American waking up one nice morning to find that the State of New York was all that was left of his country, that this remnant had become a Grand-Duchy and that all symbols of his nation had been discarded, could transfer his affections to such a monstrosity. We could not do it either. I still have a *Heimat* ("home"), yet since 1918 I am a man without a fatherland.

This dissatisfaction with a fragmentary and, in a sense, estranged country prompted me to leave Austria at the age of nineteen, to terminate my legal studies in Vienna and to take up political sciences in Budapest. I had started to write at the age of sixteen (as a Vienna correspondent of the London *Spectator*), and I had hoped to earn money with lessons and journalism in the capital of Hungary, where the traditions of the Old Monarchy were better preserved than with us. My parents disapproved of this decision, and deprived of their support I went, to my dismay, through a most wholesome period of real starvation and physical misery. Still, I succeeded in being sent at the age of twenty as correspondent for a Hungarian paper to the USSR, where I spent close on five months. Hungary had no diplomatic relations with the Soviet Union; my Austrian passport, coupled with my knowledge of Hungarian—acquired under tears—gave me the unique opportunity to get the coveted assignment. A year later I revisited the USSR illegally on another errand, but only for a short time.

These two visits to the Red Paradise gave me a first-hand experience of a Church not only in dispersion but also, partly, in the catacombs, a very healthy experience indeed! Though Hungary herself is a blend of occidental and oriental elements, my travels in the USSR, which led me to the confines of Persia and back to Central Europe via Turkey and the Balkans, confronted me, after an earlier sojourn in Eastern Poland, for the second time with forms of Christianity—even the Schism had not cancelled the legitimacy of these forms!—which were totally at variance with those I had known since my infancy. Not only sovereignty of mind, but also *distance* is necessary for knowledge, especially self-knowledge. In order to read a book one has to hold it at a certain distance from one's eyes. And prolonged absences from one's own country, one's own civilization, are *absolutely indispensable* for a real critical comprehension of the forms and ways one is accustomed to.

I was gaining new insights. Hungarian Catholicism also suffered from a parochialism similar to ours in Austria; the equation "Catholicism = Monarchy" there was even more fully in force. Now that I knew at long last what the Christian essentials really were, I rebelled violently against this formula which subordinated eternal truths no less than the Mystical Body to a political conception, actually one of the worst forms of prostitution imaginable. The whole evil of the Bonald-de Maistre position with its cleverly hidden paganism, its parochialism and false romanticism, became evident to me. In order to be "radically" Christian (the only way to fulfill the program *Omnia instaurare in Christo*) I felt that one had to divest oneself from all dead traditions, empty symbols, historic (and pseudo-historic) fixations. No

224

wonder that I started to write blistering satires against that
nauseating cocktail of a "socially acceptable" Christianity
and "upper-class behaviour patterns" so characteristic of the
Central-European scene. The "Christian gentleman," most
ludicrous of all figures (a shrewdly paganized version of the
Christian Knight), was my main target of attack. The old
cumbersome equations had to go . . .

In 1931-32 my sympathies started to grow for the concept of a "Christian Democracy" (in ignorance of the
Graves de communi injunction not to use this term in a
political sense); but I soon became suspicious of a German-
French school of thought which tried to play the Bonald-
de Maistre game in reverse; in other words, to equate
Catholicism with democracy. In subsequent years, when
political developments directed my travels to the far north
and west, I had to make the sad observation that the same
old concoction of vested interests, of sloppy thinking combined with narrowness, a total lack of historic perspective
coupled with the most odious forms of parochialism in space
and time, a real absence of world-wide experience with a
tabula rasa in linguistic matters, the whole aggravated by a
slyly camouflaged nationalism canonizing one's own political
accidentals, was busily prostituting the Church again. From
a purely theological point of view one aberration is as bad
as the other; there is the same denial of the Catholicity of
the Church and the same admission of the political money-
changers in the House of the Lord for whom the cat-o'-nine-
tails seems to be the only remedy.

Indeed to replace the human idol worship of some
"legitimists" with the demolatry of the republicans is hardly
a step in the right direction. The absolute sway of the many
is usually even worse than the absolute rule of a single man
without party support. This consideration among others
forced me, as a "liberal," back into the monarchical camp of

those supporting a truly mixed form of government. After all, most thinkers, most of the outstanding men I admired, were of the same persuasion—Bloy, Bernanos, Solovyev, Leontyev, D'Arcy, Thibon, Tocqueville, Schneider, Burckhardt, Reynold, Faulhaber, Galen, Mindszenty. As a matter of fact, only one truly outstanding European Catholic thinker is in the opposite camp, a great commentator of St. Thomas, but even he, when he was at my present age, belonged to that curious circle of the Action Française.

Meanwhile, under whatever political system, the rejection of reason and the revolt against faith is now producing results. If a native tribe on the upper Ubangi or an even more civilized nation in antiquity worshipped idols of stone, if they had no well-grounded knowledge of the nature of man, they still not only could be saved and reach eternal happiness, but they also could have had a passable collective human existence on earth. The moral trespasses and the intellectual stupidities of pre-industrial civilization rarely provoked catastrophes of the first order. Yet today intellectual ignorance coupled with our spiritual void is rapidly becoming fatal, because in the religious and the politico-ethical sphere we have experienced a frightful regression, a falling back almost to the level of babyhood, while the technical means over which mankind has "control" have received a deadly perfection. The Christianization of the world thus has ceased to be a piece of religious speculation —*it is a question of do or die* and thus attests to the truth and, even more so, to the *necessity* of the Church.

My acquaintance with Catholicism in other parts of the world has, finally, taught me that the Church in Central Europe, in spite of its lacking kinetic energy, had not been so bad as I originally thought. It has a potential dynamism which can be revived at very short notice. (Remember also the 14,000 priests, friars and nuns in Spain—

226

of all places!—who died with immense courage with hardly
a single case of apostasy.) Whatever the shortcomings of
the Church on the Danube, she never wanted to go back
to the Middle Ages, she never saw in the mere parroting of
the *Summa* the hallmark of real theology, she never considered the trespasses against the Sixth Commandment the
one and only sin, she had no limitless enthusiasm for novenas
and miraculous medals, and she always realized that the
homo Catholicus was a humorous, frank and genial creature
who had given his full assent to the Petrine notion of a royal
priesthood of *all* Christians. Of Monsignore Ignaz Seipel,
the "political Catholic prelate" we discovered, after his
death through his diary, that he had been a real wrestler
with Christ to whom only one thing had mattered: nearness
to God, sanctity. Even my own mother, haphazard Catholic
that she is, stood up wonderfully under Nazi pressure while
her "devout" children trembled in their shoes twenty-four
hours a day lest she be arrested for her cutting remarks
about the National Socialist tyranny.

As "Jesuit by birth" I had taught for one year at Beau-
mont College in England, thus prematurely terminating
my study of theology in Vienna. Soon after my transfer to
Georgetown University in early 1937 I had married Countess
Christiane Goëss, a Ph.D. who had come from a very good
family, i.e. a family which had produced numerous inmates
of concentration camps, Russian prison camps and local
jails in the fateful years of the Nazi domination and the
aftermath. My own doctor's degree (at the University of
Budapest) I had acquired before my American appointment.
Little over a year later, and a few days before I visited
Spain, the Nazis took over what was left of Austria. The
subsequent weeks, spent *in umbra mortis* on the sombre,
deserted battlefields of the Iberian Peninsula, were a time
of reflection and meditation. They had the same sobering

effects as climbing in the high Alpine regions. Austria under Nazi control I saw twice afterwards. After two confiscations, my career as a writer in the German language had come to a temporary stop; and at the end of August 1939, when my third vacation was drawing to a close, I was faced by the momentous question whether to return to the United States in order to provide for my growing family, or to drift with all those dear to me through the dark night into which we were just sailing. Even today I do not dare to say whether my return to America on a boat through Arctic waters was morally a "good thing." Europe I did not see again until the summer of 1947.

The eight years in America I spent in other universities and colleges, acting as professor, as head of a history department, as a lecturer in Japanese. The last four years I taught in Chestnut Hill College, Philadelphia, a school of the Sisters of St. Joseph. This was my happiest time in the New World. The long vacations I used to explore the country visiting all forty-eight States and Canada, my main interest being directed towards the Indians of the Southwest. I saw many sides of life in the United States, at times working on the assembly line, carrying out an assignment of the American Geographic Society in Alaska, hitch-hiking in the Rockies, studying in the Hoover Library, or campaigning for the legal protection of the Calaveras South Grove in California.

To my prolonged stays in England and, even more so, in the United States, I owe a vast amount—not only the lasting friendship of many splendid men and women, not only the opportunity to peruse the wonderful libraries of the New World, but also new ways of thinking. The languages East of the Rhine (German no less than Russian or Hungarian), owing to their wide creative possibilities, do not really foster clarity and simplicity of thought. Certainly not everything, but probably a great deal of what over here we consider to have "depth" or "originality" is nothing but obscurity of expression or plain lack of mental digestion. America, moreover, is a country of virtues which do not blossom profusely in the more easy-going orbit of the "Old Church"—hard work, discipline, readiness to co-operate on one side, a marvellous lack of envy and jealousy coupled with a moving material generosity on the other.

It is true that American Catholicism has its own special problems—mostly those of a branch of the Church in dispersion, a branch which is socially decapitated (but rapidly growing a new head), which lacks the cultural memory of the Counter-Reformation (like the Church in Ireland), a Church which occupies a position in some respects similar to that of the Netherlands and Switzerland—and one less similar to that of England-Wales-Scotland which has a Catholicism very much *sui generis*. Yet American Catholicism is a branch of the Church Universal which has a great deal to say to the world, a great deal today and even much more in the future. There are signs to this effect everywhere, small blades of grass heralding the growth of rich pastures. It is difficult to tell what aspects of American Catholicism impressed me most; the disciplined devotion of the simple parishioner, the gentle greatness of individual priests or the self-sacrificing enthusiasm of young Catholics which I had witnessed in connection with such ventures as the Catholic Worker Movement, the magazine *Integrity* or the ill-fated but truly impressive attempt to launch a Catholic daily, the *Sun Herald* of Kansas City, an enterprise which I had the privilege to watch from very close quarters. Yet I honestly believe that the palm should be given to the often overlooked contribution the female religious orders have made in the past and are making in the present. Most rarely are they featured prominently in general accounts.

Indeed, the Unknown Soldier of the Church Militant in America is not a man, but a woman with a veil.

Still, there is one mission to whose importance (or even existence) American Catholics have not entirely woken up; American Catholics *as a body* have not yet come to the realization that they—and they alone—are being called to build a bridge between the "Old" World and the New, as well as between the two Continents of the Western Hemisphere. The standard accusation against Catholics in a minority, i.e. that they owe a "higher loyalty to a foreign potentate" and that they are "not really typical of the nation as a whole"[1] has wrought great damage in many a country. This accusation is nowhere more unjust than in the case of the American Catholic whose loyalty, as Dean Sperry of Harvard has remarked, is more pronounced than that of his fellow American of other faiths. Yet the fear of being denounced as "Un-American" has prevented him from looking dispassionately at the political traditions of the nations belonging to the orbit of the "Old Church." Hence also American Catholics as a group (or even individually) do not act effectively as interpreters of the other parts of the Occident to their fellow citizens. . .

I returned to Austria as soon as I could get the permission, taking with me our American daughter born in the United States as a living link between the two Hemispheres. (She will get an education in what our friends rightly consider to be the *true* American spirit.) We had to be near those who suffered from the consequences of the crimes and follies of the victors and of the defeated. For years we lived nine miles from the Iron Curtain but then we settled down near Innsbruck in the Tyrol, halfway between Vienna

[1] *Should* a Catholic be "typical" of a non-Catholic nation? Let us ponder over this question.

230

and Paris, between Cologne and Rome, in the vicinity of
Munich and Trent, right next to a gorgeous village church
which had been consecrated by Cardinal Nicholas of Cusa,
the "first modern man." High up in the mountains, next door
to the brilliant theological faculty (Jesuit) of Innsbruck
University, we are leading a frugal life. A few weeks each
year I lecture in Germany's *Amerikahäuser* on the United
States—the American-European understanding being one
of the most burning problems of these years. Periodically I
go to Rome—to see friends, to visit the "Greg," to marvel at
the Vatican, to go down to the Mamertine Prison which, in
a sense, is the most living symbol of everything Christians
are standing for—not forgetting also the Via Sacra, the
Colosseum, the Catacombs. The hoarse cry: *Christianos ad
bestias!* in one form or the other could have been heard all
through the ages. Catholicism in the Old World has certain
marked cross-centred and death-centred aspects, and these
always attracted me magically . . . even more so than the
splendour and beauty which the Church of past ages could
muster and which, with great efforts, she is trying to revive
in a modern guise.

All these reflections have not yet touched upon the question of my personal relationship to the Mystical Body. Since
I reached something like the age of discretion I have considered myself as an active part of the Church Universal.
In the Church, morever, I have always found a complete
freedom, partly because the Church has to respect my
conscience (applied to a God-given liberty of choice, *po-
tentia ad utrumlibet*), partly because I have always realized
the wisdom of Ernst Jünger's saying: "Of all masks of
freedom, discipline is the most impenetrable." This freedom
within the Church has also startled such an acute observer
as the late Count Hermann Keyserling, who had remarked
that even the freest spirits can be at ease within the Catholic

Church. And, indeed, he who has never lived in a modern Catholic country does not fully know how sweet liberty really can be. The Anglo-Saxon, West-European type of polite agnosticism, needless to say, had never the slightest attraction for me—a cursory glance at the very people representing this flabby form of subtle despair was enough to eliminate any incipient temptation. The only intellectually respectable alternative to Catholicism I see in an atheistic existentialism of a Sartrean type with its logical ending in suicide or madness. *Dios o nada!* God or nothing.

To myself as to every sensitive Catholic the Church, of course, is *also* a cross, not only a means to salvation but also a burden and an occasion for suffering. She consists, after all, of fallen human beings and her hierarchic stratification as a Church Militant is by no means the same as that of the Church Triumphant. Hence also the frescoes in old churches showing popes, emperors, priests, dukes, monks and nuns roasting in the fires of hell. St. Peter himself, our first Holy Father, was a liar and a potential assassin. The Church founded on him is a *societas perfecta,* but, thank God, no society of perfectionists. We have to accept the fact that Our Lord chose Simon as "the Rock" and not the (perhaps) more saintly St. John. Yet Peter is fisherman and sinner, *piscator et peccator, pêcheur et pécheur.* The temptation of the sword (the ear of Malchus!) and of "diplomacy" has always been with us, and the Church has repeatedly suffered setbacks when she hoped to gain objectives by restrictive mechanical devices, thus trespassing against the precepts of charity, or by trying to be too "diplomatic" when the Holy Folly of the Cross would have been more conducive to success. "Diplomacy," furthermore, loves to wear the mask of *prudence.* I should really like to see a better understanding of the moral virtue of prudence, and a less frequent misuse of its name as a glib phrase—covering much meanness—in the Catholic jargon of our days—another one being the fear of "scandal," this term taken in a completely untheological and thoroughly bourgeois sense.

Since we have mentioned "scandal" as a non-theological concept, let it be said that the major handicaps of the Church in her existence and extension are by no means the very rare but all too human frailties of her higher or lower dignitaries, but rather failings of a very different order. Among these I would count the colossal ignorance still characterizing so many of our lay or clerical teachers, writers or scholars, an ignorance which places them at a continuous disadvantage with the representatives of other groups, Christian or otherwise. A misunderstood militant partisan spirit which is blinding and not enlightening lies at the bottom of this shortcoming. The great advantage we have, which is the possession of *basic* truth (not *all* the truth), tempts some of our men and women to fall into an intellectual high-handedness which is the mark of the half-educated. Hence also the frequent propagation of the deposit of the faith with slick phrases, clever paradoxes and "authoritative" citations which merely irritate the adversary without causing a holy unrest in his heart and mind. A careful perusal of a certain Catholic literature will lead to the discovery that some of our defenders of the Church are actually incapable of reading what has been printed black on white. They are technically illiterates because they are unable to follow an argument deviating from the clichés they have been used to. The *Catholica non leguntur* of the opposite camp finds an evil echo in ours. There is an old Roman adage which says that it is perfectly in order to learn from one's enemies; and since those outside our walls are often nothing but tragically separated brethren, there is no reason why we should not take, here and there, a page out of their books. All ways lead to Rome, and we might well translate the grand title of our Holy Father, *Pontifex Maximus* (whatever its pre-Christian connotation), as "Supreme Bridgebuilder." By building bridges, by assimilating and baptizing whatever is good, true and beautiful, we are also preserving our Catholicity.

The other failing which acts as a serious handicap is "bad priests." Again we are not alluding to carnal weakness; over my bed a relic of St. Francis Borgia is hanging, the scion of an illegitimate son of Pope Alexander VI. Yet the Borgia Pope's trespasses against the virtue of temperance were small compared with his lack of love; we cannot forget Girolamo Savonarola at the stake. Still, the appearance of St. Francis Borgia shows that God writes straight with crooked lines. The "bad priest"—as I here use the term— repeats the worst sin of Alexander VI, *Servus Servorum Dei,* which is uncharitableness. It is frightening to observe how many apostasies have their roots in an encounter with an unkind priest. Comrade Josip Broz-Tito is one of the many cases in question. It is obvious that the "bad priest" is no relative whatsoever of Mr. Graham Greene's Whisky Priest in *The Power and the Glory,* the unfortunate alcoholic servant of God with a bastard offspring. He is weak, but not wicked. As men contrast the sublimity of his station in life with the shoddiness of his behaviour, the weak priest is subject to painful ridicule, and thus we have "sympathy" for him. "Sympathy" means to suffer together; his secret tears and our sorrow will be mingled.

The "bad priest," on the other hand, not only has the arrogance of superficial knowledge and (in a very few countries) of "automatic" authority, but also, in many cases, of a celibacy not well integrated into his personality. Voluntary celibacy is spiritually of the same *basic* nature as marriage, yet it belongs to a higher order. The married person loves in his partner a Child of God, while in voluntary celibacy the person aspires to a direct love of God, sacrificing a legitimate "indirect approach" to which he has the same real right as to physical creation, "the sole earthly remedy against death."[1] Yet to man (far more so than to woman) marriage is a school for humility. Just as nobody, as the saying goes, is a hero to his valet, almost no man is held in awe by his wife. Yet the voluntary celibate is out for a greater prize, he lifts himself on a higher pinnacle, but with this elevation comes the *necessity* for a greater than ordinary humility—not to mention the more diffuse charity one expects from a person without the most immediate family ties. A priest who is neither humble nor loving—these qualities go together—takes a Prussian drill-sergeant as his ideal, not Jean Vianney, the Curé d'Ars. He implicitly denies Christ, Who washed the feet of the twelve apostles. The very large role the laity is playing today in the Church— a mere harbinger of the shape of things to come—will never obliterate this problem. The uncharitable letter, article or speech of a leading lay theologian will never have remotely the devastating effect of a rude chance remark of a village priest who, after all, daily changes bread and wine into the Body and the Blood of Our Lord, and thus represents Him in the public mind far more directly than any other person.

These reflections might create the impression that my relations with priests were none too good, but nothing could be further from the truth. North, South, East or West, we have a priesthood with admirable qualities, with high averages and with spiritual summits reaching into the altitudes of real sanctity. I was more than a quarter of a century old before I met for the first time a priest in whom I missed the

[1] Herein lies the greater sacrifice. In purely sexual matters the married Catholic today faces psychologically a far more difficult situation.

moving qualities I had come to take for granted in our clergy. This disappointment was rarely repeated. Sanctity among living Catholics (be they lay or cleric) has always been for me one of the most powerful indirect proofs of the claims of the Church—another one being the unique message of Holy Scriptures. It always defied my imagination how anybody could *not* consider them to be divinely inspired.

As to my purely spiritual relationship with the Church, I am afraid I shall have to disappoint the reader for the simple reason that a true detailed analysis of my spiritual growth I could not produce even under duress. Plain inhibitions more than sheer humility prevent me from such a performance. I have had, naturally, spiritual experiences of a general and others of a very specific sort which helped to create that state of faith which is of the "mind" and the "heart." The Catholic upbringing alone would not have been sufficient. *Gratia supponit naturam.* "Nature" was there, Grace came in time. The "inner reality" of the Faith—I may be excused for these inadequate contrived terms—I sensed when I fell for the first time seriously in love at the age of sixteen. Readers of E. I. Watkin's *The Bow in the Clouds* will easily understand me if they remember what this brilliant author has to say about the close proximity of Eros to religion. Later in my life I never had for any length of time serious "doubts" about the Faith, though I was tormented by protracted periods of absolute aridity. I then had to go on a meager, purely intellectual diet, but never gave up my religious practices. I said my prayers, went to the sacraments and patiently-impatiently waited until my train should come out from the dark tunnel. It always did. I also had during my lifetime a score of what I consider to be truly supra-natural experiences, and their memory also served as a pabulum during these lightless intervals. The

236

faith in my heart was always rekindled at very specific opportunities—in themselves anything but spectacular—and
then the old unity, peace and happiness were restored.

These pages, I am afraid, might appear to some readers
to be filled with a spirit of haughtiness. Yet in the religious
sphere I am deeply conscious of the fact that we are not
merely faced by a *Deus absconditus,* but also by an *anima
abscondita* of the individual person. Only God knows who
is truly superior to whom, only God could tell who, after
the great reshuffling of the cards, once we have passed into
a fuller life, will lie topmost, in the middle, or on the bottom.
This ignorance forces us to approach with humility every
single human being. Yet in the views and the movements
of the faceless masses divested of their personality I sense a
grave moral danger for each one of us. "To do as everybody
else does," is the lure of our age and I hold with Christopher
Dawson that the uniform injunction of Scripture is the exhortation: "Thou shalt not follow a multitude to do evil!"
Naturally, the synthesis of a legitimate (and most wholesome) pride and humility is not easily made. On the other
hand I do believe that a "robust faith" without too much
scrupulosity is something highly desirable, and that to build
one's religion primarily around a fear of sin is a travesty
of our faith. I do think that mortal sins are by no means
as easily committed as some people rashly assume. *Dilige
et fac quod vis* has been my guiding idea. This, in turn, does
not mean that I have a sense of near-perfection. I have
defended Italian Fascism a few times, and there are other
deeds, thoughts, actions I have committed and regretted,
yet whose memories evoke in me a burning sensation of
shame and helpless rage against myself.

What would happen if by some fantastic magic I were
to be thoroughly and completely deprived of my faith, my
rational religious convictions, my Catholic habits and ways

of thinking? Being a novelist, who has to "imagine things," I have sometimes asked myself this question. In a way, of course, I would be deprived of my identity. I would cease to be myself; but I am dead certain that I then would not regard Christ as "wisest of all Jewish prophets" or the Catholic Church as a "venerable old institution worthy of the sympathies of all men of good will." For such alternatives I am a little bit too logical. My poor self, emptied of all religion and cut off from Truth Eternal, would be far more beast than angel, a ruthless, shiftless, very desperate animal, a cunning and melancholic creature filled with a consuming hatred—a hatred for Christ and for His Church.

Pamela Carswell

Pamela Carswell was born in Melbourne 1918 of a mixed marriage. She was educated at Catholic and Presbyterian schools about equally, and took her B.A. in the School of Philosophy at the University of Melbourne. She spent the war years in Commonwealth Public Service; married Australian Sanskrit scholar, who has since turned stockbroker; spent a few uneventful years in London, now lives uneventfully in Melbourne; has one son.

What is the real shape of a penny? This is the kind of question which kindles philosophy students—and was, in fact, the first philosophical problem, formally presented, which ever bothered me. It bothered me very much. The argument ran like this: "A penny is round, of course," you say. Now, why "of course"? Do you ever *see* round pennies? Scarcely ever. When you look at a penny, what you see is one of an infinite number of ellipses, depending on the angle from which you view it. The chances against your looking at the penny perfectly square on— the only way it appears perfectly round—are overwhelming. So why call it round? Why pick on this particular and rare angle of vision and call it the "right" angle for viewing pennies? and so on.

The problem bothered me not so much as it concerned pennies but because it could be extended—at least in

239

philosophy classes—to throw doubt on the whole shape of life. Granted one can't look at a penny from all angles at once, it needs only a flick of the finger to view it impartially from every possible angle in succession. But when one comes to matters where "angle" is used metaphorically— when personal, political, artistic and religious "angles" are in question—spinning them round like pennies becomes difficult.

Here, there is often no universal "common-sense" verdict corresponding to "pennies are round." Philosophical gambollings over pennies seem—and usually are—frivolous. Everyone knows the things really are round, however you look at them. But where you find "angle" used metaphorically, you find phrases such as "Well, if you like to look at it *that* way . . . " and "Viewed in *that* light . . . " and "Approached from *that* direction . . . " and "From *his* standpoint . . . " and "As *I* see it . . . " all reflecting the fact that the viewpoint has a real bearing on the truth, and sometimes seeming to suggest that the truth varies with the viewpoint.

Again, you hear people say, "It would be funny if it weren't so serious," "I didn't know whether to be shocked or amused," "It's repellent but it fascinates me," these phrases reflecting the fact that the same situation may invite incompatible responses in the same person. His response will depend on how he looks at the thing, and that in turn depends on a number of factors including the sort of person he is, both generally and at that particular moment.

This state of affairs troubled me deeply when I first began thinking about it. "What is the real shape of a penny?" became "What is the real shape of the world in general?" As with the penny, there seemed to be an infinite number of shapes, many of them apparently inconsistent with the rest. This was most obviously evidenced in litera-

240

ture: the worlds of Jane Austen, Dostoievski, Hemingway, Virginia Woolf, Mauriac—each so convincingly real and complete when you are in it—are as mutually exclusive as any five pictures of human life could be. One passes freely between them, but at the thought of mixing them up imagination boggles.

It seemed to me that the same situation held, if less obviously so, in real life. Most of my views were likely to be at least comprehensible to my neighbours because we all lived in much the same mental environment: we were the products of a common educational system, read the same newspapers, recognized the same social conventions. These factors partly determined our respective "angles" long before we consciously adopted them; but they partly determined, also, the range of angles open to us: with all the effort and good will in the world, no Australian, for instance, can see that world from the standpoint natural to a Hindu.

But even Australians (or Englishmen or Italians or Swedes) among themselves—even, if you like, middle-aged, middle-class, suburban Australian housewives among themselves—contrive to take up astonishingly varied positions from which they judge and react to the world around them. Temperament, emotional capacity, mental and bodily constitution are obvious diversifying factors. Further, people's reactions and judgments are modified by a thousand quite accidental factors—by things which they happen, quite by chance, to have personally experienced, such as an alcoholic husband or losing a son in the war; by passing moods or sudden emotion; by the state of their livers, by hunger or lack of sleep, and so on.

We are appallingly limited creatures, prevented by countless obstacles both within and without us from seeing more than one segment of reality, constitutionally unable to respond fully to more than one element of what we see at a time. Experience is seldom simple. The situation confronting us at any given time may be funny, tragic, beautiful and an occasion of sin, all of these simultaneously. Whether we laugh, cry, admire or flee is up to us: what we do may be the result of conscious choice or an automatic reaction to whichever aspect strikes us most forcibly or to the exclusion of the others, but we certainly cannot respond adequately to all aspects at one and the same time.

Aldous Huxley notes this situation in *Eyeless in Gaza:*

> We look at the universe with a certain kind of physico-mental apparatus. That apparatus can respond only to certain stimuli. Within relatively narrow limits, it is adjustable. The nature of the facts which each of us perceives as primary and given depends on the nature of the individual instrument and on the adjustment we have been brought up, or deliberately chosen, to give it. . . . We can adjust our instrument deliberately, by an act of the will . . . So that one can see, for example, either irremediable senselessness and turpitude, or else actualizable potentialities for good—whichever one likes; it is a question of choice.[1]

People draw different conclusions from this. Some hug and even parade their limitations as badges of individuality: as indeed they are. "I hate poetry, aren't I awful!" declares one complacently, or (this was said to me with a delicate but unmistakable air of preening by a professor of philosophy) "I'm afraid the classical arguments for the existence of God don't appeal to me."

Others boast that they are open to every point of view (they deceive themselves) and too fair-minded to commit themselves to any one. Others again curse what they regard as their damnable facility for seeing the other person's point of view and their chronic failure to form lasting convictions

[1] Harper & Brothers, New York, 1936.

242

of their own. I know all about that group because I was in it, in the days when I worried about the proper shape of a penny.

It didn't occur to me, then, to look to the Church for any help. On the contrary: although I was as rigidly and narrowly dogmatic a Catholic as ever enlivened a free-thinkers' meeting, it was (as freethinkers believe is always the case) done with my eyes shut. I was obsessed with this question of human limitation and the seeming impossibility of ever seeing the world save through the distorting lenses of temperament and accidental circumstances; at the same time, I refused to think about my religion in the light of that obsession. So I didn't think about it, but merely hung on to it. I found it easy enough, at that time, to keep Catholicism in a separate and special category—as something to be treasured above life, but affecting only very narrow areas of life.

I came to another conclusion: that it is his very limitations which shape and enrich a man's character. The people who are given to "seeing every side of the question" are not usually notable for charm or personality. In fact, they tend to run to type and to be uncommonly boring. The man who is quite shamelessly individual, bristling with ill-grounded loves and hates, glorying in his idiosyncrasies and prejudices, is apt to have a richer and more developed humanity than, I felt, the whole passionless band of the unconvinced could muster between them.

It seemed that the very limitations which deprive us of any but a truncated and misleading view of the world are the very stuff of personality. Do away with a man's limitations and you do away with the man, no less surely than by doing away with one side of a triangle you do away with the triangle. The search for truth (so I reasoned rather grandly) could only be pursued at the expense of

243

personality, and personality enjoyed only to the neglect of truth.

That was one of my few firm convictions outside the dogmas of the Church; and of course it didn't do at all. For one thing, it didn't take into account all sorts of highly unpleasant human limitations which are not only inimical to a clear view of reality but are also dehumanizing—e.g., the capital sins. For another, it implied that reality is not a suitable human diet; and that conflicts with the teaching of the Church, which says a man is not fully man until he is united with God, Who is reality itself.

Later, I found that the answer to all these questions had been plainly at hand. They were very real problems to me at the time, and although to many they will appear commonplace or unreal or trivial, they are the sort of problems which I know do bedevil a lot of people. The feeling that nothing is certain, everything is relative to the point of view, often produces the tentative, chameleon-like person who takes his colour from whomever he happens to be with; now he agrees with one opinion, now he echoes its opposite, now he applauds a third inconsistent with either —hoping that they all are, after all, reconcilable, but hoping above all that he won't be quoted. He notes that he seems incapable of a direct, spontaneous response to anything: almost always he asks himself first, "How ought I respond to this? What is expected of me? What is the appropriate behaviour?" He feels that he is all things to all men in the worst possible sense—that he is so lacking in integrity that he is merely the sum of the different disguises he wears according to his company, that if you took away the masks there would be no face behind them.

When a man like that becomes a Catholic, the cry goes up that he has bartered his freedom for security; finding the search for truth too arduous, the responsibility for

PAMELA CARSWELL

making his own judgments and decisions too painful, he
has handed over will and intellect to the Church and delib-
erately forfeited his own large vision for the guaranteed
comforts of a magic peepshow.

If a man like that is already a Catholic, it is a fair
presumption that he has as little idea of what the Church
is as the people who invite him in the name of freedom
to leave it. It is appallingly easy for a "born Catholic" to
go through life or a large part of it having very little idea
of what the Church is. I did it very successfully in spite
of what I suppose was an excellent Catholic schooling.

The fact that the Church not only provides an answer
to this uneasy and corroding relativism, but is itself the
answer, came to me—I confess with shame—as a momentous discovery. It is often chance acquaintance with a
person or book which puts one on the track of such discoveries; in this case, it was an essay written by a priest in
pre-war Germany, Romano Guardini's *"Vom Sinn der
Kirche,"* published in England as "The Church and the
Catholic."[1] In a single page I got what I was looking for.
Guardini was concerned with just those problems which
so concerned me, but he saw them more clearly and, under
his analysis, they began to look even more formidable than
I had thought. The solution he offered was nothing new in
itself; it was implicit in beliefs I had held all my life, the
plain conclusion to be drawn from the history and nature
of the Catholic Church. But the discovery of implicit truths
is true discovery, and Guardini must have helped many to
a startlingly new conception of the Church and of themselves
as members of the Church.

This, then, is the answer I found to "What is the real
shape of a penny?" as symbolizing all those questions about
reality which seem to have as many different answers as

[1] Sheed & Ward, New York.

245

there are different people to ask them: my answer is "Its shape as seen through the eyes of the Catholic Church."

The Church is, in Guardini's words, "the whole of reality, seen, valued and experienced by the entire man." She is the whole of reality because nothing that *is*, however trivial or dissonant or commonplace, however sublime or terrible, falls outside the Church. She is, of her nature, co-extensive with all that is. And she is the whole of humanity, "the entire man"; there is no human type, no human thought or attitude or experience or emotion, which does not contribute to the Church's vision of reality. Lastly, the Church is a living organism: not an organized sum of constituent parts, but a living, organic whole, the "entire man," perceiving, judging, evaluating. This is not a fanciful theory about the Church, it is Catholic doctrine.

When the Church looks at a situation, she sees it in relation to the whole of reality. She sees it not from a particular standpoint but with a view embracing all possible standpoints. Her judgments and valuations are not conditioned by a particular culture or disposition or interest, but draw from the assimilated wealth of humanity as a whole, with all its different cultural traditions, its insights and its gifts and achievements. In this respect, the human chameleons, the sitters-on-fences, the people who aspire, *of themselves*, to escape from their individual limitations and from the "provincialism" of their native culture, are of little interest to the Church, or, therefore, to humanity as a whole. They have nothing to offer. The unique contribution which each could make—he and no other—to the Church, and so to humanity, is being neglected, whether from lack of confidence or from an impossible ambition. This contribution is one's acceptance and development of one's own distinctive character. That about a man which enables him to bring his personal stamp to everything he does is unique, given to no one else. His vision of the world is necessarily incomplete, one among uncounted millions, but it is *his*. No one has ever experienced reality in quite that way before, and to the extent that he explores and, however humbly, expresses that experience, he is adding something to human wisdom, which but for him, would be lacking.

But one cannot do this in isolation. It is a familiar comment that those who are "too much on their own" become unbalanced and one-sided, see things out of proportion. They are the people who are most helplessly at the mercy of their temperaments, and most narrowly imprisoned within the limits set by their mental and emotional capacities.

The way to freedom and personality is not easy—he who goes to the end of it is a saint; but the way is there, and even just to know that is, in itself, immeasurably consoling.

The man who is bent on escaping his personal limitations so that he may gain an all-round view of reality as a whole will succeed in the measure that he identifies himself with the Church and lives her life. And the man who is, at the same time, bent on being *himself*—who regards his character as a unique gift from God, which God wills him to bring to its full development—will succeed in the measure that he identifies himself with the Church and lives her life. To the extent that he does this he will, in Guardini's words, pass from "one-sidedness to completeness, from bondage to freedom, from mere individuality to personality." In all this I am, of course, presupposing something which, for Catholics, does not need stating: the supernatural identity of the Church and the doctrine of Christ's Mystical Body.

There are a score of very good reasons why Catholics

are Catholics—chief among them the fact that they believe
Catholicism is true. One answers people according to the
sort of answer they want, so that sometimes one, sometimes
another answer, seems indicated. "I am a Catholic because
I believe Catholicism is true" may rebuff the enquirer who
has already assumed one's good faith. Again, he may not
be interested in the intellectual grounds for the belief: "Why
are you a Catholic?" often means not "What makes you
think it is true?" but "What do you get out of it?" or "How
do you put up with it?" or "What does the Catholic Church
offer which other churches do not also claim to offer?" It
is this last query to which I might give the answer I have
just given; not because it describes the most important of
the Church's unique claims—it doesn't—but because the
unique claim which it does describe meant so much to me
personally. I think it is likely to make a surprise appeal to
a great many people and so lead to the rest.

It is *the* answer to the devitalizing malaise of relativism,
whether outside the Church or, as in my own case, within
it.

I know that "private judgment" may be defended on the
grounds that God knows and makes allowances for our
limitations. So He most mercifully does. But if one were to
reject the means He has given us to overcome them . . . ?
To the degree that a man is identified with the Church he
is, in Guardini's phrase, "emancipated from his original narrowness, made free of reality as a whole." How shall you
persuade a man who has tasted even a slight and imperfect
degree of that freedom that, in the name of freedom, he
should leave the Church?

Caryll Houselander

Caryll Houselander. *Born 1901 in the city of Bath; attended a great variety of educational institutions—a Jewish kindergarten, two convents, a Council school and a Protestant private school, the St. John's Wood Art School and St. Martin's Art School. She worked in the Censorship office during the war. In 1945 she worked in an advertising office, doing layouts. Her books are* This War is the Passion *(revised as* The Comforting of Christ*),* The Reed of God, The Flowering Tree, The Dry Wood, The Passion of the Infant Christ, Guilt. *As an artist she prefers carving to painting. A very great interest in occupational therapy—she works with the insane, displaced children and wounded veterans.*

I do not think that anyone can know the story of his own soul until he looks back at the map of his life, from God's side in eternity, and that because in everything that happened to him the mercy of God was manifest or hidden, but always there, drawing him like a magnet to Himself. His life, whether he knew it or not, was simply God's plan of love for him. So too was his individual character; if there was something that he lacked and longed for, it was because he would find it in God, and his way to God would be through that need.

Thus in my own case the Blessed Sacrament and the

indwelling presence of Christ in man give the meaning of
life to me, and satisfy my most urgent need, which is for
communion. Communion with Christ and in Him communion with all men.

The nearest one can get to that backward glance from
eternity on this earth is, I suppose, to look back across the
years to one's childhood. One sees the child one was, objectively, almost as a different person, and yet one recog-
nizes the same essential needs. Moreover one can see the
pattern that was woven by circumstances so long ago, and
the touch of God's mercy in them.

So I will look back to one Christmas Eve when I was
four years old.

The whole house was whispering delicious secrets.
Everyone was busy with the preparations, everywhere
things were hidden. There were parcels in cupboards and
under beds. I had already secretly felt them and shaken
them and smelt them. There was a huge Christmas tree
behind a screen; I had already peeped round, but could
not do so again because the grown-ups were decorating it
and would have caught me.

However, as they were so occupied upstairs I was able
to slip down to the kitchen and help myself, unobserved, to
quite a few of the dishes already prepared for the morrow.
I had dipped my finger into the trifle and managed to
hide the place with some whipped cream. I had sampled
the nuts, the *marrons glacés* and the candied fruits, and
I felt a little sick, perhaps because I had also licked my
fingers, which were sticky with gum from making paper
chains, and swallowed the dregs of the wine, which our
servants had already been imbibing in joyful if secret an-
ticipation.

I came upstairs again, probably a little unsteadily and
certainly bolder, for I peeped round the door of the for-

bidden room and glimpsed the head of the fairy doll looking over the top of the screen.

It *was* a fairy doll, not a little crowned Christ King, the Bambino who would have given Christmas its full significance. For though my family had the Christmas Spirit, which in fact flowers from the Incarnation, in full measure, they had no particular religious beliefs, and so never, at that time, dwelt on the real meaning of Christmas. The nearest we came to the supernatural was Father Christmas himself, of whom I stood in delicious awe; the fact that he was expected to visit the house tonight added a sense of mystery to the evening. We always held open house at Christmas, and the poorer and lonelier, even the more difficult or peculiar, someone was, the more welcome. Already the guests were beginning to arrive, for many would stay in the house all through the Feast, and there was a riot of kissing under the mistletoe.

Then quite suddenly and with no preparation I composed my first poem. It was an expression of the warm feeling I had for everyone else, and a longing to be wholly one of the party—

> Let's all be a jolly lot
> Let no one be forgot
> For we can't be a jolly lot
> If any one *is* forgot.

I could not write, but dictated it to one of the grown-up people who wrote it down and preserved it. Clearly at that time I was an extroverted, and normal though shy child, and I wanted to break through my shyness and be at one with other people.

A few years later that was changed. By then I had been baptized in the Catholic Church, though my mother was not yet received herself. Influenced by an agnostic friend and a Catholic doctor she had decided that her children should be brought up Catholic.

I had had very little instruction, and until I was about eight years old took scant interest in religion. I had not made my first Confession. Then I attended, by myself, a terrifying sermon at a Redemptorist mission, a sermon giving a graphic description of a soul in mortal sin, compared to a corpse in a dark room.

The effect of this sermon was almost literally to turn my character inside out. Shortly after it I became critically ill with what I suppose to have been an acute anxiety neurosis. Even before the illness I had become introverted, and developed a real or imaginary dislike, or at all events fear of, other people, whom before I had loved. I felt myself to be cut off from everyone, isolated and spiritually alone in the world, mainly I think because of the absolute impossibility for a child to put into words the acute psychological suffering I was enduring. I had then made my First Communion, and I knew instinctively that if I could receive Holy Communion again I would be cured. This was because I was certain that if Christ came to me *He* would know what I was unable to tell, *without* being told.

Ultimately I *did* receive my second Holy Communion by way of viaticum and I *was* cured. Shortly after this my parents separated and our home was broken up. This completed my withdrawal from other people. Father and mother are trustees of God's love to children, guardians of their home, the security of the house built on a rock; let the child feel betrayed by one or both parents, as in the case of a broken marriage he certainly will, and his faith in God and man is undermined.

I was sent away to a convent, where I remained for about five years, both for terms and holidays. I arrived there hard, defiant, disillusioned, determined to trust no one, to love no one, to be alone and sufficient unto myself for the rest of my life. My leaden heart, however, was swiftly molten in the fires of innumerable "inordinate affections," and my disenchantment gave way to re-enchantment that has never lost its spell. Looking back I see the touch of the mercy of God in what then seemed to be a disaster, and how even the results of mistakes and sins can be turned to fit into His plan of love.

It was a little French convent, and in it one found both the hard logic of French Catholicism and the poetry of all Catholicism; one found too both austerity and, sometimes, sentimentality. It was a real refuge for the children of broken marriages who were received at the tenderest age and mothered, sometimes even rather spoilt, by the nuns.

There was a kind of lyrical quality even in material things in that convent, a quality of purity and simplicity. The white curtains round the beds, the polished floors, even the unique convent smell of beeswax and flowers, clean linen and verbena, acted like the touch of peace on my troubled mind.

Here the seeds of faith, which had been sown on such unprepared ground and twice choked by weeds and thorns, took root in my soul.

Here too I had the first of several experiences that have made the doctrine of the indwelling presence of Christ in man a reality to me.

During the summer holidays in 1914 war broke out between France and Germany. There were only two nuns in the community who were not French, an English choir nun and a Bavarian lay-sister. Many of the older nuns in the community remembered the bitter suffering they had endured during the German Occupation of Alsace and Lorraine in 1870. They told us terrible stories of living in sewers and feeding on vermin, and I think many of them lived in daily terror of something of the same kind happening in England.

With the unbridled excitement of the French temperament the nuns worked themselves and us up into frenzies of patriotism to the *entente cordiale* and hatred for the enemy. In those days one heard nothing about loving one's enemies. As there was, at the beginning of the war, no conscription in England, the armies depended for their recruits on fierce anti-German propaganda, in which Louis Raemaekers' cartoons, showing rape and child murder and every imaginable beastliness by Germans, appeared in crude and lurid detail.

What must have been the suffering of our one Bavarian lay-sister, cut off from her own people, surrounded by her enemies, regarded by everyone as that most terrible of human creatures, a German?

Certainly at the time I had never given a thought to her possible suffering myself. But one day I saw her sitting in the "boot room" by herself, cleaning the children's shoes, and I went in to offer to help her. Only when I came close to her did I see that she was weeping soundlessly, tears pouring down her weather-beaten, rosy cheeks. Abashed as children are by grown-up people's tears, I stood for a long time looking down, looking at her lap with her beautiful, toil-worn hands folded up on a little pair of shoes in a way that was eloquent of grief.

At last I looked up and I saw that the nun was wearing the Crown of Thorns.

It was a great crown, more like a cap of thorns, covering her head, and so heavy that it bowed it down.

This and the other incidents of the same kind that follow must be explained, at least so far as I *can* explain them.

I said "I saw," but I did not see with my eyes, but with my mind, yet in great detail as one sees a definite picture. I do not claim that this and the other incidents that I will describe were visions or supernatural experiences; they are all three capable of several natural explanations; but whether they were natural or supernatural experiences does not matter at all; what matters is that it was in this way that God began to show me the Passion of Christ in man, and no doubt He did so because it was only in this way that I could apprehend it.

When I had come to regard my little French convent as my home, I was suddenly taken away from it, and because I pined openly to be back there, I was forbidden to have any communication with the nuns. I had again become ill, and with this second uprooting as well as a long illness which isolated me from other people while it lasted and left me hopelessly maladjusted to them when it was over, I felt myself cut off from other people. The wise doctor who had helped to influence my mother's decision to bring me up as a Catholic now persuaded her to a "kill or cure" method. I was sent, at his suggestion, to a big English convent. It was a complete contrast to the French one. There the accent had been on piety and embroidery; here it was on heartiness and horsiness. There individuality had been encouraged; here the ideal was to conform to a certain pattern that was supposed to be characteristic of the Order. There the accent had been on humility; here that which seemed to me in my inexperience to be "the pride of life" was encouraged. Perhaps one sentence could sum all this up—the one convent was French, the other was English.

In the English convent "Singularity" was considered among the major vices, and "Simplicity" was constantly held up to me as the ideal, but my impression was that the girls who were pointed out as "Simple," and on whom I should model myself, were not simple at all but merely brash and brainless. They were the sort of girls who were always a little out of breath and red in the face from the playing fields, who were always hungry, who always had their mouths slightly open from keenness, and who smelt of bread and butter at a hot summer picnic. Not only did I realize that it would be *impossible* for me to emulate them, but I was too conceited to want to. I *could* not have done so, because their form of "Simplicity" depended wholly on good health.

When I went to this English convent I had not only become "Singular" indeed, but odious. Before I came I had quite made up my mind to lead a solitary life, in a nursing home, or elsewhere, to become a chronic invalid if this was necessary to attain my object. Although my first refrain "Let's all be a jolly lot" still echoed at the bottom of my heart, I had become too acutely self-conscious, too aware of myself as a freak, to hope to be one of the jolly lot, and I took refuge in the most outrageous behaviour, refusing indeed to join in any of the interests of the thoroughly jolly lot that surrounded me.

I was also really bewildered. This was a rich convent, and besides that it enshrined a great deal of innocent but blatant snobbery. I was far indeed from knowing the *all-inclusiveness* of Christ, or that "Holy Poverty" can be expressed in more than one way; the height and the depth and breadth of the oneness of the Church was still a closed book to me. The fact that two religious orders could not only be not exactly identical, but almost exactly opposite in every particular, was something I could not understand, and it gave rise to doubts in my mind and to questions to which I could get no answer in the school.

One thing, however, redeemed everything that I quibbled at, the astonishing kindness of everyone, both nuns and girls. The Prefect of the school was a wise and human nun, one who was able to make the Love of God a reality, who understood even "Singularity." She was able to make me ashamed of my intolerance of the other girls and to see them as people God loved. And the girls themselves, still more surprisingly, were without exception long-suffering and kind to me. I could not have done more to provoke their dislike, I could not have behaved more offensively than I did; yet I do not remember that I ever once heard an unkind word spoken to me, let alone suffered an unkind act from anyone.

After one year in this convent, I was suddenly summoned to leave school and go home for good.

I went home to find a curious and puzzling situation. A priest who had had some considerable influence on my mother at the time when she was received into the Church had left the religious order to which he belonged and become secularized. A very sick man indeed in mind and body, he had for the time being taken refuge with my mother, in whose home he was living. I saw no harm in this arrangement, and indeed there was none. My mother had always collected "lame dogs" and always would—this was simply one of them. However, there were others, Catholics of the "churchy" type, who did not take this view. They felt that vindictive hatred that some Catholics do against a priest who they think has betrayed them, and the multitudinous tongue of scandal wagged without restraint.

I soon found myself more or less ostracized by most of the Catholics I knew, and in the egoism of youth judged them pharisees. This was further complicated by the fact that whilst most of the Catholics whom I did know, being connected with my last convent, were rich and devoid of any understanding of money, I had no money at all, and would have found friendships with my old schoolfellows, and even with the nuns, quite beyond my means. I did not actually lose my faith, but I persuaded myself that the

Blessed Sacrament (in which I never doubted) was in the hands of hypocrites, with whom it was contaminating, if not impossible, for me to be in Communion. In this, of course, I was a pharisee myself.

This conviction was greatly strengthened by the fact that the poor priest living in our home met with such scant charity. Seldom did a fellow priest visit him, even when he was critically ill, and, with one single exception, those of the laity to whom he had once ministered most devotedly either ignored him or pelted him with offensive letters.

My own life with him was unhappy, he was at the time unbalanced; but it was not what he did to me that drove me to a hopeless search for some form of Christianity other than Catholicism, but what those Catholics who prided themselves on their virtue did to him.

By July of 1918, when I had left school about a year, I had made friends of a very different kind to the Catholic ones whom I felt to have rejected me, though in fact, for motives of pride and through faults of inexperience, it was often I who had rejected them. My friends were Bohemians, artists and art students and such people, people who for the most part were as poor as I was myself. Many of them, too, were as maladjusted to society in general as I had become myself, and for these very reasons I was more at ease with them than I had yet been with any other people. Although I did not know this, and indeed thought the opposite to be the case, my mind was narrowing, my heart contracting.

Because I and many of my new friends were really aware of some crippling inferiority in ourselves, we tried to escape from this unpalatable truth by supposing ourselves superior to other people, and in revolt against all their conventions. Since we had only worn-out clothes, and for the most part could not earn enough to dress conventionally, we pretended that we wore ragged, and sometimes dirty, clothes as a protest against the absurdity of the people who dressed inconspicuously, and this attitude was carried into everything in our lives. But the shallowness of it is measured for me by the memory I have of standing in front of a wax lady in a shop window and grinding my teeth at her, not only because I, a creature of flesh and blood, could not aspire to possess a beautiful suit like hers, but because I could still less aspire to attaining her impossible wasp-like figure.

At this time I had given up going to Mass and was looking for some form of Christianity other than Catholicism. I went from one minister of religion to another, asking to be instructed in their creeds. But my own conception of Christianity had narrowed down to the size of my own prejudices and limitations. I no longer recognized Christ, excepting in people who were poor or outcast or despised, and even in them my recognition was unrealistic.

The very last person in whom I would have looked for Christ, was a king or a priest.

Then, one evening in July, 1918, the night on which the Russian Royal family were assassinated, I "saw" what I can only describe as a living ikon of Christ the King Crucified.

It was in a drab grey London street, and it was raining. Suddenly I was held still as if my feet were fixed to the road by a magnet. There in front of me, stretching from end to end of the world as it seemed, was a gigantic ikon of Christ the King Crucified. He was lifted on a burning cross, clothed in a vestment that blazed with jewels, his head bowed down under the weight of a great crown of gold. His hands and his feet were naked, and the wounds in them rubies that bled with light. His face, contrasting with this splendour, austere and simple, sharp with grief, yet with grief that was redeemed by a smile of ineffable love.

This "vision" opened my heart, as if it had been driven through and opened by a spear of light.

In what I suppose were the few seconds while it lasted, my attitude to people changed. I knew suddenly that Christ is in kings as well as in outcasts, that His Passion in the world today is being lived out in kings as well as in common men, and I had a premonition of the tragedy and the glory of His Passion in mankind that was beginning again all over the martyred world. Soon after this, perhaps the day after, I cannot remember, there was a placard at the same street corner announcing the murder of the Tsar of Russia. The face of the Tsar in the newspaper photograph was the same face as my Christ the King in the ikon, excepting that it was without its glory.

This seeing of Christ the King on the living ikon did not solve my problems or convert me then and there to my own Faith, but it broke down the narrowness of my heart and mind and all the foolish barriers I had set up between myself and other people.

I will not dwell on the years which followed—about two years, I think—excepting to say that the necessity to earn my living, which had become acute, and for which I was hopelessly unqualified, did very much to force me to overcome my shyness and introversion. Psychological conflict is always *within oneself,* the problems of hunger and clothes to wear and a roof over one's head, throw one *outside* of oneself. They compel one, too, to realize the dependence of everyone on each other. In its most crude and primitive form this interdependence is a hint at the meaning of the Mystical Body of Christ. I regard it as yet another touch of God's mercy, therefore, that at this time I *had* to concentrate all my energy on earning the barest of livings. This forced me to make many contacts with all sorts of people, and to realize the interdependence, and to some extent the solidarity, of the human race.

Then the third "vision" came upon me. Please remember I only refer to these incidents as "visions" for want of another word; they were *seeing* certainly, but seeing not with the eyes but with the mind. Perhaps they could be described more truly as "knowing," except that the knowledge they gave was not such as could be wholly assimilated at once, but it was rather like a tiny little seed sown in the mind, which would increase and flower only through years of prayer and of study of the doctrines of the Church, which invariably endorsed them.

Very well, at this time I was living perilously—I had failed to be convinced by any of the clergy who had instructed me. I knew enough about Catholic doctrine to realize that, so far, I had heard nothing true or beautiful that was not contained in the Catholic religion, and that the rest, which was obviously not true or beautiful (such as puritanical hatred of pleasure) was *not* part of Catholicism. Cut off as I had been for a long time from the sacraments, and inevitably losing the habit of prayer more and more, I was a ready victim to every influence, and still more to every temptation that assailed me.

So far, unfaithful though I was, I had done nothing to cut myself off completely, and perhaps irrevocably, from the Church, but now I felt tempted to do so. My position seemed to me to be hopeless—the borderline state in which I lived, not finally and absolutely out of the Church, but definitely not "in" it, offered no happiness, no satisfaction of any sort—I had almost made up my mind to take the drastic step and do something that would separate me from the Church once and for all, when the third "vision" came to me.

I was travelling on an underground train. The train was

261

packed by workers going home at the rush hour. Every sort of worker. Dapper little clerks in pin-stripe city trousers and black coats; weary, rather anæmic typists; bristling, upholstered, successful business women; pallid office boys; blowzy cooks, foot-sore waitresses, "washer-ups," and charwomen. There were also little school boys with yellow bony knees, red noses, and their satchels slung over their shoulders. It would have been difficult to imagine a more ordinary, a more daily crowd of people going home in a train.

Suddenly I saw, not with my eyes, but with my mind and more vividly than one can see even the most wonderful picture, that Christ was in them all—that they *were*, in some way outside of my understanding, Christ.

In every one of them Christ's life was being lived out. In some of them His Passion, in some of them His fatigue, when He sat, worn-out, by the well in Samaria and handed His work of conversion to the poor sinful woman, who quibbled about giving Him a sup of cold water to drink. In some of them the child Christ, in some Christ the home-less wanderer, in some Christ crucified or Christ in the tomb.

If I wrote a whole book on this one "showing" alone, of Christ in man, I still could give no idea of it, because it not only included everyone living at that time, but the whole world. I had the feeling that all who *had* lived and who *would* live were there.

From the moment that I had this "vision" of Christ in men—in *all* men—I knew, though I could not at that moment have said why, that my search must end where it had begun, in the Catholic Church.

The vision itself faded, and in all the years that followed I could see Christ in man only through a blind act of faith. But if the vision had gone, the knowledge had not, and at the least touch of the Holy Spirit it has flowered again and again.

262

Perhaps the nearest I can come to saying what this has meant to me, and what the Church means to me, is that, helped by continual study of the doctrine of the Mystical Body of Christ, I realize more and more intensely that Christ has put Himself into *our* hands. That we are in the hands of God, immensely consoling as that is, does not take my breath away, like the fact that *God is in our hands.*

Perhaps that is why the memory of my first Christmas poem is associated in my mind with the idea of the indwelling presence of Christ.

Christ *could* have become man, had He so chosen, without the help of a human creature, but He chose to depend for His Humanity on Mary, His Mother. He chooses for His life in the Blessed Sacrament to depend on human creatures—day after day He is born again on the altar in the hands of men—in the hands of men He is carried in the Blessed Sacrament to the sick, to the dying, to the imprisoned. He depends upon the co-operation of men to give Himself to them in all the sacraments.

Above all—in His indwelling presence in men, in His Mystical Body, He is our gift to one another—He has put Himself into our hands to be our communion, our oneness, with one another.

Perhaps the nearest I can come to saying why I am a Catholic is that I realize more and more that in Christ everyone is included, and as Joan of Arc told us, "Christ and His Church are one."

Hilaire Belloc[1]

The question which I am set to answer is, "Why am I still a Catholic?" These are my terms of reference. To these terms of reference I will write: giving as best I can the statement of why the individual who writes these lines accepts, maintains and will to the best of his ability, God willing, defend the Faith. And I mean herein by the term "the Faith," both that which teaches and that which is taught: the religious organization in communion with the Bishop of Rome as its supreme and infallible Head on earth, and the doctrine and discipline emanating from this organization.

Now writing as I do to the Terms of Reference, and therefore necessarily in a fashion wholly personal (Why *I* accept the Faith?), certain provisos are necessary.

First, the thing being personal, there will be a great deal that is personal. That is unpleasant but under the conditions, inevitable. Secondly, I may, or rather, certainly shall, fall into certain repetitions of matter I have written elsewhere. I will avoid these as much as possible; but to avoid them altogether is impossible, because I have been writing upon this very subject (under many aspects, it is true) for perhaps thirty years.

Thirdly, I humbly provise (if that be English, which I doubt) that my personal statement here is not to the

---

[1] From *Why I Am and Why I Am Not a Catholic* (London, Cassell, 1931), pp. 87–108.

264

prejudice of a thousand others. My own reasons are of less value than those of better men, than those of men who never express themselves (many millions of them), of men enjoying or suffering spiritual knowledge far more profound.

Fourthly, the Church being what it is, nothing I say must be taken as representative. The largest and truest lines of affirmation or evidence probably escape me. I may be drawn, by what our forefathers well called "the imbecility of private nature," into statements of little or no value, or of worse than no value. Let no one think I pretend to a full, the best, or even a sufficient statement. It is no more than my individual confession.

Lastly (I need hardly say it, save that so many modern readers do not know what the Church is, nor the nature of adherence to her doctrine), any chance words in this poor essay are wholly subject to authority. If I misstate a point in theological argument I accept its correction at once at the hands of authority.

I, then, who must here present my argument, have these personal advantages and limitations.

In the first place I was baptized into the Faith upon my birth, and have known it all my life. Next, I have spent my life, for the most part, with people not of the Faith. Next, I have, though baptized into it and familiar with it from my earliest years, in some sense also discovered the Faith—but this line I will not pursue as it is somewhat intimate and hardly to the point; unless, indeed, it be to the point to tell those who read me and who are balancing, that I also have balanced.

But more important than the foregoing personal points is this personal point: I am by nature sceptical; that is, my inclination or appetite is for intellectual process, for analysis, for discovering the nature of things by the reason rather than by vision. All men know (or should know) the advantages and disadvantages of this weakness or talent in a man. It imposes a certain dryness: it may lead him astray through deduction from insufficient premises. To use the common metaphor, it neglects the heart and lays too heavy a load upon the head. On the other hand, it leads to unshakable conclusions, it establishes perfect discoveries. Scepticism assured leads to confidence absolute. In general this temperament leads to the disadvantage of restriction, the advantage of certitude, for others as well as oneself.

I have before me two tasks, which I will call, for convenience, Positive and Negative. These words, "Positive" and "Negative," are often abused. They are obviously relative in any connection, for what is positive to one aspect of a question is negative to its opposite. To use them as though they had final meaning is silly (as it is silly to talk with final meaning of "destructive" criticism and "constructive" criticism); but if we define our terms, these words "Positive" and "Negative" have their use.

I mean here by "Positive," all those arguments in favour of the Faith: the reasons I find for accepting it. I mean by "Negative," my reasons for not accepting such arguments as I am familiar with upon the other side.

In either category I shall distinguish (I hope not arbitrarily) between major and minor considerations. For it seems to me that there are both in the attack upon the Faith and in the defence of it, certain large determining propositions, few or single in number, which I will call "Major," and a host of other converging lesser propositions supporting either side, which I will call "Minor."

Thus in a discussion upon identity in a Court of Law, whether John Jones be John Jones or another, the main Positive point is the recognition of John Jones by a number of witnesses with an experience entitling them to affirm; while minor considerations would be questions of handwriting, or tricks of habit, etc. On the other side, the main Negative point may be a mass of evidence to the death of the said John Jones, and minor considerations would be the disputing of his handwriting, the authenticity of photographs, etc.

The Major argument for an acceptation of the Faith may be stated thus:

The Faith solves the principal problem presented to mankind. It would be truer to say that it solves the problem which is not only principal, but, like the Faith itself, unique. The problem which the Faith solves is not one of many, which vary only in degree of importance. It is rather a Problem of a different category altogether from the rest: to wit, "What is the nature and the fate of man?" Since we are men, this alone really matters.

Someone having lost his memory, and finding himself alone in a locked room, may interest himself in the wall paper, the pictures, and a slight itch upon his left arm. But the business of knowing who he is, how he got there, and what is likely to happen to him when he gets out, is on a different plane altogether. He will certainly begin with the large question before (perhaps in despair of answering it) he amuses himself with the wall paper and the pictures, or even bothers about his left arm. It would be a truer parallel, seeing what the development of a human life is, to say that, on coming to himself, he might first, in a silly sort of way, begin noticing the wall paper and the pictures, and only as he became fully conscious would pull himself together and consider the only real problem before him. For that is what happens to us in human life. As children we only notice what is around us. Even as young men the chief affair may not occupy our minds. But when we come to maturity of thought, that chief problem must inevitably occupy our minds; and if we leave the great questions for a jaded interest in lesser things, it is only because we have despaired of an answer.

As we examine the great Problem (its best formula is "What, whence, whither?") we have certain foundations upon which to build. We have certain directives towards a solution.

We have the sense of right and wrong, the sense of honour and dishonour, the sense of pleasure and pain, the strange paradox of mutability coexisting with a necessity for permanence—nay, an acute appetite for permanence.

What is the meaning of these things? It is one answer to say "They have no meaning"; but it is significant that man has never sincerely accepted that answer. He has always corporately and individually attempted a system; in societies through many generations, and moment by moment within his own soul, he gropes for something which should give him some answer. They who have replied that no answer is discoverable have themselves given an answer; but never was there a man yet, still less a society—that is man collective, and possessed of collective wisdom and an inheritance—who did not attempt an answer. Every man propounds a philosophy. For the word "philosophy" signifies the love of wisdom; that is, the love of knowledge; and that is, the solution of questions in their order. Now, necessarily, the solution of questions in their order points, as a first step to be taken, to the solution of the Prime question, "What? Whence? Whither?" before we can attempt any other.

Every man, I say, propounds a philosophy. The Sophists indeed propound none openly, and what they call their "philosophies" or "systems" are but games; yet they also are men, and therefore each of them has some philosophy in his heart, commonly of despair, sometimes more puerile than despair; though what each propounds to his school is but a system, an opinion, or an arabesque drawn on the window pane to correspond to the outlines of reality out-of-doors; at the best a half solution, a guess which may be modified, at the worst a mere negation; never, never an *answer*. And of this kind have been all the belauded names of the last hundred years, from that of Kant to that of the recently fashionable Bergson.

But what of *philosophy*? What of an *answer* to the main problem?

Were there a system which could flood with light the darkness of these torturing doubts, and make us know what we are and whence we come and whither we go, it would indeed be worthy of acceptance. It would immediately take precedence over all other affirmations, however well proved, upon such petty things as our bodily life and our passing environment in this world.

If Materialism could give a sufficient answer, we might rightly exalt it to the highest place, for it would at least establish a certitude; though that certitude were but nothingness and despair. It would be a determining Ideal and final. But Materialism does not sufficiently reply. It does not assuage the thirst for real knowledge. It stops short at "How?" (and not nearly enough even of "How?"). It is quite dumb upon "Why?"

Any system, I say, which could give the oracular reply would be blessed of all men, even though it were but a system. But wait a moment. Can any mere system give a reply?

Here we touch the very core of the affair. Man is an organism. All that is organic is complex. The full reply must meet the general nature of man. A merely mathematical reply will not suffice, nor will an emotional divorced from the intelligence. The full reply can only come from something consonant to the noble complexity of man.

Man is a Person; by nothing less than a Person alone

269

can he be guided. He has ears to hear—but nothing that he hears will satisfy him unless it proceed from a speaking soul, expressing will, intelligence, full being, in articulate words. There is that in man which, when he demands a full solution (I mean a *sufficient* solution, a harbour, a repose in conviction), requires something responding to himself; I say, again, a Personality, a Voice, an Organism, a Being. We look about, not for a theory but for a thing. In our search for that which can tell us in gradually convincing fashion "Things are thus and thus; such are you; such is the world," we expect, we cannot be content without, a living authoritative and intelligible Voice and Person.

Now the Catholic is that man who has heard such a Voice, who has come across such a Personality, and who is (most rationally) satisfied with its credentials.

Man is not satisfied by an emotion alone; he is not content with a rational process alone; he must have both in unison and manifestly interdependent. He is illumined by the unexpected synthesis wherein all his ultimate demands are satisfied, and the great Question is answered.

It is no objection to this experience when men say, "That Voice I have not heard; that Personality I have not met; with that Organism I have no real acquaintance; that Society is outside my experience." The only true countervailing objection would be, "All this I also knew, but it did not satisfy me." Now *that* objection—and this must be carefully weighed—is not to be found. Men lose the Faith, indeed, as one may lose his sense of taste, or any other of the lesser approaches to reality; but when this calamity falls on them never do they cease to remember with anguish the sense of perfect adjustment whereof they have been deprived.

I have in other places used various metaphors to describe the event, the meeting, the realization of home.

One of these metaphors I happen to cherish particularly. Perhaps it will be of less value to others: perhaps of more value to a few. I have compared the world to those pictures which were drawn in a distorted perspective by the artists of the later Renaissance and the eighteenth century, in which pictures all appears meaningless until you put your eye into a particular position, from which all suddenly falls into order, and you see a reasonable, well-proportioned scheme. The Faith so solves the world.

Another of those metaphors is that of groping in a dark room. You take for granted, from all you know of rooms and from the nature of things, that there is a door, or a window: some entry, some exit. Were there not, you could not be there. No sense proclaims it. There is no sound. All is blackness. You experiment; you feel; you find. And having found, you have no doubts at all. "Here is the door."

Parallels and metaphors are but aids to thought. They cannot of themselves convince, nor am I here occupied in convincing others, but only in making it clear how the Faith comes to, or, having been always accepted, is confirmed in, a man. It is a coming on reality. It is a grasp of things as they are. And if anyone then add, "But, why do I not perceive as you do?" I suggest this answer, "Have *you*, then, found reality?" I think not.

To this main proposition there come in a flood of minor considerations which will, I am afraid, have greater effect upon the modern mind than exposition of the major point. In another generation I would not have lingered upon them; for, in other and stronger generations, men preferred wrestling upon main points. But for what they are worth, let me tabulate them.

We who are of the Faith note that with the Faith there has arisen and continued what is manifestly the highest of human cultures. The expressions of the human spirit

271

have in that air obtained and maintained the sublime. Ruins
of the past proclaim that truth; relics of old efforts, tradition, and existing characters in the present.

The test of human happiness (the test of tests), if we
are to descend to mere pragmatic proof, tells the same tale.
So does the test of human dignity. So does (and this will
seem strange, I think, in the ears of most English readers,
though it is a commonplace abroad), the test of science
and discovery. Truth confirms truth; and it is both singular
and arresting to note how, for nearly three hundred years of
rapidly advancing achievement in the lesser forms of reality,
physical science and the rest, the Catholic Church has found
itself supported. The first achievements of research—hurried,
insufficiently confirmed—have almost invariably risen at
issue against the Faith. Without exception—I say, without
one single exception—the definitely proved conclusions of
physical research (even on that insignificant level) have
been compelled to withdraw from the attack, or better still,
have occasionally confirmed the immortal thesis.

Shall I advance lesser arguments still? What of the completeness of the Catholic affirmation? That completeness
might be man-made. That vast and exactly consonant body
of moral and transcendental theology might conceivably be
of human manufacture. But in what other instance has man
done such a thing?

Or shall I advance the unique Individuality of the Faith?

It is not true that the Church is but one of many warring
creeds and varying religions. There is but one Authority
on earth which claims to reveal to men their nature and their
destiny. All else is opinion, habit of life, unreasoned affirmation or partial pickings and choosings from the entire Faith.
All else either borrows from that central thing (remaining
schismatic or heretical) or is separate from it, yet not
conclusive.

272

And this leads me to another consideration which should be of profound effect with any man who understands the nature of his fellow men; I mean a consideration of the hatred and attack to which the Church is subject. Herein you discover that strong argument which runs from Tertullian to Newman through sixteen hundred years. "If there were on earth something which compelled men to the Divine, something which was the very voice of the Divine, how should we men, being what we are and know ourselves to be, being what we are and knowing ourselves to be capable of what we are not, being what we are and angry with our own defects—how should we receive It? With obloquy, with persecution, with defiance, with continual reaction against it." So it is with the Faith, and with the Faith alone, as a permanent historical phenomenon.

Many other hatreds there have been, many alliances and counter alliances; but one note runs through the whole of history, wherever this Person has been felt, this Visage seen, this Voice heard; the note of violent antagonism, provoking sporadic, often belated, but sufficiently heroic defence.

And on that minor argument of the tests by which we might know what such a Divine Society would be *if* such a thing existed, what of its Claims? It would claim absolute right. It would claim to speak with the Voice of God. It would demand (in its own sphere, though only in its own sphere) obedience. It would, *alone of things on this earth,* refuse to compromise. And by that test also the Faith is the Faith.

And here, to end up with, is another minor argument, which will appeal less perhaps to others than it does to me. It appeals to me strongly because I feel it in every line of good verse, in every excellent room or monument, in every phrase of good music, in every admirable character; I mean the argument from Proportion.

273

Nowhere else, in all the experience of mankind, will you discover universal Proportion as you discover it in the doctrine of the Catholic Church. Though it applies to the whole of human life, it does, in every relation, keep the normal—which some have translated "the Mean." It does so in the relations of parent and child, of husband and wife, of the propertied man and the destitute, of the citizen and the Christian (I mean of our duty to the Prince and our duty to God). It does so in that most difficult of all actual problems, the management of appetite.

The flesh is good. But the flesh can devour a man. If anyone can tell me where in the whole world there is another authority which decided rightly upon this awful crux, I shall listen with interest. Hitherto I have heard of none. I have met those who have told me that the crux may be neglected, and I have seen madness and terrible death ensue. I have heard those who have told me that it may be evaded; and I have met men contemptible thereby. But nowhere, save within the walls of the Holy City, have I seen the affair put in its just relations, leaving man, though fallen and always suffering, at least neither tortured, nor a sensual fool, nor a slave.

Perhaps if I were conducting this exposition of what is (I beg you to remember) a personal argument, and in no way a general one, upon general conversational, familiar lines, neglecting ultimate principles, I would lay more insistence upon this point of Proportion than upon any other. That which will give us Proportion even in temporal affairs has been discovered and is here to our hand. Men have achieved Proportion outside the Faith in one department at the expense of another. They have had the grace given them to satisfy the human spirit to the full in column and arch—and meanwhile to despise justice. They have had exactitude of law and have meanwhile despised beauty.

They have had a just arrangement of property, and meanwhile have lost culture. But in the Catholic scheme there inhabits a certain balancing, compensating spirit, which though it can never constrain men to achieve perfect proportion, for men are fallen, does make them approach to such perfection sufficiently for the right conduct of life.

And here let me tell you another little point in connection with Proportion. The Catholic scheme (which those who desire to avoid the term Catholic call also by the uncertain title of Christian) will give you that final complement of Proportion which is called Humour.

Let me turn now to the negative affair.

There is one outstanding major argument against the Catholic Church, which, to all men of intelligence, comes first. It is this: Why should this particular affirmation be true?

"There are a myriad trees in the wood. What is there special about this particular tree? There are a myriad guesses at an insoluble problem. Why do you call this guess a solution? You have affirmed the thing to be unique. I recognize" (says the instructed opponent—the uninstructed I neglect) "that it *is* unique. You are right when you say it is something quite unlike any other thing and cannot be put into a category with others. It is not" (he admits) "one religion out of many, still less one creed out of many." (Indeed, being instructed, he knows that even the Catholic Creeds do not pretend to be a full exposition of the Faith, but only special definitions answering special denials.) "The Catholic Church *is* striking, individual, something apart. But to say that is not enough. *That* does not make it what you claim it to be, the actual Voice of God upon earth. Indeed to men like myself and a host of others, it is no more than one, perhaps the most sympathetic, perhaps the most arresting, but not upon that account the most convincing, of I know not how many structures of the human imagination."

Now to this major argument (which alone I respect among the unnumerable propositions against the Divine origin of the Faith) there is no answer save that of the Faith itself. To the main agnostic argument, to Lucretius as to Huxley, there is no answer save the answer of appreciation, acceptation, discovery, and the experience of what Chesterton has justly called "the Thing."

That is why Faith is Faith. Were it other than Faith, the mass of men would accept or all men would reject. Being what it is, many, even of those who approach, reject; many accept; the rest remain ignoring.

That one Particular Man out of incalculable millions should alone have been also the Incarnate God; that one Organization out of I know not how many myriad organizations should alone be absolute in authority; that one connected and multiple set of statements—however closely interdependent, however widely ramifying—should be an ultimate philosophy; these are not affirmations which can be proved by the deductive reason, nor can they be put to such tests as will be immediately accepted by all rational beings.

Against *that* affirmation "Your Particular cannot take the place of the General," there is, I take it, no answer but the Faith itself. There is no answer, in other words, save that convergence of experience in morals, in intelligence, in appetite, which brings us into, or maintains us in, the Household whereof the inhabiting spirit is a lively, a triumphant, a divine repose.

You are of that Household or not of it. But approach it, examine it closely and after so doing, decide.

Of the minor negative points, perhaps the most important today are the arguments drawn against the Faith from history and from what is called "pre-history"—though I would like to make the exception here, that pre-history is not history at all, but guesswork upon matters very little known.

The argument from real history is of two kinds.

The first is what I may call the Protestant argument. It is the argument that the Church *was* founded by Jesus Christ, who *was* God, who *did* intend to create a society among men after His own image, but that (though He so intended) everything went wrong. Some say it went wrong at Pentecost, others at the conversion of Constantine; others again, with the Papacy of the monk they call Hildebrand, but we St. Gregory VII; others, again, with the excommunication of Elizabeth Tudor; others in the rejection of Mrs. Eddy.

To all this, if you will pardon me, I will pay no attention. Others can deal with it better than I, for I am afraid that I despise it with such a wholehearted contempt that I am unfitted to deal with it.

No one can doubt the existence of an historical, visible Church. If it have not authority, *all* doctrine fails; for from that body all doctrine has proceeded. No Christian doctrine has any other historical basis as dogma.

But the second argument from real history is of more weight; it is that history shows the whole affair of the Church to have been man-made. "The earliest documents," it says, "the now lost original memorials underlying our existing texts (which are corrupt) presented a young Jewish teacher who said vague things of a common morality, and was put to death either because he conflicted with government, or because his ideals were too high. These, later, were embroidered on by various hands. Then we get accretions upon accretions: the supposed Divinity of the said young

277

man, and all the Christian theology, spun out henceforward from empty brains."

I can't agree. The first documents are *not* of the sort presupposed by this hypothesis. Any man who has ever written a book knows that they are homogeneous, save for trifling textual discrepancies, and every man who can read at all knows that they are direct, sincere, and overwhelming. Everyone who knows enough history to be worth arguing with knows that there proceeded from the very origin of the thing the Christian Church, and that the Christian Church had authority, claiming such from its founder. You are free to say that the origin was a myth, or an illusion, and only Faith can answer you; but you are not free to say as an historian that, at the very origin, the Church was not founded, or that all the great development does not start from that one seed. The Gospels proceed from the Church: not the Church from the Gospels.

As to pre-history (in which is included the observation of many savages) the whole argument against the Faith lies in this, that men follow certain lines in religion, and that because the Catholic Church follows those lines in an exalted way, therefore it is man-made. I don't agree. I say that if God intended to reveal Himself to man, and to give man an institution whereby that revelation would continue and have body and form, substance, continuity, life, that institution would incorporate those things which man either remembered or had groped after or in his intimate nature desired.

It is a very old quarrel, and there is no solution save the Faith. You either look at the thing one way, or you look at it the other. But there is this much quite certain, that *if* there be a Divine Institution on earth, then its consonance with human habits, traditions and adumbrations of the truth, are not against the claim of that Institution, but heavily in its favour. You may call Our Lady the Egyptian Isis or the

Chinese Mother-Goddess, but *if* the Incarnation is true she is the Mother of God, and worthy of our worship.

On the old minor argument from the supposed superior prosperity and happiness of the non-Catholic as against the Catholic culture I will not linger. Today one can only laugh; though in reading the cocksure nonsense of forty years ago and the timid objections of Catholics living within the anti-Catholic culture, one might also weep.

To the argument that the Catholic Church destroys freedom in the intelligence or in the character I am afraid I can only answer with a similar contempt. I know that all contempt is acid, and that no man drinks it to his profit; but it is honest truth that I cannot brew any other liquor out of such materials. Within the Catholic culture alone is general freedom of discussion to be found, because within that culture alone are first principles, constantly demanded, and because in that culture alone is Reason the ultimate test. In practice it is within the Catholic culture that you hear matters debated fully, with such a contempt for rank and wealth, the power of the police or of the popular press or of the lawyers, of common labels and uninvestigated affirmation, as a non-Catholic culture can hardly conceive. If you doubt it, read the press and the books of our contemporary world in various nations. Take specimens and decide.

As for character, within the Catholic culture still flourish the saints.

There is my little apologetic. I know it to be grossly insufficient. If I could have drawn a picture of that Face which commands us, written a score of that music which we hear, or presented a map of that country which we see, I should have done better.

To do that is quite beyond my powers. I cannot reveal the Church. But there She stands. *Stat et stabit. Manet ac manebit: Spectator orbis.*

279

Date Due

A 27'57			
Demco 293-5			